LOMBARDI

AND

LANDRY

LOMBARDI AND LANDRY

How Two of Pro Football's Greatest Coaches Launched Their Legends and Changed the Game Forever

ERNIE PALLADINO

Skyhorse Publishing

Skyhorse Publishing books may be purchased in bulk at
special discounts for sales promotion, corporate gifts, fund-
raising, or educational purposes. Special editions can also be
created to specifications. For details, contact the Special Sales
Department, Skyhorse Publishing,
307 West 36th Street, 11th Floor, New York, NY 10018 or
info@skyhorsepublishing.com.

Skyhorse® and Skyhorse Publishing® are registered trade-
marks of Skyhorse Publishing, Inc.®, a Delaware corporation.

www.skyhorsepublishing.com

10 9 8 7 6 5 4 3 2 1

Library of Congress Cataloging-in-Publication Data is
available on file.
ISBN: 978-1-61608-441-7

Printed in the United States of America

A la famiglia
Sempre Famiglia

CONTENTS

PROLOGUE

EVERYBODY STARTS someplace.

Even the greatest generals were, at one time, someone else's right hand. Sherman served Grant, MacArthur served Pershing, Eisenhower served MacArthur. They all had their beginnings answering to somebody else.

So it was with Vince Lombardi and Tom Landry. Just as none of history's stars arrived on the scene as full-blown leaders, two of the NFL's greatest coaches also had to serve their professional apprenticeships somewhere, under someone. Theirs came with the New York Giants under Jim Lee Howell. The lessons Lombardi and Landry learned between 1954, the duo's first year together, and 1959, Landry's final year in New York, carried them both into historic head coaching careers in Green Bay and Dallas. The responsibilities they held molded them into true leaders of men. The professional and personal setbacks and challenges each man faced steeled them for the adversity they would later encounter as head coaches.

They came to their respective success through hard work and God-given mental acuity. But there was a bit of luck involved, too. Had they worked under a boss other than Howell, who delegated responsibility to them on a level never seen before and rarely seen since, only smaller worlds might ever have heard the names Lombardi and Landry. Lombardi's legend might have been swallowed up by the vast landscape of college football or the small private sphere of banking; Landry's in the oil business. A few hundred people might have remembered them as astute givers of loans or as innovative oil rig designers. But Howell's managerial style allowed them to ascend to a much larger stage, where millions could appreciate the yield of their efforts weekly.

One remains a constant presence in the Super Bowl trophy that bears his name; the other set the standard for long-term coaching success in the modern era, and neither would have had the opportunity to make their mark if not for Howell's faith in them, and for their ability to fulfill Howell's sole command—win.

He left Lombardi and Landry to take care of strokes both broad and minute, and they each delivered masterpieces.

The idea for this book sprang from a 2010 magazine article I did on the Giants' great defensive lieutenants. The progression to head coaching success and, sometimes, greatness, was much the same for Bill Parcells, who served as Ray Perkins' defensive coordinator in the early eighties, Bill Belichick, whom Parcells later molded after being promoted, and John Fox, who led the Giants defense under head coach Jim Fassel from 1997–2001.

This is the story of the professional beginnings of two of the greatest generals in NFL history. Their apprenticeships came at a time when being a pro football assistant was a part-time job done with full-time effort, when the sport itself completed the transition from a grungy, tramp-player Wild West show trying to horn in on college football's Broadway, to autumn's true national pastime.

The era, head coach, and lady luck all combined to make Vince Lombardi and Tom Landry who they were, and who they would eventually become.

None of it would have happened if not for the events of 1953.

INTRODUCTION

FIRING STEVE OWEN was the toughest thing Jack Mara ever had to do. He loved the old man. How could he not? Owen had steered the New York Giants through the last twenty-three years, won them 153 games, taken them to eight NFL championship games, and won two titles including the fabled "Sneakers Game" against the Chicago Bears in 1934. The whole Mara family admired everything about the man who had served the team's founding father, Tim, and his two sons, Jack and Wellington, since he came onboard in 1926 as a bruising two-way tackle, one year into the franchise's existence.

By 1953 it was time to go, though. Things had changed, speeded up both socially and competitively from the era the fifty-five-year-old Owen had known. The game was quickly moving from the straight-ahead, head-busting, territorial ground battle Owen prospered in as player and coach to a complex contest of speed, maneuverability, deception, and scoring. The game had passed him by, many in the press asserted. He was stubborn and slow to change, the critics said, and they were not wrong. While the rest of the NFL probed the perimeters of formations for opportunities, Owen's philosophical compass still pointed north and south on both offense and defense.

Despite the criticism, nobody really blamed Owen for his inability to adapt. North-South was what he knew, what his game had been for so long. As a player in 1927, he had stood strong in a sixty-minute fistfight against Red Grange and the Bears. The 13–7 win in late November, combined with a 14–0 win over the New York Yankees the following week gave the Giants a first-place finish. In the young NFL, there were no championship playoffs. Finishing on top of the regular-season standings was as good as it got. The Chicago game sealed Owen's reputation as a give-no-quarter, ask-no-quarter player. Playing next to Cal Hubbard on the defensive line, the future Hall of Fame duo held off the Bears with a ferocious goal line stand to maintain a 7–7 tie that eventually allowed the offense to convert a fake punt and the 58-yard completion which came off it into the winning touchdown.

Owen and his offensive counterpart Jim McMillen, who later gained fame as a popular pro wrestler, sat exhausted in the dirt for more than five minutes after that game, barely able to muster enough energy to shake each other's hands. "It was the toughest, roughest football game I ever played in," Owen recalled years later.

That bloodbath sat long in the tobacco-chewing, gravel-voiced coach's past by the end of 1953, though. America and its National Football League were on the move. The three-year, undeclared war in Korea had wound to an uneasy conclusion. Dwight Eisenhower had taken over at 1600 Pennsylvania Ave. at the dawn of "an era where nothing happened," unless one counts the escalation of the cold war, the horrific aftermath of McCarthyism, racial unrest, and the rise of the Brooklyn Dodgers to World Series champions. The women of the country had started doing their laundry in new time-saving electric washing machines and their cooking on electric stoves. Ribbons of asphalt spread like tentacles across the nation, and people used the fast-developing interstate highway system to heed Dinah Shore's urgings to "See the USA in your Chevrolet." And none of the wise-ass athletes who came out of college ogling Marilyn Monroe or the vets who survived bloody front lines from Okinawa to Inchon had much patience for loudmouth Depression-era guys like Owen telling them what to do and how to do it.

On top of that, the Giants weren't winning, having slipped to a lousy 3–9 record in 1953. The media had long ago pegged Owen as strictly a defensive coach, a claim the gruff leader angrily disputed. But now, even that unit failed to produce. It gave up 277 points, almost 3 touchdowns, and a field goal per game. And Owen took the downfall as hard as did the Polo Grounds faithful and the Mara clan.

The worst part, though, was the lack of offense despite the presence of such talent as Charlie Conerly, Kyle Rote, and a promising second-year pro named Frank Gifford. Only four times did Owen's team score more than 16 points, and two of those outbursts came against the even-sorrier (1–10–1) Chicago Cardinals. What's more, the defense accounted for two touchdowns and a safety amid the paltry 179-point total.

The Giants of 1953 were not just bad. They were boring.

Clearly, the time for a fresh start had arrived. With television still in its infancy and just beginning its national reach in 1953, the Mara family could never have envisioned the impact the new medium would have on the NFL five Decembers down the road. But they did know this was the time to act, before the family business to sank into a prolonged coma.

So Jack, speaking for his brother, Wellington, and his father, Tim, made the move on December 6, 1953, that many sportswriters thought he should have made years before. He brought Owen into his office after that day's 62–14 loss to Cleveland and told him he could have any job he wanted in the front office.

But, Jack said, Owen would no longer coach. The Giants, Mara explained, needed a shot of younger blood.

"It was the toughest thing I ever had to do," Jack said. "Steve was like family."

The toughest thing, yes. But also the wisest. And not just because the Maras stayed in-house by promoting Owen's old defensive end and assistant, Jim Lee Howell. The real genius rested with the Maras' choices of assistants. With Vince Lombardi running the offense between 1954 and '58, and Tom Landry running the defense from '54 to '59, the thirty-nine-year-old Howell had the greatest right hand and left hand who ever worked under any head coach at any one time.

Their collaboration produced the first half of what history came to regard as the Giants' golden age, a period from 1954 to '63 where the Giants reached the NFL Championship Game six times and won it all in 1956. Howell would never suffer a losing season, something no other coach in the league from 1954 to Howell's retirement after the 1960 season could say. In fact, he remains the only Giants coach in the franchise's eighty-five-year history with more than two full years of service to never have a losing season.

In just a few years, Lombardi and Landry would begin Hall of Fame head coaching careers with different teams. Letting Lombardi, then Landry, go a year apart to the Green Bay Packers and expansion

Dallas Cowboys (originally dubbed the Rangers) would be one of the great mistakes the Giants' brain trust ever made, a mess created in part by ownership's frugality. Had Jack Mara been less concerned about his head coach fulfilling the final year of his contract and more in tune with the future, the Giants might have avoided a seventeen-year malaise that started four years into Howell successor Allie Sherman's contentious eight-season reign. The remnants of what Lombardi and Landry built allowed Sherman to reach the championship game his first three years, but intra-squad squabbles and an eventual sell-off of personnel led to the Giants' unfortunate demise.

The most ironic part of it was that the affable (to the public) Howell once told reporters he'd thought about stepping down as early as 1957. He stayed for a shot at a second title and the chance to go out on top. If his team had beaten the Baltimore Colts in the famous overtime championship game of 1958, "I would have quit," he said.

Instead, Howell stayed and Lombardi left for Green Bay. And then they let Landry go to the upstart Dallas franchise right after the 1959 season, just before Howell let Wellington Mara know in no uncertain terms that he was ready to hang up his whistle. Only a year before, Mara had complained about how ill-prepared he was for the initial stage of the draft—in those days, the first four rounds of the thirty-round draft were conducted in December—and half-jokingly asked Howell if he'd ever thought about giving up coaching to help with personnel matters upstairs.

"I'd quit right now if I had another job," Howell replied.

The Maras' reluctance to replace Howell before his contract ran out cost them dearly.

The changing philosophies of the game and the nation had brought the two geniuses together in the first place. Pro football had grown so complicated by the early 1950s that the head coach could no longer see to both offense and defense and still handle all the details that surrounded a football team. The head coach's job was just beginning to evolve into an executive-type, general overseer position, a sea change Howell inadvertently and unknowingly helped popularize. Howell owned a 1,200-acre livestock farm with his brother in his native Arkansas and had plenty of experience operating a business, which is exactly how he told the Maras he wanted to run the Giants. From the time he took the head coaching job a few days after Owen's final game, a 27–16 loss to the Detroit Lions, which Owen coached out of a sense of duty, Howell presided over an enterprise, not a football team. He watched over the big picture while Lombardi and Landry (who was still a player) served as the brains of the operation. In a very short amount of time, Lombardi and Landry were wielding unprecedented power in an era where few assistants held any sway with the head man.

A defining story of the Howell era occurred in 1956 when Kyle Rote happened by the coaching offices at the Giants' training camp at St. Michael's College in Winooski, Vermont. He looked in one room and saw Lombardi hard at work breaking down film. He looked in another and saw Landry peering at the film screen.

"I continued on down the hall and saw Jim Lee reading a newspaper," Rote said.

Howell often joked that his main job was to "pump up the footballs." But give him credit. He not only had the smarts to recognize the talents of the two very smart people who worked under him, but he had the humility to step away and let them work their magic as well.

There was certainly magic to be made, and it was needed. Paul Brown and his Cleveland Browns had quickly entrenched themselves in the NFL and were tearing up the league. Since joining the NFL in 1950 with the Baltimore Colts and San Francisco 49ers as the only surviving franchises of the All-America Football Conference, Paul Brown's gang had won the conference title every year. Quarterback Otto Graham led an offensive group that also included Lou Groza up front and at kicker, Dante Lavelli at end, and a bruising fullback named Marion Motley in a harrowing balance of rushing and passing.

It wasn't the kind of deep passing game the Los Angeles Rams employed, with their alternating quarterbacks, Bob Waterfield and Norm Van Brocklin, a funny-gaited flanker named Elroy "Crazylegs" Hirsch, and a fleet end in Tom Fears. Those guys flung it all over the field, which served the dual purpose of winning games and entertaining a Hollywood crowd that had no patience for muddy, grind-it-out football. Instead, Brown's game combined power running with a short, controlled passing scheme.

The greatest of all Brown's weapons was still earning his thirteen varsity letters in football, baseball, and lacrosse at Manhasset High School on Long Island at this time. But Paul Brown had drawn the curiosity and consternation of NFL strategists long before Jim Brown ever lined up in his backfield. And the ones that alternately copied and refined the coach's innovations, or successfully defended them, were on their way to Jim Lee Howell's staff.

Once Lombardi and Landry finished with their dissection of (and thievery from) Paul Brown's playbook, the Giants were able to break Cleveland's 6–1–1 stranglehold on them to win five straight times, including a 10–0 shutout in an Eastern Conference playoff game in 1958. In eleven meetings from 1954 to '58, Landry's defense would hold the Browns to an average of

18 points per game, well below the 25-point average Cleveland held against the rest of the league over that span.

Luring Lombardi was the real trick. He was busy assisting Col. Earl "Red" Blaik at Army, and he had options. Air Force had even thought about hiring him as their head coach. The Maras never considered him for the top job, since Lombardi had no pro coaching experience and doubts lingered that Wellington Mara's forty-one-year-old Fordham University classmate could provide the disciplined leadership the family wanted. As history showed, it was a huge miscalculation, and it was harder on the Giants' franchise than it was on Army. Had Lombardi stayed, he might have succeeded Blaik, the target of the Maras' affections from the beginning.

Landry was the easier get, as he was already there. Since his arrival in 1950 as one of the dispersed New York Yankees of the AAFC, the former University of Texas defensive back had led an All-Pro life in Owen's Umbrella defense. He had done remarkably well on the field, despite his admission that he'd never run a 100-yard dash faster than 10.3 seconds. Landry made up for that by studying film, noting the tendencies of each player. By knowing an offense's tendencies, he could predict where a receiver might be at any time, and then get to the spot before him.

His work habits reaped tremendous results. By the time he stepped off the gridiron for good after 1955, the admittedly slow-footed Texan had nabbed 31 interceptions, 3 returned for touchdowns, in seventy career games. He picked off 8 passes in 1951, '52, and '54, ranking him among the league's leaders.

Owen was the first to notice Landry's impeccable football intellect. Though Landry wouldn't become an official coach until Howell took over in 1954—first for two years as a twenty-nine-year-old player-coach—he had served Owen unofficially in that same capacity since he was twenty-five out of sheer necessity.

Owen's vision leaned more toward broad strokes than details. So when the coach came up with a defensive innovation such as the Umbrella alignment, which utilized a 6–1–4 setup in which the defensive ends would alternately stand up and drop into coverage or go into their three-point stances to rush the quarterback, it was left to others to figure out the finer points of the scheme. The others, in this case, was Tom Landry.

Gifted with a sharp mind that had already earned him an engineering degree, Landry could root out exactly what Owen wanted.

"Steve Owen was not a great detail man," Landry said. "He'd just do things like that and figure you would work out the details for yourself on the field. I learned much of my coaching by playing under him because I had to work out the details of what he meant."

Even more important, he could teach them to the rest of the team.

"I can remember being in training camp and Owen would be up at the chalkboard, going over a defense," Wellington Mara said. "Suddenly, he'd just stop and say, 'Tom, come up and do this. You know more about it than I do.' It was during those times when Tom was still playing that he was also becoming a coach, whether he knew it or not."

Landry had been thinking on his feet well before he'd ever met Owen, and he'd continue to do so long after the old coach was dead and buried. His overall intelligence had gained him entrance in 1943 to pre-flight school in San Antonio, followed by pilot training and assignment to a bomber crew in the Eighth Air Force. And his quick mind and analytical brain eventually saved his life, and that of his crewmen.

Flying out of Ipswich, England, on one of his thirty missions over German factories and refineries—five more than the Army required for discharge—his plane suddenly began sputtering and losing altitude over German-held Belgium on the return flight. The plane appeared to have run out of gas, and had sunk to a thousand feet amid heavy flak.

The pilot ordered the crew to bail out. But Landry, the co-pilot, looked over at the instrument panel just before he started heading for the door. Working on a hunch, he calmly reached over and adjusted the fuel mixture. The engines started up again, the plane got back to England, and the whole crew was saved from death or, at the very least, interment in a prisoner of war camp.

"I just realized something might be wrong with the fuel mixture," Landry recalled. "I wasn't sure. It just came to me that the mixture might be off. It was just one of those things."

That same composure also saved Landry and his family in 1995. While piloting a private Cessna over Ennis, Texas, Landry's engine stalled. Without a hint of panic, he set the plane down on a dirt field next to a high school. Police later reported that Tom and Alicia Landry and two other relatives walked away uninjured. The Cessna was undamaged.

Cerebral. Matter of fact. Unaffected. That was Landry's personality, and it was these traits that eventually led to the "Plastic Man" moniker the Cowboys' Duane Thomas derisively hung on him years later. But make no mistake, the man Howell and the Maras picked to handle the defense had a tough-as-nails side to him, too.

Landry had played the 1950 American Conference playoff game against Cleveland with a shoulder so severely injured that the trainers refused to shoot him up with painkillers for fear that he'd wreck the joint completely. But Landry's work in that 8–3 loss to the eventual NFL champions helped foster its legend as one of the greatest defensive battles in pro football history. "Tom was hollering and yelling and screaming when the offense was on the field," Wellington Mara said. "And he had tears in his eyes. When a Cleveland tackler hit one of our players who appeared to be out of bounds and Tom interpreted this as a cheap shot, he rushed over and was all over the guy and ready to fight before they separated them."

Landry also got into it with running back Glenn Davis during a preseason game against the Rams in 1951. Landry worked on Davis the entire afternoon until Army's former Heisman Trophy winner finally beat him by 10 yards for an easy touchdown. Landry kept running, though, even after Davis crossed the goal line. As Landry neared, Davis threw the ball at him and sprinted toward the bench, with the irate defensive back closing fast. "I knew he wanted to punish me, so I heaved the ball at him and I yelled, 'You wanted the ball all afternoon, now you've got it,'" Davis later recalled. "He was so mad, I'll bet he'd have killed me if I hadn't made it to the bench."

Landry's ascension to the coaching ranks seemed a foregone conclusion given that, really, he'd been coaching for Owen, anyway. Moving him into his initial spot as player-coach was easily done, as the strict contractual dividing line between coach and player would not be drawn until after Dan Reeves served as a player-coach for Landry in 1971. (It would be thirty-two years before the next player-coach came along in Denver Broncos cornerback Jimmy Spencer in 2003, and there hasn't been another since.)

Lombardi was another story. He had desperately wanted the Giants' head coaching job after assisting Blaik since 1949. He had pretty much seen it all and done it all at Army by the end of 1953.

Off the field, Lombardi had a major role in redirecting his players' focus from the sad Korean War fatality dispatches that listed several of Army's former stars. Though he never served in the military like Landry, Lombardi did briefly travel to Korea to meet the troops. While visiting a position close to the front lines, he wound up scared and shaken as an enemy bomb exploded nearby, interrupting dinner and splattering baked beans over the top of his head.

He had watched Blaik's soulful struggle and near-resignation in the face of a cheating scandal in 1951. Lombardi, being a civilian, never could understand all the fuss. He knew well that the crimes the cadets allegedly committed against West Point's honor system were common occurrences in most of the country's schools. He stood beside his boss morally. And then he stood beside him physically when Blaik announced amid applause from a group of his sportswriter friends at Mama Leone's Restaurant in New York that he would indeed stay at Army.

In the aftermath, Lombardi worked his connections with New York's Catholic hierarchy to find spots for several of his expelled players at Manhattan College, Iona, and his alma mater, Fordham.

Blaik's ultimate decision to remain at Army, much influenced by the urging of his great benefactor, Gen. Douglas MacArthur, marked a turning point in Lombardi's career. "If I ever needed a lesson, and I guess everybody does sooner or later," Lombardi said, "I got it with Colonel Blaik. Red showed me . . . what could be done by perseverance."

On the field, Lombardi was already espousing the qualities of teamwork and syncopated football that would define his head coaching career.

He'd learned a lot of that during his playing days at Fordham, where he served as one of the fabled "Seven Blocks of Granite" until his graduation in 1937. His playing career actually ended with commencement. Lombardi was good enough as a college player, but far from pro material. In fact, Class of '37 mate Wellington Mara served as sports editor of the school yearbook, *The Maroon*, and never wrote about Lombardi. He was clearly the seventh block. Any accomplishments he may have had were overshadowed by the exploits of his 1936 teammates Johnny "Tarzan" Druze, Leo Paquin, Alex Wojciechowicz, Ed Franco, Al Barbatsky, and Natty Pierce.

In today's parlance, one would say Lombardi's biggest asset was his motor. He had a great one, and a temper to boot. It galled him when his teammates did not play as hard as he did, and he'd let them know it. He also soaked in the intricacies of precise blocking and sure tackling taught to him by his coach, "Sleepy" Jim Crowley of Notre Dame's "Four Horsemen" fame, and his line coach, Frank Leahy. And from those he found what he called football's Fourth Dimension.

Material, coaching, and schedule made up the first three. "The fourth is selfless teamwork and collective pride which accumulate until they have made positive thinking and victory habitual," he said.

Lombardi transferred all that to West Point. He became among the first to institute blocking rules for his linemen. A steady flow of communications to Leahy, by then coaching Notre Dame, brought more complexity to the offensive backfield.

Lombardi yearned to run his own show, though, and truly believed the Giants were calling with his opportunity. He was forty-one, with a wife and two children, and it was certainly the right time in his life to move up.

Unfortunately for him, the Maras would have had to break some social and cultural ground to do that, and the family wasn't as forward-thinking as one might like to believe. Lombardi was working-class Italian all the way, and he suspected issues more cultural than strategic stood in his way. He once opined to Wellington Mara in 1955 that, having lost out on several college jobs, he might never get his chance because of his heritage.

The owner didn't really buy the notion, but he didn't argue with Lombardi, either. Fact was, most Italians of the 1950s had yet to break through the cultural ceiling. They didn't run things; they worked for other people.

If you needed a wall built, the Italian stone masons who came over in the wave of turn-of-the-century immigration were the best around. Anybody who appreciated good food knew the wonders Italians could perform with tomatoes, garlic, and olive oil. Italians could fight in the boxing ring, as the great champions Rocky Marciano and Carmen Basilio proved. They could certainly soldier with the best of them and earn the Medal of Honor, as Marine Gunnery Sgt. John Basilone did on Guadalcanal and Iwo Jima.

But run a country? Run a company? Run a team?

Hardly. Of the twelve teams that comprised the NFL in 1954, only three had ever employed Italians as a head coach—Green Bay (Gene Ronzani from 1950–53), Pittsburgh (Luby DiMeolo in 1934), and the Cleveland Rams (Buff Donelli in 1944). It would be six years before the nation elected its first and only Roman Catholic president, and his descendents came from Ireland at that. Italians controlled Mulberry Street, sometimes brutally. Wall Street, though, remained a bastion of Anglo-Saxon Protestantism.

There were the exceptions, of course. Fiorello LaGuardia had run New York City as its mayor from 1934 to '45. Another Italian named Vincent Impelliterri had beaten out two other Italians for the same office in 1950, and he'd reign until 1954. And Rhode Island Democrat John Orlando Pastore, the first Italian elected to the U.S. Senate, was four years into a twenty-six-year run when Lombardi lodged his concerns to Mara.

The age of political correctness was still two generations away. Joe DiMaggio might have been the Yankee Clipper to his fans, but inside the clubhouse he was known as the Big Dago; Daig to his teammates. Big band leaders Tommy and Jimmy Dorsey had advised their singer—a fellow named Frank Sinatra—to change his name to something more acceptable, like Frankie Satin. And when Lombardi followed his usual strategy of pulling quarterback Don Heinrich for Charlie Conerly after the first quarter in one 1956 game, an enraged Heinrich blasted, "You guinea sonofabitch!"

That wasn't Lombardi's first brush with prejudice. He faced it directly during his days at Fordham, once while courting his future wife, Marie. He had arrived at a hotel for one of Marie's sorority dances when a group of fraternity brothers eyed Lombardi and his friend walking through the door. "Who's the little wop?" one frat boy asked, at which point Lombardi turned and slugged the guy in the mouth.

After practice one day in 1936, Lombardi and Fordham end Leo Paquin were showering when a second-string end and another man walked into the small shower room, the second of which was of a darker complexion. The second-stringer called to the swarthier fellow: "Hey, come here. Stand alongside Lombardi. I want to see which one of you looks more like a nigger." Lombardi decked the loudmouth. Upon hearing about the incident, coach Crowley suspended both men, though the pragmatic Crowley made sure Lombardi, a starter, would be available for that Saturday's game. The other, more expendable guy, sat until the following week.

While timing was probably Lombardi's biggest obstacle to a head coaching job, Lombardi wasn't wrong in citing his heritage as an underlying issue. His experience seeking the open Wake Forest job during his Army tenure offered direct proof that at least certain parts of the country were as prejudiced against the Italian as it was the African American. Other Blaik assistants had gotten jobs that year, and Lombardi's interview at Wake Forest had gone so well that he thought he was a cinch for the job. But as long-time Newark *Star-Ledger* columnist Jerry Izenberg recounted, Lombardi was anything but a lock.

"A guy down in North Carolina called," Izenberg remembered, "and said, 'Vince, I have to tell you, I don't want you to play out a charade. They had several number of people interview and you were one of them. But they are not going to give this job to anyone whose name ends in a vowel.'"

There were few positive examples of Italian advancement the aging assistant from Sheepshead Bay, Brooklyn, could lean on for moral support. Even in the movies, he was likely to see his people portrayed as mobsters, even though less than one-tenth of one percent of Italians were involved in criminal activity at the time.

Italian Americans were still getting their hands dirty. But Lombardi wanted much more than that. He was devastated when he learned the Maras had an assistant's job in mind for him. He put them off just long enough to first ask Blaik for a raise. An extra $1,000 would keep him at West Point, where he would most likely serve as Blaik's successor-in-waiting.

When the colonel told him a raise was out of the question because he had maxed out on the school's assistants' pay scale, Lombardi took the Giants' offer. But even then, the Maras wouldn't make it official until Lombardi quelled their concerns that he and Howell might not get along. Howell had preferred Owen's old backfield coach, Allie Sherman, for the job. A week-long visit between Christmas and New Year's to the coach's farm in Lonoke, Arkansas, bonded the men, a task made easier when Howell assured Lombardi between down-home servings of wild duck and wild rice that the offense was all his. Ultimately, coaching freedom was the path to Lombardi's heart, but a tasty meal made for a nice paving stone. "You can't buy anything like this anywhere," Lombardi raved of the meal.

With that, Lombardi became a Giant. Howell's coaching treasure chest would soon overflow with creative offensive formations, defensive innovations, and most important, victories.

The creation of a winner didn't happen organically, though. It took Howell's organizational skills to pull things together at first, and then keep them running smoothly as his two brilliant though competitive underlings vied for his attention.

"At the beginning, we all got together," Howell said. "I delegated the authority—the offense to Lombardi, the defense to Landry, the other jobs to Ken Kavanaugh and Ed Kolman. Then we had to get together a lot and work on that. But after a while, everything fell into place."

Howell did not completely detach himself from the strategic end of things. He would run his game plan meetings like a corporate board meeting, listening to suggestions from his staff and approving or overriding them as he saw fit. But once those meetings ended and the practice week began, he left it up to his assistants to teach and implement their strategy.

Come Sunday, Lombardi and Landry would handle most of the play-calling. But it was Howell who made the key decisions, like sending Pat Summerall out for a long, snow-swept field goal attempt to break a 10–10 tie with Cleveland and force a conference playoff game in 1958.

Howell took the blame for the losses. Lombardi and Landry got credit for the wins.

"I want them to have the initiative to act on their own and the confidence that comes with getting the credit for doing a good job," Howell said. "When you call Vince Lombardi the offensive coach, he's just that. He's in charge of designing our offense and carrying it out."

Both assistants could further delegate the teaching if they so desired. The former defensive back Landry wasn't always comfortable imparting advice to defensive linemen, for example. So once future Hall of Fame defensive end Andy Robustelli came aboard in a 1956 trade with the Rams, Landry had Robustelli teach the techniques Landry devised each week.

Both Lombardi and Landry were responsible for the pacing of practice and for handling the occasional personal problem.

"If you're a defensive end like me [and you've got a problem]," Robustelli said, "you go to Tom Landry, who's the defensive coach, and you know he's got the authority to handle it. If you think they're running you too hard, slip him the word the boys need a blow. Tom'll do something about it. On some other clubs, they don't listen to their assistants."

Were power measured in inches, Howell gave Landry and Lombardi yards of it. But that led to occasions where each wanted miles. Power meant not money or prestige, but practice time in an age where thirty-three-man rosters and players with multiple responsibilities made full-unit work difficult and, at times, logistically impossible. It was sometimes a challenge for Howell to balance the week, so neither of his stars' rather sizeable egos came away bruised. "Everybody worked so hard," Howell said. "Landry would be in my office one minute asking for more time in practice for his defense, and Lombardi would walk in the next minute asking for more time for his offense. They were always fussing."

It was a small headache when weighed against the rewards.

In Vince Lombardi, they had an offensive genius who would bring to the Giants the Power Sweep Paul Brown had used to terrorize an entire league. He already had four pieces of what would become a legendary offense in running back Gifford, end Rote, quarterback Conerly, and left tackle Rosie Brown. But then so had Owen, only the old coach didn't quite know the offensive talent he had in Gifford when the Giants made the glamour boy from USC their first-round pick in 1952. Gifford had played both ways his first two years under Owen, performing at a Pro Bowl level in the defensive backfield yet only occasionally saw action at halfback. Eddie Price was the Giants' main ball-carrier before Lombardi arrived and changed Gifford's life.

"The day Vince Lombardi took over the offense in 1954, he came up to me and said, 'You're my halfback,'" Gifford said. "Before then, I was used mostly on defense and only sometimes as a halfback. I hardly ever came out of the game."

Now exclusively a one-way player, Gifford would run behind the pulling Rosie Brown in Lombardi's variation of the Power

Sweep that would propel both players into the Hall of Fame. Lombardi would later take the play with him to Green Bay, where Paul Hornung would run it to achieve legendary status.

Lombardi also made Conerly a more efficient thrower. The quarterback had thrown 303 passes for 13 touchdowns and a whopping 25 interceptions in 1953. He would never reach those levels in attempts or interceptions under Lombardi. Conerly's attempts dropped to 210 in 1954, with 17 touchdowns and 11 interceptions, and they dropped even further the following year, to 202, with 13 touchdowns and 13 picks. His completion percentage rose marginally, from 47.2 in 1953 to 49.0, 48.5, 51.7, 55.2, and 47.8 during the Lombardi era.

A lot of those were short throws to Gifford, the team leader in receptions from 1955–59 and, in 1954, to split end Bob Schnelker. Lombardi also had Gifford throwing the ball on the option. Gifford would continue that for his remaining career as a running back—he converted to wide receiver after losing a year and a half because of his fabled collision with Philadelphia's Chuck Bednarik in 1960—and he'd finish his career with 14 touchdown passes, still a record for a non-quarterback.

Lombardi had an immediate impact on the team's offensive production. The Giants scored 293 points in 1954, a huge increase from the 179 Owen's last group produced. Under Lombardi, they never scored fewer points than the 246 they put up in 1958.

In Tom Landry, the Giants had a man who would change the entire language of defense. He was like Dante with a chalkboard, moving football nomenclature from its simple, vulgar terms into the complex but more easily managed syntax of the modern era.

Landry was the first to designate formations by color: "Red Left" if the halfback lined up to the left of the fullback in a split backfield, and so forth. He named the linebacker positions after females, such as Sarah, Meg, and Wanda for strong side, middle, and weak side. Those names would also come into the play-calling, with calls like "StormSarah," or "BlitzWanda." A call of Mambo, Combo, or Tango would shift the defensive backfield accordingly.

He was the first to talk about frequencies, the fruits of his intensive film study that revealed what kind of play was likely to be called on second-and-seven with a split-back formation, or on third-and-short out of an I-formation.

"No one had ever done it," Sam Huff said. "Tom Landry was the first to do that. He was calculated."

Landry was also hard-working. It was nothing for him to put in eighteen- to twenty-hour days watching film in the office or at home, logging percentages of passes versus runs out of various formations, while also observing players as a card sharp might eye his foes for any physical tells—a head-nod here, a subtle shifting of weight from one foot to the other there.

In that, Landry fashioned himself an acute observer of the human condition.

"You can rely on some players giving you a real good tip-off," Landry said as he prepared for the 1959 NFL Championship game against the Colts. "Others you can be sure won't give anything away. Then there are those that lead you on falsely. That's why it's a never-ending job, studying the characteristics of individuals.

"One tip-off can stop what can become a big play for the other side. But I've never seen it so sure that you can bank on it one hundred percent. We couldn't watch one man, even if he's a notorious tipper-offer, and rig our defense by his actions.

You must plan your defense overall to get the most effective results."

Landry's biggest development was the 4-3 inside and 4-3 outside alignment: four men up front, three linebackers, all acting differently depending on formation and game situation. He wouldn't have all his pieces in place until 1956, but the strategy's beginnings took seed in 1954 as he looked for an alternative to the Umbrella and Eagle defenses the dominant Browns exploited regularly.

The Philadelphia Eagles had actually begun replacing a linebacker with a defensive back standing at the line on passing downs, giving their defense a 4-3 "look." Landry turned that into four down linemen, with the ends responsible for peeling off into the flare areas on passing downs, while a mobile middle linebacker stepped up to handle the running game.

"What everybody was doing was forcing the play back inside," Wellington Mara said. "But Tom came up with the idea of defensing the end run inside-out, stopping opponents up the middle with the idea that pursuit would take care of the outside.

"Simply, Tom was talking about today's 4-3 defense, where the four defensive linemen are charged with the responsibility of keeping the five offensive linemen from having a clear shot at the middle linebacker. Jim Lee Howell accepted the theory, and the rest is history—the 4-3 defense."

Though he wouldn't get his main cog, Huff, in there until '56, Landry's theories, like Lombardi's, paid off immediately. In 1954, the Giants finished second in the league with 184 points allowed, third with 195 first downs allowed, and third at 3.2 average yards per rush. The following season they finished third with 223 points allowed, second with 77 first downs rushing, and second at 3.4 average yards per rush. The defensive backfield came alive in '54 with a league-high 33 interceptions. Landry and Emlen Tunnell, who had come to the organization in 1948 as an undrafted free agent, each had eight picks that year.

During Landry's time in New York, his defenses averaged just 194 points allowed per season, well under the 215 league average over that span. In 13 games against the vaunted Browns, Cleveland managed only 16 points per game, a far cry from the 25 they averaged against everyone else.

All of that lay in the future, however. In the offseason of 1953, after Jack Mara fired the man he admired, respected, and loved, no one knew what Jim Lee Howell and his pair of unknown assistants would produce. Lombardi had yet to become an offensive genius. The unit that would eventually be called "Landry's Legions" had yet to ferment. All anyone knew at that point was that both Lombardi and Landry had unbounded energy, an incredible capacity to learn, and the freedom to employ new ideas.

They were of two temperaments; "different as daylight and dark," Howell said. He could not have known it at the time, but Lombardi and Landry's differences proved to be their greatest strengths.

1

STRANGE BEDFELLOWS

AS DIFFERENT AS daylight and dark. Jim Lee Howell couldn't have pegged Vinny Lombardi (he wasn't really known as Vince until he reached Green Bay) and Tom Landry any better. Nor could Wellington Mara have described them more accurately than when he claimed one could hear Vinny "from five blocks away," but you couldn't hear Landry from the next chair.

Together, they formed an intellectual dream team—the brainiest, most strategically sound, and academically able set of assistants anywhere. But it easily could have gone the other way, for theirs was not an easy partnership. Better to describe it as complicated. Given their diverse personalities and an inborn competitiveness that pitted each against the other as much as their upcoming opponent, they could have been at each other's throats every day of the five seasons they spent together. If not for Howell's adept handling of his two budding Einsteins, the whole arrangement might have failed.

"[Their relationship] was good-natured, I think," said Vince Lombardi Jr., who witnessed their interactions from the training camp sidelines. "I don't think it was in bad faith or anything of that nature. But, of course, while the offense did well, the defense was really the core of that team in many respects. So I'm sure there was some of the pushing and pull of that.

"I think they got along. I think there was respect. But I don't think there was a closeness there. No."

Vince Jr., of course, viewed their relationship from the eyes of a teenager. Alicia Landry had a much different view as the wife of the defensive assistant.

"Vinny was a lot lower-key as an assistant than when he went to Green Bay as a head coach," she said. "He was a jokester, and I thought the world about him.

"But they were competitive. Each had the offense and the defense, and they each wanted their half to be better. But Marie and Sue Howell and I all got along great, and we were all sure that all three of [the men] were equally important."

They could not have been more different in temperament, character, or even spirituality. Though both were God-fearing men, they wore their religion in different ways. Landry was a church-going Methodist who would come to a life-altering epiphany while attending Bible classes after the 1958 season. Lombardi, born and raised in the Roman Catholic Church, took Holy Communion daily for as long as he could remember, and helped priests as an altar server well into adulthood. "They probably could have gone to church together," Frank Gifford said.

The difference was that Landry found peace with his Lord, while Lombardi found both comfort and conflict.

In the quiet of his bedroom, inside the walls of the church, and out on the street, Lombardi asked his God questions that, more often than not, went unanswered.

He wanted to be a good father to son Vincent and daughter Susan. He wanted to be an attentive husband to Marie. But how could he with the hours his job required? There was always the next opponent to prepare for, the next film to study, the next practice to run. How could Lombardi bring a priorities list that read "God, Family, Football" into balance so the family would not feel lonely and forgotten?

He wanted to be a good man, made in his God's image. *Love thy neighbor.* But he coached a sport that fed upon violence. *Hit the hole! Knock that linebacker into next week!* And he coached that violent sport with vigor. Yelling. Cursing. Many of his players eventually recognized he loved them, that the abuse was designed only to make them better football players. But still, there was a brutality to it all. In later years, Packers tight end Gary Knafelc would say Lombardi worked his players so hard that "when he tells you to go to hell, you look forward to the trip."

Lombardi prayed for patience.

"In many respects, my father wasn't always pleased with who he had to be to be successful; the demanding and the pushing [that it required]," Vince Jr. said. "The time he spent in conversation with his God was an attempt to reconcile the two—what he knew to be a good person and what he knew he had to be to be successful. The conversations with his God were, in many respects, an attempt to come to some kind of reconciliation."

Whether Lombardi ever did find that balance between God and football is debatable. He never did subdue his temper, a major reason why colleges never warmed to him as a potential head coach. He never did find the patience for which he prayed. But he did find a way to relate to his players, and many of them, like Gifford, came away loving him for making them great.

During his Green Bay years, Lombardi rode noted hell-raiser Paul Hornung relentlessly, fining him untold amounts of cash. But he turned the womanizer's life around, and Hornung never forgot it. Hardly a letter writer, Hornung did express his gratitude in a missive to his coach as Hornung prepared to leave Green Bay for expansion New Orleans on February 23, 1967:

"I want you to know that I have always felt closer to you than any coach I have ever had or ever hope to have. I believe the greatest thing I have learned from your 'Football' has not only been the idea of winning, but WHY you want to win! Each and every ballplayer who has had the opportunity of playing under your guidance in some ways will always try to mirror some part of your personality."

In his first year with the Giants, Lombardi was almost universally disliked among the team's veterans, some of whom had dealt with far worse than some ill-tempered coach while serving in World War II. The yelling didn't really register much with Charlie Conerly, who had his rifle shot out of his hands by a Japanese sniper during the Marine invasion of Guam in 1944. Who did this big-mouthed guy think he was, full of bluster but devoid of any pro experience? Did he really think that rinky-dink Army offense was going to work? Gifford, who later became one of Lombardi's greatest friends, called him "loud and arrogant, a total pain in the ass."

Though the bombast continued, Lombardi adjusted. After some initial, failed attempts to gain their trust that first camp, Lombardi visited some of his key players and asked for help. What plays did they like to run? What were they comfortable with?

To Lombardi, winning was far more important than getting his own way.

"We would listen to him and he would listen to us," Conerly said.

He made accommodations to age and skill sets. He bent. And in return, the players gave him their loyalty and attention. Though he would become more aloof from the players as a head coach, with these Giants he drank, played cards, and communed as a human being.

While the players still caught a heaping helping of his tyrannical manner on the practice field, they eventually became comfortable enough with him to exact their own form of revenge. More than once, Lombardi walked into a meeting room only to find the chalk he had meticulously laid out beforehand had vanished. The players roared as their foil spat accusations and expletives before a hurled chalkboard ended the entertainment portion of the day.

Adaptability became Lombardi's greatest strength.

"He was one of the few coaches who could coach individually," Gifford said. "There were great coaches over the years who couldn't change his tactic because of one guy or his attitude. You can't coach individually because football's a team game. But he was great that way. He could make players play who wouldn't have played for somebody else."

Balancing football and family was even harder. Lombardi was often distracted, so much so that he'd sometimes walk into the wrong house as his mind drifted deep into the Xs and Os. But he wasn't so distant that he couldn't dole out punishment to a rebellious teenager who had just brought home a bad report card. A substandard grade—young Vincent received his share— might get him grounded for the next marking period. Breaking a house rule might mean the abrupt introduction of his father's hand, a favored punishment in many households of the day.

"Somebody tried to tell me I was abused as a child," Vince Jr. said. "I said wait a minute. If you mean that when I broke a rule of the house I got spanked, yeah. But I'm not dumb. I learned pretty quick—don't break a rule, you don't get spanked. Those are good lessons, ones I'm not sure the next generation is teaching their kids."

He'd bring his son to training camp to serve as a ball boy. Vince Jr. would catch it there, too, just as bad as the players, if he didn't round up the balls fast enough. About the only peace he found was on the sidelines on game days, probably because his father was focused on other more pressing matters, like beating an opposing defense.

For his daughter Susan, who struggled with a learning disability, Lombardi would often brush her hair at night, counting the hundred strokes with her. When together in the car, they'd play games where they each picked out letters in street signs.

Lombardi had no shortage of love for his children, or for Marie, despite their loud and frequent arguments. Time was the issue. Time would always be the issue, for Vince Lombardi was driven to coaching excellence. He wanted nothing more than to become a great football coach.

God, Family, and Football remained in constant conflict.

"Sometimes, he'd forget those priorities," Vince Jr. said.

Tom Landry was quite different in that respect as well. Landry had come to coaching quite by accident, and never truly expected to become much more than an assistant until the Murchison family offered him the head coaching job of the expansion Dallas Cowboys after the 1959 season.

"He never intended to be a coach," Alicia Landry said. "He was going to go into industrial engineering, but [the Giants] asked him to be a player-coach and he enjoyed it. And then they asked him to stay on as the defensive coach."

The balancing act wasn't that difficult for him.

"He always said God came first, and then family and football," Alicia Landry said. "Of course, during the season, we kind of waited a little bit. But he did all of his after-hours work at home. You read about coaches who spend the night in the locker room. Tommy thought those who spent too much time there weren't working on the right thing.

"He made an absolute effort. We had breakfast together every morning and dinner together every night. He stayed up late and watched film and worked on his game plan, and it worked out really well. I never felt we were deprived of our father and husband because he made a big effort to stay part of the family.

"He had breakfast, he went to work, he came home for dinner, and he went down to his study and he worked there. I wanted to go down and watch some films with him, but he kept running them back and forth just when they'd get interesting. It drove me crazy."

Trips to New York's museums and Central Park from the Concourse Plaza Hotel, the social hub where the Landrys and many of the Giants took up their in-season residence just steps from Yankee Stadium, became regular events for the family, which at the time included Tom Jr. and daughter Kitty. Another daughter, Lisa, would arrive in 1958. Tom Jr. often played catch with Kyle Rote Jr. in the sprawling park.

For the children of a football coach, the upbringing could not have been more normal, a feat engineered by a couple of even-handed parents. Tom Jr., being only five years old when his father joined the coaching ranks in 1954, did not go to training camp like Vince Jr. did, however.

Other than that, Landry made it a point to be around.

"I think they had it as normal as anybody could have," his wife said.

Their marriage had a storybook quality to it that endured through six decades until Landry's death in 2000. They met only because of the insistence of Alicia's friend, a member of a University of Texas sorority she had pledged as a freshman in 1948. But once they did, they were destined to be together.

Love at first sight?

"It almost was," Alicia said. "We met on a blind date arranged by one of the actives. I had pledged a sorority, and this girl, Gloria Newhaws, her boyfriend was Tommy's best friend. And I refused to go. And she said, 'Well, you're going because you're a pledge and I'm an active,' so I went.

"I just thought he was great. We dated after that. Even after we were married, we had a date one night a week. Thursday night was my night."

Date night lasted all the way through his coaching career with the Cowboys and beyond. And when his teams traveled, Alicia came along, even if it was just to the Bear Mountain, New York, training grounds the Giants occasionally used during the regular season.

"We had a fantastic time together," she said.

In his own way, Landry was just as deeply religious as Lombardi. Methodists don't carry rosary beads, but Landry held a deep belief in God throughout his life. His father was the superintendent of the Sunday school of the mission church that stood across the street from his house, and young Tom was no stranger to their services.

He and Alicia went to church every Sunday. But in the offseason of 1958, Landry got involved in a Bible study class in Dallas at the invitation of a friend. At first, the man of great intellect questioned the veracity of the Scripture passages the group read, discussed, and reread. Eventually, he even came to question whether he truly believed and accepted Jesus Christ's words and message.

So Landry started researching Christ, looking for the impact of Christ's life much like he looked for strengths and weaknesses in his defensive schemes. What he found was the man's influence on millions of people. And there was a peace to that which he never found as a casual churchgoer.

It took Landry more than a year to conclude that bringing Christ into his life was more important than football. But once he made that choice, he became an active Christian, eventually chairing the Billy Graham Crusade that opened Texas Stadium in 1971 and witnessing frequently before organizations like the Fellowship of Christian Athletes.

He remained the same quiet Tom, however.

"He wanted to turn his life over to Christ, and so he did," Alicia said. "But he was always nice and good and honest. It wasn't any huge change in his personality as far as I could see. I'd always seen that side of him."

Devotion was never an issue for either Landry or Lombardi. Nor was carousing.

"I'd gone to the same church since I was four years old, and I'm not drawn to people who carouse," Alicia said. "Most of our friends are wholesome, and most were Christians.

"Vinny was a devout Catholic, and he wasn't cheating or drinking, either. But his voice was louder."

*   *   *

Lombardi and Landry never socialized together. Lombardi spent most of his off hours in the house he bought for his family in Oradell, New Jersey. As much as Landry was also devoted to his family, he could just as easily be found on the golf course, where the coach settled even deeper into his quiet universe.

"We played a lot of golf together," former Giants public relations director Don Smith said of Landry. "He was a pain in the ass. He used to be my partner, and it was hard to get anything out of him that might help the match."

That might have been due to Landry's "do unto others as they would do unto you" life credo. He didn't particularly like taking advice from those who knew less than he did, which by his reckoning was just about everyone. Even as he aged, his self-confidence on the golf course, racquetball court, or film room remained so high that one proffered advice at one's own risk.

"He was so quiet," said Dan Reeves, Landry's former Cowboys running back, offensive assistant, and frequent golf partner. "In golf, he wasn't going to be telling you all kind of things. If you asked him something, he'd give you an opinion. But he fought it because he didn't want somebody else telling him what to do. You'd better not say, 'You know, Coach, you better keep your head down on that one.' You kept your mouth shut."

In 1989, the year after new Dallas owner Jerry Jones fired the only coach the Cowboys had ever known, Wellington Mara's son and eventual successor, John, and three of his brothers found themselves in the same grouping as Landry at an NFL Alumni Best-Ball outing at Quaker Ridge Golf Club in Scarsdale, New York. John had just scored himself a piece of personal history, holing an eagle from 120 yards out. Flushed with excitement, John and his brothers frolicked with high-fives all around as Landry sat placidly in his cart. Finally, the old coach looked up.

"That was exciting," Landry deadpanned.

And that was Landry all over.

"Very quiet," John Mara said. "Lombardi was not that way. Very gregarious. Talkative and loud. Two completely different personalities."

But Landry was quite different at home. Alicia Landry remembered her husband as an intuitive, interesting conversationalist. Humorous, even. Not withdrawn by any means.

"He really wasn't," Alicia said. "He was very witty and very smart. I think smart people are witty because they get it. But he was very witty, very interesting. He was just a different person at the training table than he was at the dinner table."

In the locker room and meeting room, Landry could be an aloof character—all business. And most of that business was focused on those who were healthy and playing. His wonderful defensive tackle Dick Modzelewski remembered one week when he was injured and certainly out for the next game. Modzelewski found himself standing at adjoining urinals with Landry, heeding nature's call.

Landry acted as though Little Mo wasn't even there.

"I guess because I wasn't going to play, he didn't really have anything to tell me," Modzelewski said. "Yet [the previous] week, when I played, he had plenty to say to me."

Only when he stepped outside football did Landry open up, even to people like Frank Gifford, who would eventually become a lifelong friend.

"I don't mean to sound cold, but he was kind of cold," Gifford said. "In person, I know he wasn't like that. I had kids and he had kids, and we all lived in the same hotel. Out of the football field and out of the locker room, Tom and I would take our strollers and we'd stroll with our kids down the highway and we'd talk. He was a different person then.

"But when he was standing up there telling us what to do, he was a different Tom, a different personality."

Remembered Alicia Landry, "He was a good strategist and probably would have made a good general. And he was a leader. Somebody once asked him what it took to be a leader and he said, 'I don't know. I guess followers.'"

*   *   *

The one quality Landry and Lombardi did share—and revel in—was competitiveness. Be it football, golf, tiddlywinks, whatever, they both possessed an unquenchable desire to win.

Out of season, Landry wouldn't even consider playing his first round of golf until he took five or six lessons, fearing he'd look less than competitive on the course. On the racquetball court, his matches against Reeves and another Cowboys assistant, Landry's former great tight end, Mike Ditka, took on mythic proportions. "You could see he was ready to whip us," Reeves said. "He'd get that square-jawed look. He was under control, but you could tell he was burning up inside. Beat you? Heck, yeah, he'd beat you. He wasn't going to meet us out there just to get exercise."

Then there was Lombardi, ever fighting opposing linemen despite a significant weight disadvantage, beckoning any under-performing Fordham teammate to raise his intensity level. Card games like Hearts turned into one-man laugh-fests as he slipped his opponent the deadly Queen of Spades. The high school basketball squad at St. Cecilia's, his only head coaching job before arriving in Green Bay, might've outshot him in Horse, but Lombardi would never let them forget about the one circus shot he swished.

When it came to football, the performance of the two coaches' individual units became their ultimate measuring stick. Each became a major pain in Howell's ear while promoting the offense or defense, lobbying for more time, more attention; a punt instead of an offensive play on fourth-and-short or, in one instance, a risky play instead of a field goal on fourth-and-10.

There, in keeping Landry and Lombardi on a peacefully even keel, Jim Lee Howell's true genius emerged. He wasn't a fantastic game coach. He wasn't a great strategist. He never garnered undying love from his players. But without a head man like Howell—a boss willing to hear out both sides but strong enough to break a tie knowing full well he'd bruise one of his assistants' egos—Lombardi and Landry might well have become football's version of the Hatfields and McCoys.

Howell spread around just enough responsibility—and praise—to his assistants to make them feel fulfilled and impor-tant in their roles. Those two needed the validation, too, given their high opinions of their own football acumen. Howell recog-nized their talents, and then stayed out of the way.

"Isn't that what you'd want to do?" John Mara said, para-phrasing his father's reminiscences from that era. "Don't let your ego get in the way. Who would do that today, not let their egos get in the way?

"To me, he did a masterful job. There were mixed reviews of Jim Lee Howell from the players who played for him, but my father always felt very strongly about him. That's why we hired him for our front office after his coaching career ended. He was better as a coach than as a personnel director. But I think history shows he did a masterful job holding it all together, keeping the egos in check."

Though they spent hours together going over game plans and developing plays, there was a palpable tension between Howell's lieutenants. It never turned into outright animosity, but they each had their own strong opinions about how things should go. Neither was shy about telling Howell, either, though Lombardi was, of course, the most demonstrative in that area. The hot-blooded Italian gave Howell the full treatment in the final minutes of the final regular season game of the 1958 season, when Howell shrugged off Lombardi's demand to go for it on fourth-and-10 against the Browns and instead ordered out Pat Summerall for a 49-yard field goal attempt in a blizzard at Yankee Stadium. Lombardi stepped away from Howell and stood, arms folded petulantly, as Summerall kicked the Giants out of a 10–10 deadlock and into an Eastern Conference tie with the Browns, forcing a conference title playoff the following week.

Opinions differ on the level of friendship Landry and Lombardi shared. Summerall said he never saw the two exchange more than three words at any one time in the single season both men coached him; Don Smith remembered that "they kind of lived with each other."

If they weren't exactly buddies, at least they got along. That was a good thing, too. Years later, the NFL would see how warring coaches could destroy a team's fortunes. Buddy Ryan's attempted knockout of his offensive counterpart, Kevin Gilbride, on the Houston Oilers sideline in January 1994 was clearly a low point for a franchise that would sink to 2–14 the following season and relocate to Tennessee four seasons later. Head coach Tom Cable added to the embarrassment of the already pitiful 2009 Oakland Raiders when he allegedly sent defensive assistant Randy Hanson to the hospital with a broken jaw, and was then sued by Hanson.

Lombardi and Landry never let their emotions fly that far afield. But if Howell had not been decisive as an arbiter, tense friendship could have given way to open hostility. Had that happened, the many late-day meetings where Lombardi and Landry bounced ideas off each other might have taken on a far different tone. It may well have impeded the Giants' rise out of the morass of late-Owen era mediocrity. There likely would have been no success, no golden age. So if Howell had to sublimate some of his own philosophies to keep the peace, the boss had no problem doing so.

"Howell was smart enough to keep those two at bay," Smith said. "He knew he had a good team there, and when you have that you want to keep things going. He'd keep the harmony so the two of them wouldn't be at each other's throats. He might suggest some things, like put this guy here, or do this on this play, but for the most part Lombardi and Landry ignored him."

Howell often had his hands full dealing with the normal emotional swings of the season, especially with regard to Lombardi. Where Landry affected the quiet, analytical façade of a college intellectual, Lombardi's emotions undulated like waves in an ocean storm.

When things went right with the offense, out came the jovial Vinny; the Brooklyn working stiff who loved a good joke, laughed easily and long and hard, didn't mind imbibing the occasional drink or three, and slapped the back of his players. But when things went bad, as they occasionally did over the course of a season, a depressed, angry Vinny would take over. A rough offensive outing could send him into a two- or three-day funk, where he would skulk around the coaching rooms with nary a word to Howell or his defensive counterpart. Landry hung the nickname "Mr. High-Low" on him "because when his offense did well, he was sky high; but, boy, when they didn't do well, you couldn't speak to him."

Howell wasn't above taking a playful poke or two at Lombardi during the down times. He once found his assistant prowling a roof, deep in angry thought, after a poor day at training camp. Thus did "Somebody find Vinny a roof!" become a common cry for Howell.

Lombardi would complain to anyone who would listen if he thought something was off kilter. It was a trait he carried over to his head coaching career, as Dan French remembered from the week the Packers' rookie coach spent training his team in Bangor, Maine, in prelude to their 1959 exhibition game there against the Giants. French, then a twenty-five-year-old towel boy and general gofer during practices, became a personal sounding board for Lombardi when his players made mistakes. French also stayed well within earshot to hear the coach's on-field corrections. "He swore like a drunken sailor," French said. "I told people then I didn't think he'd last as a football coach."

*   *   *

Whether by loud, crude cajoling or calm explanation, both men were tremendous teachers. Different, certainly, but both extremely effective in his own manner.

"Tom never swore," Landry's star middle linebacker Sam Huff said. "He was so good. He was so believable. What he told you, what he put up there, you could do. He always said, 'If you do what I tell you to do, we can control the game. Don't guess. You gotta believe in what I'm telling you,' and you did."

When things went wrong, it only took a mere glare from Landry to let the player know he'd sinned.

"[He] never screamed," Huff said. "[It was] just the way he looked at you. When Tom Landry looked at you, it was a stare. It was like, 'God damn, you know better than that.' He just looked at you, like, 'You know I taught you better than that.'

"Tom always said, 'Anytime you can't do what I'm asking you to do, you let me know.' You do what he taught you to do, it was easy. He gave you the keys, he gave you the formation and everything. He was a master teacher."

Even the spectacular stop, if done outside the scheme, would garner a rebuke.

"I remember making a tremendous play on my own, outside the defense," massive defensive tackle Rosey Grier recalled, "and he said to me, 'You made a great play, but nine times out of ten you miss it. If you play the defense, it's always covered.' So not very long after that, I had a chance to do the very same thing again and I let it go to test his theory. So I let [the runner] go and Harland Svare made an incredible crunch on that back. Right then, I began trusting the defense. But he also made a point of telling me I made a great play."

Wellington Mara likened them both to college professors in their blackboard presence. The only difference was that Landry's intellectual approach made it seem like he was teaching the top 10 percent of his class, while Lombardi's earthier, repetitive method seemed directed at the bottom 10 percent.

Landry was satisfied that only three or four people in the room truly understood what he was talking about. He would rely on them, especially brainy defensive end Andy Robustelli and Huff, once they arrived in 1956, and Emlen Tunnell before them, to get the message across to the less-astute defenders. Yet there weren't many of those. The difference between the smartest guy and the dumbest in Landry's classroom wasn't as wide as one might think.

"He made you smart," defensive tackle Dick Modzelewski said. "His schemes were so easy. When we were playing the Browns, he'd have a Browns Special. That was the huddle call. You lined up in a formation and Sam would call out the numbers. It would be a 4-3 outside. They wound up in another formation, it would be something else. Yeah, you had to think, but not a whole lot. All you had to do was beat the hell out of the guy in front of you and go get the quarterback."

Once he got to the Cowboys, Landry gained a major say in personnel decisions, and player intelligence became a major criteria for him when assessing talent. The complexity and the language of his schemes, both offensive and defensive, dictated that even his weakest link pick up the main concepts quickly. Like Paul Brown before him, Landry turned intelligence into a measurable in his scouting reports, weighing it just as equally as a player's height, weight, and 40-yard dash time. In the early 1970s, he became the first coach to employ the now-standard Wonderlic Classic Cognitive Ability Test as part of the drafting criteria.

As it happened, the Giants defenses under Landry became one of the league's most intelligent units, especially once cerebral players like Robustelli, Svare, and defensive back Jimmy Patton came aboard.

Many eventually transferred their brains from the playing field to the sidelines. Robustelli served as player-coach once Landry departed for Dallas, and eventually went into the Giants' front office. Svare first took over Landry's job, and later became a head coach with the Rams and Chargers. Sam Huff was a player-coach with Lombardi's Redskins. Dick Modzelewski became a defensive assistant with the Browns. Em Tunnell went on to Lombardi's staff in Green Bay, and then returned to the Giants. Dick Nolan went on to assist Landry in Dallas, after which he embarked on an eleven-year coaching career with San Francisco and New Orleans.

"[Landry would] teach people what to do and how to do it," Huff said. "Everybody says conditioning, conditioning, conditioning. It's not. It's intelligence, intelligence, intelligence. You outsmart the other guy. You out-hit him, you outperform him.

"He gave you keys. You're here, and there's number 32 [Jim Brown]. 'He's your man, Sam.' One-on-one. That's the way it was."

Landry convinced his players of the absolute certainty of his keys. If the offense set this way, this would happen. No question.

"He was going to be a great friend of mine, but I remember him chewing my ass off after I'd made great plays," said Frank Gifford, who went to the Pro Bowl as a defensive back while playing next to Landry his first years with the Giants. "If I hadn't made a great play, they would have scored, but I was in the wrong position.

"One time, we're looking at the film and he kept running it back and forth, back and forth, back and forth, and he kept saying 'Look, the D-back is playing here, where should you be?' And he kept going back and forth. I felt like just walking out. But I began to understand it, and the next few years you saw how great he did, and then he went on to Dallas and put the same kind of material into his defense and they dominated everybody."

Lombardi and Landry

If, in rare instances, something unforeseen happened, Landry would fall back on one of his favorite expressions: "You react like a football player."

Lombardi was different. He would go over and over his nuances until everybody understood. And if they didn't, he'd simplify them.

One of the first changes Lombardi made upon his arrival in '54 was the installation of a system of automatics—audibles as they're called today. His original trigger involved simple addition. If the quarterback called "41" in the huddle, a run up the middle, and he later recognized the defense was set up to stop it, he could call out "eight!" at the line. That made the new play "49," one of the end runs in the Giants' playbook.

Lombardi explained it over and over again until one player piped up, "Jesus Christ! Do I have to carry an adding machine with me?" Lombardi threw his chalk down and screamed, "You are without a doubt the dumbest bunch of supposed college graduates I've ever had the misfortune to be associated with in my life!"

With that, he stormed out of the room.

He didn't come back, either. The players sat there until Howell happened by, noticed the unattended blackboard, and dismissed the players for the day.

The next day, Lombardi returned with a brand-new plan.

"All right," he stated, "for you dummies who can't add or subtract, we're going to make it easier for you."

Lombardi then explained a system that used an indicator number. For instance, if the indicator was the snap count "2," the next number would be the new play. In other words, if the huddle call was "41 (middle run) on 2," the automatic call at the line would sound like "Two! Forty-nine! Hut, hut!"

The snap count remained Lombardi's preferred audible trigger throughout his coaching career.

He kept his terminology simple. Colors denoted formations, as in Brown for the fullback setting up directly behind the quarterback, and Red for split backs. The holes were numbered outward from center, odd numbers to the right, even to the left. The ballcarriers also received numbers; 2 for the left halfback, 3 for the fullback, and 4 for the right halfback. So a play such as "36" would be a handoff to the fullback designed to hit outside the left tackle.

Repetition was key—everywhere. Lombardi would stop practice to correct a player, or the entire unit, for failing to run plays correctly. No one was immune, be he Frank Gifford, Alex Webster, or any blocker. Webster, especially, repeated plenty of plays with Lombardi's voice reverberating through his ear holes; a game day monster, his practice habits left much to be desired. But Lombardi saved his harshest methods for a small-school end who, years after the Giants cut him, would make a Hall of Fame impact with the Jets.

"The first whipping boy we ever had was in '58," remembered Ray "Whitey" Walsh Jr., a teenage ball boy at training camp and son of the Giants' business manager, Ray Walsh Sr. "It was Don Maynard, who came out of Texas Western [now UTEP]. It must have been a very small program. He didn't know how to run patterns, he couldn't get lined up right. That used to drive Lombardi crazy, if you couldn't get lined up in the right spot. He'd always figure, you could adjust him from there, but if he couldn't even line up right, you can't do anything.

"And he couldn't get the right number of steps or yardage before he made his cut. At one point, Vinny takes Maynard by his hand and walks him through where he wanted him to go. 'Come down here, SIX YARDS!' And everybody's watching. The guy must have felt like a jerk. I don't think he was really dumb. He was just from a very small program and didn't know what all this big-time stuff was about. But I distinctly recall Vinny taking Maynard by his wrist and walked him right where he wanted him to go. Did the pattern. "SIX YARDS, MAKE A CUT!" I was embarrassed for the guy. I was only sixteen."

*   *   *

Lombardi and Landry each came to their methods long before they ever signed on with the Giants.

Landry developed his analytical nature while growing up as a shy kid trying to overcome a speech impediment in Mission, Texas, deep in the Rio Grande Valley near the Mexican border. Though always ambitious, he stayed much to himself until high school, where he blossomed into the class valedictorian and a member of the National Honor Society.

He wound up at the University of Texas, where he pursued a degree in industrial engineering with an eye toward entering the oil business. His distinguished hitch flying B-17 Flying Fortresses during World War II interrupted his education, but he returned after his discharge in 1946 to complete the final three years of his degree and playing career. In 1946, his only year under the legendary coach D. X. Bible, then in his final season at Texas, Landry was introduced to the tireless preparation and work ethic Bible touted that, with a little help from a beating at the hands of the Cleveland Browns, would become the cornerstones of his coaching philosophy. He met his wife, Alicia, during that time. But for the most part, he could best be described as a quiet loner. If a football player could ever be described as a bookworm, Landry was it.

His interest and training in industrial engineering was the tipoff to his personality, though. Taking classes at the University of Houston during the AAFC and NFL off-seasons, he earned a master's degree in the subject by 1952. By nature, engineering is an analytical field that deals not only in the need to build something, but how to build it. Through painstaking breakdown of a mountain of studies and statistics, the engineer anticipates how stresses such as wind, rain, even the ground upon which he builds, will affect his structure. And then he must give his structure the flexibility to move with and counteract the stresses. Sometimes, the structure neutralizes the stresses by working with them, rather than pushing against them.

At the same time, the engineer has to manage his workers to function as one.

Landry applied many of the same principles to football.

"I think my post-graduate training, which stressed coordinating people, helped me as a coach," Landry said. "My approach was to blend players together as a single unit to establish a strong, solid defense. Under my plan, we hold a position and don't try to force through a block when it's not going to work. That way, a player controls a specific area."

In other words, take the path of least resistance. Use leverage rather than strength. If a tackle angle-blocks the defensive end to the outside, throw the blocker outside rather than try to muscle him back inside. Know where the blocker is going in the first place, so you know how to react once the contact comes.

From his playing days into his coaching career, Landry watched hours upon hours of film, looking for the leverages, the angles, the tendencies. Intelligence and positioning, not brute strength, were the girders. Study, preparation, and analysis were the rivets that held it all together.

The films showed him that each offensive formation had a limited number of options. If the halfbacks were split behind the quarterback, a team might run a trap up the middle, go around the end, or run misdirection. Line up the fullback behind the quarterback with the halfback on the tight end side, and the fullback was more than likely to get the ball.

Once the defense knew the keys, it knew where the play was most likely going. A defender could then beat the offensive player to the spot and stop him.

Landry not only came up with keys, but he also became the first coach to chart frequencies. For instance, how many times would an opponent run off right tackle on second-and-short, or throw on third-and-5 or less?

"Frequencies was a key word with him," Huff said. "'From this formation, this is where they run.' He gave them a color. The split backfield was the Red formation. The fullback in his regular position and the halfback beside him was the Brown formation, after the Cleveland Browns. If they switched backs, it was a Green formation, or a Blue formation. You identified formations by color. First time it was ever done.

"Then you had frequencies where they ran the ball or threw the ball from those formations."

Landry wasn't the only one studying films. He made his players watch and chart, too. The smarter ones, like Robustelli and Huff, learned much from filling up the blank sheets Landry gave them with offensive plays and their defensive solutions. The object was to take the guesswork out of defense.

It took some getting used to, since Landry had turned the previously accepted philosophy of "see, chase, and tackle" on its head. He asked his players to sit back and read the formation, get into position based on the pre-snap information, and let the play come to them. Today's coaches might call it a read-and-react system, a much-tried defensive tactic that often fails because the personnel is either not smart enough or not disciplined enough to execute it. That's why Landry needed smart players like Robustelli and Tunnell to carry it out. (It's also why Tony Dungy's read-and-react Tampa-2 coverage needed heady folks like cornerback Ronde Barber, safety John Lynch, and linebacker Derrick Brooks to be successful.)

For doubters of Landry's system—and there were some players who needed convincing—Landry could just point to himself as proof that it worked. He was never fast, but his intense study habits enabled him to beat his receiver to the spot for either a jarring tackle or an interception. He'd intercepted 8 passes on his way to All-Pro designation in 1952 because of his individual film study, and was never more efficient than when he and Tunnell worked Steve Owen's Umbrella Defense to perfection in a 6–0 shutout of Otto Graham and the Browns in 1950. Benefiting from a pass rush that kept Graham on the run, Landry made one tackle after another on luminaries Mac Speedie and Dante Lavelli. Both were far faster and more agile than the defensive back. But he understood that, if played properly, Owen's 6-1-4 Umbrella alignment and its system of dropping defensive ends into passing lanes would run the Cleveland receivers into double coverage.

Landry taught his defensive backs the same things he taught himself. The running backs, not the quarterback, will tell you where the receiver is going. If the back was going outside in the flat, the receiver was going inside. It was all there on the endless film footage. It never varied. The receiver never ran a sideline route if the back flared into the flat; the end always went inside. And if the back went inside, the receiver always went outside. So if the back heads inside, jump the outside route. Anticipate it. You'll be right. If the back goes outside, be more aggressive inside. Expect it. You saw it on film, and the film never lies.

The intellectual flow between Landry and his players never ceased. When Landry rented a Stamford, Connecticut, home from one of Robustelli's friends in 1957, he and the defensive end drove to Yankee Stadium together for the next three seasons, discussing defense the entire trip. Robustelli would later say he never learned as much about strategy as he did during those drives. "No one on the Giants knew Landry and his system better than I did," Robustelli remembered.

During the 1956 season, Landry lived at the Concourse Plaza Hotel, down the street from Yankee Stadium, as did Huff and several other Giants players and their families. It wasn't unusual for Landry to call Huff's room and ask what his middle linebacker was doing.

"Watching television."

"Good. I'm glad you aren't doing anything. Why don't you come up to my room and look at some football films with me? There are some things I want to show you."

Thus did Huff begin his postgraduate work in offensive prevention as projected images flickered on Professor Landry's living room wall.

Lombardi was a far different creature, though just as effective a teacher. He, too, would study hours of film. But his educational and early professional background made him more of an old-style rote teacher.

The son of an immigrant butcher in Sheepshead Bay nearly became a priest. Upon completing the eighth grade in 1928, Lombardi enrolled in the Cathedral College of the Immaculate Conception, otherwise known as Cathedral Prep. There, he studied such subjects as Latin, Greek, and geometry. The disciplined repetition of the lessons, plus the never-varied routine of the Roman Catholic Mass he would attend every morning for the rest of his life, influenced his approach.

The words of St. Paul, particularly his first letter to the Corinthians, had a profound effect on Lombardi's life on and off the gridiron. It drove him to be the best coach he could be. It drove him to push his players to fulfill their potential. It made him great, though at the cost of making him deeply flawed in his single-mindedness.

"Do you not know that the runners in the stadium all run in the race, but only one wins the prize? *Run so as to win*," St. Paul wrote. "Every athlete exercises discipline in every way. They do it to win a perishable crown, but we an imperishable one. Thus I do not run aimlessly; I do not fight as if I were shadowboxing. No, I drive my body and train it, for fear that, after having preached to others, I myself should be disqualified."

Run so as to win. It was a message not of winning, and certainly not of the running game Lombardi would make his trademark, but of self-discipline. And Lombardi applied it to every facet of his life. Journalists would later ascribe the phrase "Winning isn't everything, it's the only thing" to Lombardi, but the coach always maintained he was misquoted. What he really said was "Winning isn't everything, but *making the effort to win* is."

The effort comes through discipline, in every walk of life. Discipline, like winning, comes through habit. And Lombardi was all about habit.

Mathematics is discipline. If A equals B and B equals C, then A equals C. The area of a circle equals 3.14 times the radius squared. It never changes. Repeat it. Commit it to memory and you'll have it forever.

Faith is discipline. *Kyrie eleison, Christe eleison.* Lord have mercy, Christ have mercy. Whether the priest muttered his Latin prayers into the altar or, as in Lombardi's post-Vatican II later years, recited them in English facing the parishioners, the liturgical structure never changed. The prayer Lombardi said while gripping the rosary beads he kept in his pocket and his car every day of his life never varied—"Hail Mary, full of grace . . . Pray for us sinners . . . Now and at the hour of our death, Amen." The words and their meanings remain constant. Repeat them. Memorize them and forever walk the path to salvation.

The same held true for plays, as grizzled lineman Jack Stroud learned in one of Lombardi's first chalkboard sessions in 1954. Frank Gifford recalled the coach's lesson to Stroud. "This is the 26-Power play. The 26-Power play. Do you have that, Jack? The first step is for the right guard to pull back. He must pull back, must pull back, must pull back. He must pull back to avoid the center, who will be moving to the off side. So the first step is for the right guard to pull back. Got that, Jack? The first step is back."

Practice it. Memorize it. And victory is yours.

Lombardi never did complete Cathedral Prep's six-year program that led to ordination. By 1932, he'd realized he did not have the priestly calling. But his dogmatic education continued, first at St. Francis Prep in Brooklyn, and then at Fordham University, where the good Jesuits were all about mental discipline.

The Fordham curriculum did not encourage independent thinking. Students took their lessons and then were tested, tested, and tested some more.

Graduation from Fordham did not bring an opportunity in the NFL for the undersized, 180-pound guard. So, after bouncing around semi-pro ball for two years, he got a job at St. Cecilia's High School in Englewood, New Jersey. Lombardi spent eight years there, teaching physics, chemistry, and Latin. He coached the line as a top football assistant under Fordham teammate Andy Palau, and served as head coach of the basketball team. He became the Saints' head football coach in 1942.

Lombardi brought to the Saints the new T-formation, which he taught himself from a pamphlet co-written by Bears coach George Halas and Stanford coach Clark Shaughnessy. He did it through repetition, as he would with all the other teams he coached throughout his career. The players' first exposure to the T came not during afternoon practice but in the morning, as Lombardi pulled a few boys out of class to run through the new plays in the gym.

He won big at St. Cecilia's—thirty-six games in a row and six New Jersey championships—and then he went off to Fordham to coach the freshman team. All the while Lombardi worked on refining the T, hammering into his players all the little details that made it unique. He spent hours every day breaking down the formation for his players—from the snap, to the number of inches and the number of steps that determined where each back lined up, to the timing. Over and over and over again. It was all technique, muscle memory learned movement by movement, like a Latin scholar translating Cicero word by meticulous word.

The method didn't change when Lombardi got to Army. A converted defensive lineman named Robert Haas remembered how Lombardi made him repeat a trap block ten times in a row, yelling at him the whole time, until he got the idea. Once he got it, there was a pat and a hug. "There was a love involved in the teaching," Haas recalled.

And so it continued, be it running through plays with cleats and pads or taking notes in the classroom. Lombardi was the Jesuit professor, breaking complex thoughts down to their simplest terms so everyone could understand them.

He kept his playbooks small, too. Lombardi wasn't a big believer in complex offenses. Executing a handful of plays perfectly was his major tenet. With the Giants, the Halfback Option and the Power Sweep became staples.

Just as well. Given his teaching style, if his playbook was any more expansive his players might never have gotten out of the meeting room in time to practice.

2

THE MASTER AND HIS DISCIPLES

IF IT WEREN'T for Paul Brown, there may never have been a Vince Lombardi or a Tom Landry. At least not a Lombardi or Landry who coached professional football franchises.

Like a mother raising children, Brown and his methods and strategies provided both men, in very different ways, their professional football compasses. He pointed them in directions neither had considered before, and the destinations those directions led them to influenced each man's head coaching career in profound ways.

Brown knew the league as well as he knew his own team, and he recognized the head coaches and assistants who had true, forward-thinking philosophies. In Landry and Lombardi, he saw the two men who were truly responsible for the Giants' success.

"There weren't so many assistant coaches back then," said Mike Brown, Paul's son and the president of the Cincinnati Bengals. "My father understood where the real horses were who were pulling the wagon. There was no doubt in his mind about that. It was just a fact.

"It's not that he disrespected Jim Lee Howell, but he had unusual regard for those two. That wasn't generally the case that he'd single out a single assistant coach. It's fair to say my father would have known and ranked in his own mind every assistant coach in the NFL. He just knew who they were and how they operated and what they did."

Like so many nurturing mothers, Brown had his favorite son. The great Cleveland coach forged a lifelong relationship with Lombardi.

After Lombardi took the Green Bay job in '59, they often visited with each other, ate dinner together, swapped stories and player information. There were many late-night phone calls between the two. It helped that they were not in the same division or, eventually, in the same league, as Brown went off to the AFL's upstart Bengals in 1968 after a five-year absence following his firing from the Browns after the 1962 season.

"[Lombardi] and my father both had a good sense of humor, which people don't attribute to them," Mike Brown said. "They think of them in other terms. They enjoyed telling stories like guys do. Stories about football. Stories about life. They were comfortable with that kind of exchange."

The two went beyond conversation, creating a sort of pipeline for castoff talent between Cleveland and Green Bay.

And when it came to having Lombardi's back in the face of unwanted publicity, Brown became his closest ally. One story has it that long-time *New York Post* reporter Leonard Schecter once wrote a profile of Lombardi for *Esquire* magazine that was so harsh—it compared his treatment of players to a general's ruthless use of troops in battle—it nearly drove the Packers' leader out of coaching. When Schecter showed up at Cleveland's training camp to do a story on Brown, the coach recognized him during a media conference.

"Are you the one that wrote that story on my friend, Vince Lombardi?" Brown thundered.

"Yes," said Schecter.

"Get out!"

Brown never became that close with Landry, however.

"In terms of personalities, Landry was a lot like Brown, though not quite as stiff and set in his ways," author Jack Cavanaugh said. "Landry was more flexible. Brown was a martinet. [Brown] was a tough coach and had a huge ego. Landry never had a big ego."

Aside from a few words before a game and their short, heated exchange during Landry's playing days, there is no record of a true personal friendship between Landry and Brown.

"He didn't have quite the relationship [with Landry] that he had with Vince," Mike Brown said. "I couldn't tell you why. I don't mean anything in the least critical of Landry. He was a great coach and an exceptional person, too.

"These were unusual people. They had a work ethic and carried themselves at a high level and achieved. They made the game better. All three of them made the NFL. These guys were big figures."

At the time of Lombardi's and Landry's apprenticeships with the Giants, though, no figure loomed bigger than Paul Brown. From his days coaching Washington High School and Ohio State, the legendary Great Lakes Naval Station squad during World War II, and the Cleveland Browns of the AAFC and the NFL, the imperious Brown became known as an innovator of strategy and preparation, a perfectionist for execution, and an aloof, hard driver of men.

He didn't respect many people. But if a coach did catch his eye, he could become that man's staunchest supporter. It happened that way with his own assistant, Blanton Collier, who Brown urged to come back from the University of Kentucky to succeed him when Art Modell fired Brown at the end of the 1962 season. It happened with Lombardi from afar, as Brown eventually went to bat for him in a big way when the Green Bay job came up after the 1958 season.

"My dad had a remarkable number of coaches who worked for him who went on to become NFL head coaches," Mike Brown said. "And he recommended people. People listened to him. Vince was one that, I know, he recommended with enthusiasm because he thought he deserved it. He thought he was good and had earned it."

From Brown, Lombardi learned strategy. From Brown, Landry learned the value of preparation.

*　　*　　*

Few coaches of the day had the mental wherewithal of Paul Brown. He was what one might call a gridiron intellectual. A former quarterback at Washington High School in Massillon, Ohio, he succeeded Harry Stuhldreher after Stuhldreher joined Jim Crowley, Elmer Layden, and Don Miller to form Notre Dame's vaunted "Four Horsemen" backfield. Brown went on to Ohio State, and then transferred to small-school Miami of Ohio when he realized his 145-pound frame wouldn't hold up to the rigors of the Big Ten Conference.

As a senior in 1930, Brown qualified for a Rhodes Scholarship, but he had married his high school sweetheart, Katie Kester, the year before and deemed it necessary to find a job. He started his coaching career at the Severn School in Maryland, eventually moving on after two years and a 16–1–1 record to his alma mater, Washington High. In nine years there, he posted an 80–8–2 mark, which included a thirty-five-game winning streak. From 1935 to 1940, Brown's teams were voted to six straight Ohio poll championships and outscored opponents 2,393–168 over that period. His 1940 team outscored its opponents 477–6.

It was at Massillon that Brown's innovative nature took root. Every aspect of Massillon's football program was planned, from how each section of practice would be conducted to classroom lectures and film work. He also made sure that a cadre of assistant coaches would install his system in Massillon's junior highs so the players would already know it when they reached high school.

Brown arrived at Ohio State in 1941 and won the Buckeyes' first national title in 1942 despite fielding a team of three seniors, sixteen juniors, and twenty-four sophomores because of graduation and military duty.

Uncle Sam caught up to Brown in 1944. Reclassified 1-A and assigned to the Great Lakes Naval Station just north of Chicago, he coached the Bluejackets and their collection of college and professional all-stars-turned-swabbies to a 15–5–2 mark against other service and college teams.

Among the collection of Great Lakes talent was one Marion Motley, who would later become a Hall of Fame fullback for Brown's Cleveland Browns and one of the first African-American players to compete in the All-America Football Conference.

Brown could have gone back to Ohio State after the war, but instead he decided to link up with the Cleveland franchise of the upstart AAFC. He was still in the Navy when he signed on as vice president, general manager, and head coach on February 8, 1945. The winner of a name-the-team poll by the Cleveland *Plain*

Dealer was the Browns, a tribute to the coach's well-established popularity around Ohio. Brown originally declined the honor, but then agreed to it when a local businessman claimed rights to the alternate choice, the Panthers. (The Cleveland Panthers had been the name of a failed football team from the 1920s.)

Once ensconced in Cleveland, Brown's genius clicked into full gear. He called all the shots, and that included picking the players. He was the first to quantify intelligence when scouting for the draft, something both Landry and Lombardi would later demand when drafting for their own teams. It was no coincidence, then, that Landry's Giants defense was one of the most intelligent units in the league.

"We wanted our players to be intelligent, fast, coachable, to have good size and a good character," said Brown, who became the first coach to use intelligence tests on prospective players. "In other words, be solid citizens and solid football players."

The most solid in Brown's cerebral world had to be the quarterback, the offensive linemen, and the linebackers. The quarterback needed the smarts because he had to control the offense. The guards, tackles, and center had to be quick-witted because of the split-second blocking adjustments they'd make upon the snap. And the linebackers had to have the brains to handle the most complex defensive positions on the field, which require a mixture of line play, sideline-to-sideline pursuit, and pass coverage.

Paul Brown's game stepped away from the sixty-minute rumbles of the old days and became one of speed as well as power. By the time a young fellow named Bill Walsh became Brown's offensive coordinator with the Cincinnati Bengals in 1968, Brown's methods had long since changed the game. And Walsh, moving on to Stanford and the San Francisco 49ers, eventually would evolve it further with the pass-oriented West Coast Offense, patterned after Brown's original concepts.

"It used to be more brute force on the opposition, a matter of trying to outdo one another," Browns fullback Ed Modzelewski said. "That was the old timers. It became much more finesse. They'd put oats in our water so you wouldn't drink, but Paul Brown was of a different theory."

Entirely different. Though Brown's offense would eventually feature arguably the greatest running back of all time in Jim Brown, he relied just as much on the passing game. Small wonder, then, that Brown signed Otto Graham as his quarterback. Known before the war as one of the brainiest college football players in the country, Graham had played tailback at Northwestern, where the school record he set for total career yards would stand until 1964.

But Graham's quick mind and strong arm led Brown to switch him to quarterback, a decision that proved wise as Graham became the greatest passer of his generation, throwing 174 touchdowns in a ten-year career and thrice leading the league. Additionally, he rushed for 44 touchdowns and scored two others on an interception and fumble for 220 total career scores.

Brown surrounded Graham with tremendous offensive talent, from fullback Motley to ends Dante Lavelli and Mac Speedie, and flanker-halfback Dub Jones. He protected Graham with the likes of Lou Groza and Mike McCormack, linemen whose 4.8 clockings in the 40-yard dash are still impressive by today's standards, where the average lineman runs in the low 5.0s.

Jones could run a 4.5. Graham could escape any jam. Lavelli and Speedie could beat just about any defensive back downfield.

Brown's philosophy resulted in a "wide open" offense, an engine that was as sleek as it was powerful. And it was never displayed to better effect than in the Browns 1955 NFL championship game win over the L.A. Rams. In Otto Graham's final game, Brown employed a revolutionary two-flanker offense to chew up a surprised defense starring future Giants defensive end Andy Robustelli, 38–14.

Brown sought out speed on defense as well. Bill Willis, Brown's fabled middle guard, had a sprinter's background (as did Motley and, later, Jim Brown).

"All players must be fast and quick," Brown said. "I was a self-styled 'speed freak.'"

Speed. Power. And most of all, precision.

"Cleveland always was a well-conditioned team, methodical and precise, and almost perfect in what they did," Robustelli said. "Play execution was their hallmark. They were never the toughest physical team, but being so precise and talented they didn't need to win on toughness."

Brown demanded excellence of his players both on and off the field. On the road, he made them wear business suits, a demand Lombardi would later mimic as he reversed the casual, anything-goes-but-winning culture of the Green Bay Packers.

The precision of his team's game day execution began on the practice field, where Brown dictated the smallest details, like the exact height he required players to raise their legs on leg-lifts during warm-ups. But he showed a human side, too, as when he drew heat from other players for letting Jim Brown cheat a few inches. "How could I criticize someone who had just carried the ball twenty or twenty-five times two days before and had taken such a terrible beating in helping us win because he didn't raise his legs six inches higher than anyone else?" Brown asked, bringing the debate to a dead halt.

He noticed everything. Even the earliest risers couldn't put one past Brown. Rams coach Joe Stydahar tried. Before the 1951 championship game against the Rams, Cleveland billeted at the Green Hotel in Pasadena and was practicing on a nearby open field when Brown noticed a couple of Rams scouts running reconnaissance for Stydahar. So Brown set his defense up in a six-man line and threw in a bunch of other twists to fill the scouts' notebooks.

It was all a ruse. Brown never used any of it in the game. The Rams eventually won 24–17 on Norm Van Brocklin's fourth quarter touchdown throw to Tom Fears, but it took them more than a half to sort out the real scheme.

*   *   *

Tom Landry's first encounter with Paul Brown wasn't a particularly pleasant one. But it was certainly educational, so much so that it caused Landry to rethink his whole philosophy of playing defense.

Landry was a rookie in 1949 with the old New York Yankees of the AAFC. The only reason he went with the Yankees instead of the Giants, who drafted him as an eighteenth-round "future" pick in 1947, was because the Yankees' offer of a $2,000 signing bonus and $7,500 base salary doubled what most established players in either league made. With graduate school tuition bills coming from the University of Houston, Landry went with the money.

He began the season as most rookies do, as a backup. But an injury in the secondary turned him into a starter just as the much-feared Browns came up on the schedule.

Otto Graham saw the kid, raw with talent but basically clueless as to the vagaries of the Browns' offense. And the pass master showed no mercy, challenging Landry with both Dante Lavelli and

Mac Speedie throughout the game. The two ends sliced and diced Landry, racking up more than 200 receiving yards between them.

Landry, duly chastened, swore then that such a humiliation would never occur again. Not to him.

"The primary lesson learned that day served as the very foundation of my philosophical approach to playing and coaching pro football," Landry said years later. "Any success I ever attained would require the utmost in preparation and knowledge. I couldn't wait and react to my opponent. I had to know what he was going to do before he did it."

Without even so much as shaking the great coach's hand, Landry had been given a life-altering introduction to Paul Brown's genius. For as unprepared as Landry was, that's how ready the Browns were to adjust a game plan to exploit an opponent's unexpected weakness.

Building upon the gospel of preparation his old Texas coach D. X. Bible espoused, Landry took his preparation level to new heights. He dedicated himself to film study, watching for hours as he noticed formations, tendencies, even little tells that would tip off his man's plans on any particular play.

The object was to beat his receiver to the spot, and then deliver such a jarring hit that said receiver would think twice about coming his way again.

"I had an acute hatred for receivers," Landry said. "If a guy caught a ball against me, I'd try to hit him so hard he wished he hadn't."

Landry learned his lessons well, and in 1950, his first year with the Giants, he helped shut down Graham and beat the Browns twice, 6–0 and 17–13, behind Steve Owen's revolutionary Umbrella Defense, before Cleveland produced an 8–3 win in the American Conference playoff.

Brown was busy learning his own lessons, however. After 1950, he added a quarterback draw to the mobile Graham's repertoire. That took advantage of the natural gaps that opened across the front as the Giants' defensive linemen and linebackers backpedaled into pass coverage.

That, in part, led Landry to create his coordinated defense. Accounting for all the gaps was key. Every man needed to work his responsibility. Two steps in the wrong direction, a single departure from an assigned gap in an attempt to make a big play for somebody else, could mean the difference between a tackle for loss and a big play for the offense.

But mere coordination—epitomized by Landry's eventual development of the 4-3 inside and 4-3 outside alignments that changed football—wasn't enough to stop the Browns. For that, Landry had to develop his imagination, too. He had to think along with Brown, a mighty challenge for even the best of them.

Brown soon started combating the growing popularity of zone coverage schemes by rolling Graham out of the pocket. That not only gave Graham time to find his speedy receivers downfield, but also added a run option.

Given the speed at which the Browns' offense operated, the more twists Brown installed, the dizzier it made defenses.

"That was a time we were riding high and we had great receivers: Lavelli, Speedie, Dub Jones," Mike Brown said. "If they were reincarnated today, believe me, they'd play for any team in the NFL . . . They were fast, they were good-sized guys. Smart and exceptional receivers.

"We did things throwing the ball that were just ahead of the times. So it was pass and trap and draws and screens. The theory was, if you want to rush us, fine, we'll screen, we'll draw, we'll trap. If you choose to lay back, we'll throw. Those teams were very successful."

So Landry had to evolve his theories of keys, tendencies, and individual responsibilities even further to account for situations that before were rarely considered viable.

He started thinking outside his own box.

"Coordinated defensive thinking didn't work against the Browns' great offense," Robustelli said. "Because the Browns were our chief rival in the conference, Landry had to develop his coordinated defense; we had to find a way to beat them before we could win any titles.

"Tom later said he had to match wits with Paul Brown, and in doing so, Brown forced him to become a better coach since Tom had to develop a system that neutralized everything Cleveland did so well."

Dick Nolan, a rookie defensive back in Landry's first year as player-coach in 1954, knew exactly what that was all about.

"We'd get in the defensive huddle, and Tom would call the defense," Nolan said. "He'd look over at me and say, 'Dick, if they put the flanker out in front of you, then you key the fullback and, if the fullback swings out, the flanker will run a down-and-in, so be ready.'

"He was usually right."

Brown and Landry had one other thing in common: their respect for the kicking game. Landry came by his naturally. As a player he was a great punter in addition to being an outstanding defensive back. But it was only later on, as Howell's assistant, that he immersed himself in the science of placekicking. As the Giants' only defensive assistant, he also took on responsibilities for the kicking game and thus became one of the league's first legitimate special teams coaches.

Brown came by his love of the kicking game as a function of his overall coaching personality. As he moved away from the rough-and-tumble past, he became one of the few coaches to realize that settling for a field goal on a stalled drive down the field was not unmanly—a prevailing sentiment among old-style coaches—but beneficial to team morale and the scoreboard. And Brown had one of the best placekickers ever—Lou "the Toe" Groza—to do his bidding.

Despite going undrafted coming out of Ohio State, Groza produced 1,608 points (including 264 field goals) in a twenty-one-year Hall of Fame career, all with the Browns. That stood as an all-time record until field goals became commonplace. But from 1950, Groza stood among a handful of kickers who tried as many as 20 field goals in a season, a testament to how Brown would gladly settle for three points than nothing. Groza led the league four straight seasons between 1950 and '53 in field goal attempts, compiling his all-time high of 33 in 1952. That was eight more than second-place kicker George Blanda of the Bears attempted that year. And it stood as a record until Baltimore's Steve Myrha attempted 39 in 1961.

By then, virtually every regular kicker in the league had attempts up in the 20s. But during the years Landry played and assisted, no more than half of the dozen teams sent out their kickers with such frequency. Still, it's no surprise that Landry's two main guys, Ben Agajanian and Pat Summerall, finished among the leaders in attempts while under his charge.

Groza, who was also an All-Pro tackle, rewarded Brown's faith on many occasions, but one in particular. His 16-yard field goal in the final seconds won Cleveland the 1950 championship over the Rams.

Groza's square-toed shoe became a regular sight on game day, and from 1950–55, so did the special tee and long tape he used to measure his steps into the sweet spot of the ball. The tee and tape vanished in '56, however, thanks to the passing of the Lou Groza Rule, which prohibited any artificial aid for kickers on field goal attempts.

By the time Summerall reached the Giants from the Chicago Cardinals in 1958, Landry was deep into the science.

"He approached kicking like an engineer," Summerall recalled of his first practice sessions with Landry. "When I worked with Landry during practice, if I missed in one direction, he would say, 'Well, this is what happened,' and he'd identify exactly how the movement of my kick had led the ball off course. He'd tell me, 'Keep your head down,' 'remember your straight follow through,' and 'lock your ankle,' which is hard to do.

"He'd tell me how far to stand away from the ball [a step and a half]."

The instruction didn't stop with Summerall, however. He would drill center Ray Wietecha, telling him how many revolutions the ball should make before it reached holder Charlie Conerly. And, of course, he'd keep an eye on Conerly to make sure he spun the laces out. Summerall said that in all the time he kicked with Conerly, he never saw the laces.

Quite simply, not a lot of coaches had that kind of knowledge in those days, or the deft holding ability of a Conerly. Summerall certainly had never encountered it as a Cardinal.

"You're not kidding I was lucky," Summerall said. "I was lucky in that I had the best holder in the business, too, Charlie Conerly. It was usually the quarterback on the Jim Lee Howell teams." Even as Landry left to start his head coaching career, he was still teaching Summerall.

"When he was going to leave and go to the Cowboys, he called me to his apartment and said, among other things, 'When you miss to the right, this is what you do wrong. And when you miss to the left, this is what you do wrong.'" Summerall said. "And he said 'Don't kick without supervision, without somebody who knows about your kicking, because you'll develop bad habits and that doesn't help anybody.' That was valuable."

Oh, about that Graham fellow. Landry made sure the quarterback got his for the shredding he handed that rookie defensive back. One game shortly thereafter, Landry found himself zeroing in on Graham, who had broken into the open field on a keeper. The collision was so loud, the whole stadium heard it.

So did Paul Brown. As Graham staggered off the field, Brown stepped off the sideline and yelled, "Cheap shot, Landry! Cheap shot."

Landry turned to the coach, very satisfied with himself. "You know better than that, Paul."

*　　*　　*

Though little direct evidence exists, it wouldn't be a stretch to say that Landry also noticed what was happening with opposing defenses, even before he officially became a coach. The NFL has always been a copycat league, and ideas spread and evolved as quickly in the 1950s as they do now. So it is quite likely that Landry noticed how Paul Brown used middle guard Bill Willis.

Willis was one of those rare specimens—not very big at 6-2, 210, but possessing sprinter's speed and a rather disagreeable disposition when placed on a football field. Paul Brown had coached the two-way lineman at Ohio State and deemed he was better suited for defense. Brown wasn't wrong, either. In his first pro scrimmage ever, Brown lined up his undrafted rookie in the middle of a five-man line. Willis blasted over the center four straight times and buried Otto Graham. Brown's assistants thought he was simply jumping offside, but film review convinced them all that Willis was just that fast.

Brown signed him to a contract that night.

Willis went on to be named All-League seven times in an eight-year career that stretched from 1946 to '53. His touchdown-saving tackle in 1950 preserved Cleveland's 8–3 conference playoff victory over the Giants. He was quick, and he was as sure a tackler as any in the NFL at the time. Eventually, Brown found another way to utilize his star's speed.

As teams began emphasizing the passing game, Brown started standing Willis up two yards behind scrimmage. From there, he might fall into coverage that much easier. But, as the air game became more complex, Brown started "shooting" his linebackers through the frontal gaps to drop the quarterback before the ball ever got in the air. Thus, the blitzing linebacker. And Willis was one of the first to do it regularly.

It worked, too. In the first dozen years of the Browns' existence, they finished first in the league in overall defense five times and second five times. Willis was a big part of the reason over the first eight years.

Landry advanced that same tactic a step further in his 4-3 defense by permanently planting Sam Huff there as a middle linebacker.

Huff may have been the NFL's first true middle linebacker, with others like Detroit's Joe Schmidt and Green Bay's Ray

Nitschke to follow. Some maintain that Chicago's Bill George was really the first true middle linebacker—and therefore the father of the 4-3—because he began dropping back in 1954 after noticing quarterbacks were dumping the ball over his head when he battled the center head-on. But because Brown used Willis as part of a formal strategy, Willis must be looked upon as the direct ancestor of the position. It was Brown's brainchild, and there is no reason to believe that Landry wasn't at least slightly influenced by Brown.

As part of his preparation, Landry asked questions, seemingly millions of them.

His classroom presence as a player became legendary, even before he started his unpaid career as Steve Owen's strategic interpreter. Once defensive tackle Dick Modzelewski got to the Giants in 1956, he immediately relayed some of Landry's characteristics to his brother Ed, then a Browns fullback.

"Most guys play ball and they know their position. But Dick said Tom Landry was so far ahead of everybody else," Ed Modzelewski said. "He reminded me of [future four-time Super Bowl-winning Steelers coach] Chuck Noll, a teammate of mine with the Browns. When we got in a meeting with Paul Brown, he wanted to know a little more than the average ballplayer.

"They were in-depth. They wanted to know about what this guy does, what that guy does, what's the reason for this, what's the reason for that. I knew Chuck would be different because he looked at football different, more in-depth. That's the same thing Dick would tell me about Landry.

"It was much more cerebral than it was before. Paul Brown was that way, too. He didn't want to leave the game on the field.

By the end of the week, we were only working fifty-five minutes on the field [in practice]. Tom Landry was that way, too."

*   *   *

As soon as Vince Lombardi left Army for Jim Lee Howell's Giants, he began breaking down every Giants game film from the previous two years. The 41-year-old assistant knew the professional game would be far different than the college game, but he never knew how different until he laid eyes upon the projected images of the Giants against the Cleveland Browns.

The gap in strategy was, quite simply, tremendous.

"The big point I realized was that whatever formation I used," Lombardi said, "I had to have a flanker-back. You had to have the threat of a pass. Everyone in the league was using flankers."

Brown's flanker was Dub Jones, and there were few examples of a finer one. In his eight seasons with the Browns, Jones became the ideal backfield complement to the hard-running Motley. He could run like a halfback, but also catch the ball from either the line or the backfield.

The so-called flanker back then was different than the flankers of today. The present-day flanker is generally the "Z" receiver, a pass-catcher who lines up off the line on the strong side, almost even with the quarterback. He is often found in the slot between a split end and a tackle, or as a third receiver in a three-receiver "bunch" formation opposite the "X" receiver, or split end.

(There are exceptions, of course, such as Washington's Chris Cooley, a modern-day "H-back" whose deeper backfield positioning makes him more of a throwback flanker.)

In Jones's case, he was more of a halfback who was asked to run between the tackles as well as catch passes out of the backfield. The threat he presented, along with the deep routes of traditional ends Dante Lavelli and Mac Speedie, made the Browns' passing game that much more effective.

Lombardi installed Frank Gifford as his halfback as soon as he took over in 1954. In tabbing Gifford, Lombardi not only grounded the future Hall of Famer in one spot, but also immediately added a pass-catching dimension to a graceful runner who could work both the inside and outside with equal ease.

Gifford was a natural choice in Lombardi's eyes, not just because of what he saw on film, but what he saw from the Army sideline during his assistantship under Red Blaik. The Cadets had played Gifford-led USC at Yankee Stadium in 1951, and Lombardi well remembered the halfback who ran all over his team for 138 yards on 26 carries in that 28–6 mud-fest.

Gifford also went 2-of-7 passing for 50 yards, and kicked four extra points in the game.

"Watching Gifford, I remembered that great day he had against us, not only as a running back but as a fine passer," Lombardi said. "Since the Giants ran from a T-formation and the halfback option is basically a single-wing play, I had to figure out how we could utilize Gifford's tailback talents."

Lombardi found a way to cash in on Gifford's arm, too, in the halfback option he installed immediately. Unlike Jones, who only threw three passes in his eight-years with Cleveland, Gifford was always an airborne threat. That by itself moved Lombardi's theories a step beyond Brown's.

Gifford didn't mind one bit. After former head coach Steve Owen bounced him between the offensive and defensive backfield his first two years in the league, Gifford found great relief in concentrating on just one side of the ball.

"Steve Owen didn't know how to use anyone," Gifford said. "All he believed in was defense, and he had a pretty good defense with Landry and this big defensive tackle we had [Ray Krouse]. We had pretty good guys, with me and Kyle Rote.

"We were so terrible in '53, I wasn't going to play anymore. I had a contract with Warner Bros. and I was making money. I was so tired of it. I wanted to go back and get my degree. I'd had enough of that. I didn't come out of the last five games. Played offense, defense, when Landry got hurt I had to punt. We just didn't have any players. We were terrible. We were getting beat up by everybody, and I said, 'Who the hell needs this?'"

The halfback option became Lombardi's pet "gadget" play, and he used it with great effectiveness. Gifford threw 35 passes, completing 15 for 538 yards and 10 touchdowns and 3 interceptions during the Lombardi era.

"Vince liked his halfbacks to do a lot of things," Gifford said.

Lombardi also tinkered with the positioning of his flanker. Most of the NFL at that time operated out of the popular T-formation without a formal tight end. Brown's "T" lined up Jones inside the strong-side end in passing situations. Lombardi often moved the split end in "tight" to the strong-side tackle, thus creating the forerunner of the tight end. The flanker lined up outside the end in what amounted to a three-receiver set.

The strategy eventually evolved into one with an outside rushing element that led to his famous Power Sweep, the basis of which came from watching Rams films from the early fifties. Though he installed it immediately into his playbook in 1954, the sweep didn't really take hold until the Giants lured Alex Webster out of the Canadian Football League in 1955. In Webster, he not only had a tough runner, but also a halfback-fullback type who reveled as much in laying out a defender as in catching a touchdown pass.

Lombardi's sweep actually started as a melding of the coach's T-formation philosophies developed under Blaik, his other great role model, and the A-formation he played at Fordham.

"I knew Vince wanted me because I fit into his T-formation," Gifford said. "It was basically the old single-wing. All we did was pull the guards on the sweep, all the things he did at Fordham. He just brought it up to date and put it in the T-formation. He was always ahead of everybody. We'd do it for a year, and then everybody would copy him. We had, at that point, the most innovative coach in all [of] football."

By the time Lombardi got to Green Bay, his sweep had evolved into offensive system unto itself. Not just about pulling guards and running to daylight, it involved seemingly hundreds of options at every position, each a coordinated reaction to what a defender might or might not do.

Legend has it that Lombardi once lectured about the guard's role in the sweep for eight hours—nonstop—at one of Cleveland assistant Blanton Collier's clinics. That's 480 minutes on just the guard, not the whole offense.

His notes indicate the kind of kind of precision he demanded in the sweep.

"As soon as he gets the ball from the quarterback, the halfback seats the ball and comes under control with a light belly or dip so he can key the block of the tight end on the linebacker or whoever is playing over the tight end," Lombardi wrote in the posthumously published *Lombardi on Football.* "The halfback must now make a decision on whether to go inside or outside of the tight end block.

"If the back comes across the line too fast, he will be unable to cut back inside—he'll cut off the guards or beat the guards out to their blocking areas. If the linebacker is driven outside, the halfback cuts inside. If the linebacker moves to the inside, the back continues outside of the tight end block."

The play, Lombardi continued, opens two rushing holes, but possibly more because of the halfback's hesitation before starting his outside journey.

"If the defensive end makes a violent move outside, the belly allows the halfback to push off the outside foot and shoot inside the defensive end," Lombardi wrote.

With such obsession with detail, is it any wonder that Lombardi and Brown would grow close despite coaching on opposite sidelines of the era's most heated rivalry?

But Lombardi could actually do Brown one better in the teaching department. His earthy methods paid off in Green Bay where Fuzzy Thurston, pulling right from his left guard spot, had a rough time blocking the correct defender on one of the sweep calls.

"Fuzzy," Lombardi said, "if you see a helmet, hit it. If you see an ass, make a left!"

Thurston said he never missed that block again.

Brown and Lombardi shared enough personality traits to gravitate toward each other. Though Lombardi's chalkboard style might have been less professorial than Brown's, his overall teaching style was similar.

Lombardi insisted that his players write down everything he said, from broad strokes to minor points. So did Brown.

Hall of Fame coach Don Shula, a Browns defensive back in 1951 and '52, said Brown's insistence on his players writing down his every word, and his ability to demonstrate how to run those plays on the practice field, influenced him more than any other coach.

And then there was the drilling and testing, testing and drilling.

"You learned by listening, writing, practicing, and doing," Shula said. "That pretty much was the basis of my philosophy when I went into coaching."

The same echoes come from Lombardi's players.

"I can tell you any defense they play and how to block it, still," said Lombardi's former Green Bay tight end Ron Kramer years after his playing days had ended. "That's mostly due to Vince Lombardi's thoroughness."

3

SUMMER 1956—SEEDS OF SOMETHING SPECIAL

THE 1954 AND '55 seasons had gone well enough. The Giants were winning again, going 7–5 in Howell's maiden voyage and 6–5–1 in 1955. But they were more building years for Lombardi and Landry than anything else, an opportunity to put new offensive and defensive philosophies to work and add some missing components.

The clock was ticking, though. The Giants had not attended a league championship game since a 24–14 loss to the Bears in 1946, and by the summer of 1956, the franchise had grown restless. Even though Jim Lee Howell's new two-year contract demonstrated the Maras' faith that they had the right man for the job, nine seasons without a postseason appearance made the hunger gnaw that much more.

But there was major change in the air as training camp opened at St. Michael's College in Winooski, Vermont. The Giants had compiled the league's best record over the final seven games of

'55, a 5–1–1 run that included a 35–35 tie with eventual champion Cleveland. This sparked expectations for the upcoming season, and even the team's matinee idol running back decided to give it another shot after spending the offseason grappling with thoughts of retirement.

Frank Gifford had been used and abused by Steve Owen, and his first two years under Lombardi's command hadn't totally convinced him that the offensive assistant's collegiate theories particularly jibed with the pro game. But '54 and '55 did show him that good things were possible. Especially the way the '55 season ended.

"All of a sudden, everyone felt good about the way things were going," Gifford said. "I think we got that more from Lombardi than anybody. We'd had some good games in '55. We'd tied Cleveland. And we'd played good in Detroit, and they had Doak Walker and Bobby Layne. That's when we came together. Detroit was the defending [Western Conference] champions and they had some great players, and we beat them in Detroit. I remember that because I bought a Pontiac there and drove it to California. Saved $1,000. I needed it."

Detroit was experiencing a down year and would finish at the bottom of the conference at 3–9. But still, beating them was an encouraging sign for the Giants.

"I don't know if I'd have played anymore if I hadn't felt so good about that year," Gifford said. "I'd done a pilot for a TV series, and I'd worked in a lot of movies. I'd worked my way around that world. Financially, it was more beneficial for me than playing football. So even then, I was thinking about forgetting it. Wellington Mara really talked me into coming back, and I'm glad I did because the next year we really turned the whole thing around."

If a handicapper would have gauged the Giants' progress at the end of '55 in terms of a horserace, he'd have put Lombardi's offense ahead of Landry's defense by a length. The Giants were running a wide-open offense, and it manifested itself with 15 plays of 40 yards or more in 1955. The offense averaged better than 25 points per game in those final seven contests.

The defense lagged behind that year, allowing a respectable though unspectacular 223 points. Landry used his new 4-3 inside-outside alignment more and more, but he remained in search of that standout middle linebacker to really make it work. Meanwhile, he also spent time grooming defensive back Jimmy Patton to take his place in the secondary. The tutoring would produce a truly wonderful successor to Landry. But at the time Landry transitioned from player-coach in '55 to fulltime assistant in '56, the Giants went as Lombardi's unit went.

History would deem this all very fitting, for Landry would forever find himself chasing Lombardi. Vince was technically the first assistant Howell hired. His unit was the furthest ahead in two years of production. He'd be the first to leave. And then, as a head coach, he'd be the first to win a championship and, once the Super Bowl came into existence, the first to win that game, too.

The Hall of Fame? Lombardi beat Landry to Canton, too. By nineteen years.

But Landry and Lombardi were still cutting their professional coaching teeth when the team headed north to Winooski Park, following two years at Willamette University in Salem, Oregon. The Giants trained far from their New York base in those days simply because the Polo Grounds and, starting in 1956, Yankee Stadium, were occupied by the baseball Giants and Yankees. The football Giants would spend the entirety of their six-game exhibition season on the road, and then play their first three regular-season games on enemy turf while the baseball season wound down.

These extended road segments were old hat to the players and coaches, so little fuss was made about them. But there was something about this first camp at St. Michael's College that brought immediate optimism—Tom Landry's defense had finally arrived.

Even before the first whistle of training camp blew, a glance at the list of defensive talent gave rise to unbridled expectations.

"I'm sitting in the stands, [and] I see this beautiful blonde woman walking by," said newly arrived Dick Modzelewski. "It's Ann Mara. We're talking, and I said, 'I think this year we're gonna wind up winning the whole thing.' I had that feeling because I'd been traded to a good ball club and a good organization. It wasn't even the first practice. Why I said that, I have no idea."

Perhaps it was because he'd seen just how busy Ann's husband had been the past two years. Wellington Mara had spent the '55 and '56 off-seasons picking up some missing pieces, mostly on the defensive side. As Howell had said several times the first two years, he always knew the Giants could score. The question was whether they could stop someone at a key moment. Clearly, the defense needed further help to make it one that, this season, would draw never-before-heard cheers of "Dee-Fense! Dee-Fense!" and "Huff-Huff-Huff-Huff!" from the growing Yankee Stadium crowds.

Indeed, Howell rarely worried about the offense at this point. He was an offensive guy, to the extent where he now drew the opposite criticisms the media had leveled against his coach and predecessor, Owen, for being too defensive-minded.

Slim Jim may unwittingly have promoted their description of him as knotted to the offense's apron through a 1954 sideline conversation with Lombardi that hit the newspaper columns. While watching the Packers abuse Landry's defense with a huge passing attack in the final preseason game, Lombardi moaned to Howell, "This is awful. We gotta stop this somehow."

"What do you suggest?" was Howell's simple response.

The Giants wound up winning 38–27 to set up a 6–2 start. If not for injuries to Gifford and receiver Kyle Rote in the ninth game on the same play—when the running back's knee collided with Rote's head—the Giants might have gone all the way that year. Instead, they lost Gifford for the season with a knee injury and Rote for two weeks with a concussion. With basically their entire offense gone, the Giants dropped three of the last four games.

Still, the offense averaged 28 points in those first six victories, a huge improvement over the previous year's league-low production of 179 points. Howell, according to *New York Times* columnist Arthur Daley, had become the Admiral David Farragut of the NFL—"Damn the torpedoes! Full speed ahead!" Where Howell's defense-minded predecessor had gone on record as saying he'd rather win a game 3–0 than lose 38–36, Howell seemed all about scoring, which put him directly in Lombardi's corner.

That changed in 1956. By the time camp opened, the Giants' thirty-three-man roster had turned over from the year before to include ten new players, with many dotting the defense. The addition of Andy Robustelli, Sam Huff, Jim Katcavage, and Modzelewski made for an ideal situation for Landry; together they formed the most physically gifted set of individuals in the NFL, guided by what had quickly become the league's most creative defensive mind.

The great influx of talent began with the 1955 draft, when defensive tackle Roosevelt Grier arrived in the third round from Penn

State. He enjoyed a solid rookie season, though his teammates and coaches had to tolerate an exuberance that caused him to overrun the occasional play. But of greater concern were his apparent deficiencies in overall motivation and self-discipline. Grier, who in later years would become an ordained minister, a jazz musician, and would venture boldly into the less-than-macho art of needlepoint, reported to Winooski Park at nearly 300 pounds, far from the 275 the coaches had dictated. This was an era where even one of the biggest, meanest men in the league, such as Baltimore's Big Daddy Lipscomb, barely pushed the game day dial to 300.

Grier was up there, though. And as far as head trainer Sid Moret was concerned, he was in the right place to be overweight.

"We're lucky we're in Vermont," Moret was heard to say one day. "We can go to the border and weigh him on the truck scales."

The 1955 draft also brought Landry's on-field successor, Patton, destined to become one of the great defensive backs in Giants history. Fast and smart, Jimmy Patton would tie Otto Schnellbacher's franchise record with 11 interceptions in 1958, a mark which stands to this day.

The 1956 draft brought Landry's middle linebacker, Huff, and defensive end Katcavage, in the third and fourth rounds, respectively. And trades in April and July 1956 brought defensive tackle Modzelewski and the real brains of Landry's entire outfit, Robustelli.

Drafter Wellington Mara hadn't exactly ignored the offense, either. Fullback Mel Triplett came in the fifth round in 1955, and Mara enticed running back Alex Webster to make his way down from the Canadian Football League that same season.

But outside of those two, Lombardi simply used the resources of his first two years to create a powerhouse offense.

Frank Gifford, now a one-way player and occasional kicker, had come via the first round of the 1952 draft. With Triplett and Webster joining Gifford and Eddie Price, who led the '54 Giants in all-purpose yards with 555 rushing and 352 receiving, Lombardi now had two interchangeable, fresh backfields to keep relentless pressure on defenses.

He had moved linebacker Ray Wietecha to center to add more blocking to a line already benefiting from a mobile left tackle in Roosevelt Brown, a twenty-seventh-round gem plucked out of Morgan State in 1953. Brown was fast, athletic, and bruising, just the kind of player Lombardi needed to pave the way for his backfield. And with Wietecha's revolutionary no-look snap—he is believed to be the first player to perform it—eliminated the need to move his head from between his legs before getting into a blocking position and gave Lombardi a quicker line off the snap.

The Giants had gotten Kyle Rote in the first round in 1951 by sheer luck. The draft in those days was done as it is today, in ascending order according to record, with the worst selecting first. But there was also a so-called "bonus pick." Each team pulled a piece of paper out of a bag for a shot at the privilege of having the very first pick in the draft, regardless of finish. Jack or Wellington Mara usually put their hands in the bag and never won. So, as a change of pace, Wellington suggested Steve Owen do the picking. Sure enough, Owen plucked the lucky ticket, and the Giants fulfilled the pundits' collective prophesy that Rote, Heisman Trophy runner-up to Ohio State's junior halfback Vic Janowicz, would go as the top overall pick.

The SMU star had arrived with the Giants as a back. Bad knees had turned those duties into a real struggle, so much so that trainer John Johnson often had to strap up both knees in order for Rote to make it to the field. "You'd wonder how he could run at all," said Johnson.

But by 1954, he had turned into an end, not by Lombardi's doing, but by Landry's. "I'd run patterns against Tom in practice from my position which, basically, was a halfback split out wide," Rote said. "I suppose I'd run pretty good patterns and [caught] the ball fairly well, so one day in practice Tom stopped me."

"Hey," Landry said, "why don't you try it at end? I think you'd do a good job there."

It turned out to be a fateful suggestion, as Rote became one of the pre-eminent ends of the era. Howell called him "the most spectacular football player in the country" during the '56 season. "He can run and catch passes, and nobody can cut like him."

Eagles coach Hugh Devore was just as effusive the week before their regular-season matchup that year, calling Rote "another Crazylegs Hirsch."

No such praise would have come his way if the astute Landry hadn't made his suggestion.

"Tom knew I couldn't run out of the backfield anymore because of my knees," Rote said. "I just couldn't do it. When I moved to end, it was the biggest break of my football career."

Playing at end, Rote's knees no longer endured the pounding of a back running between the tackles. He could just run straight ahead and make the occasional cut. Even at that, he'd come out heavily taped, and the trainers had to work extra hard to keep him going.

Charlie Conerly's career was already well under way by the time Lombardi came on the scene. The thrower from Ole Miss—later to become cigarette advertising's first Marlboro Man despite the fact that he'd never ridden a horse before—had established himself as an elite passer under Owen since 1948. Never quite as flashy as Bob Waterfield or Norm Van Brocklin in Los Angeles, never as efficient as Otto Graham in Cleveland, and certainly never as mobile as, say, Washington's tiny Eddie LeBaron, Conerly simply went about his business in a low-key manner that befit his Southern humility. His career had had plenty of ups and downs. At one point, he incurred one of the many jeerings he took at the Polo Grounds as he played through a shoulder separation. When he finally apprised Owen of the injury, the coach nearly jumped out of his trousers.

"Why didn't you tell me?" Owen asked.

"Why bother?" Conerly replied. "I was the only quarterback you had. The others were injured, and I figured I was better'n none at all."

Conerly had plenty of bad periods as Owen's offense sank deeper into the morass, and the fans let him hear it over and over again. At times, he might have been the most disliked athlete in New York, though he rarely departed from his friendly, though quiet, demeanor.

Of anyone on the offense, however, Conerly may have been the most resistant to Lombardi's theories, especially the ones that combined the quarterback and the concept of running.

"Vince had put an option series and a belly series in the play-book," Gifford recalled. "We'd come off the field during an exhibition game that first year and Vince would ask, 'Why isn't Charlie running the option?' And somebody would say, 'I don't think Charlie likes it.'

"We knew it might have worked at Army, but not in the NFL because guys like [Bears end] Ed Sprinkle, [Eagles end] Norm Willey, and [Eagles linebacker] Tom Scott didn't just hit the quarterback, they demolished him. Charlie didn't want to be demolished, and Vince gradually got the idea."

Lombardi received one other major piece for his program in 1955.

Webster, a bruising fullback, had been playing in the Canadian Football League since 1953. In those days, it wasn't just NFL castoffs who made their way to Canada, but talented players, too. The CFL, in fact, had quite a little war going with their neighbor owners as it signed young roster-worthy players away from the NFL. Paul Brown had lost his great receiver, Mac Speedie, to the Saskatchewan Roughriders in 1953. Webster, a New Jersey native drafted by the Redskins the same year Speedie left, signed with the Montreal Alouettes.

Seeing that Eddie Price was about at the end, and dissatisfied with his blocking anyway, Wellington Mara figured he could use another running back. So he looked north, said, "Let's stop the nonsense," and lured Big Red to the Giants. Through 1964, the 6-3, 220-pound Webster muscled his way to 4,638 rushing yards and 39 rushing touchdowns, both of which still rank fourth on the Giants' all-time list.

* * *

Lombardi had the total package. Running, passing, blocking. And by 1956, he'd have added one more weapon, a bit of strategy he carried the rest of his career—the Power Sweep. He'd begun perfecting it as the '55 season wound down.

"What a difference it made for us at the end of the 1955 season," Howell crowed to reporters.

Lombardi had taken components of the T-formation and the Giants' old A-formation and added a double-team blocking element to it. Two running backs, usually Webster and Gifford, would line up split directly behind the quarterback, with one of them taking the direct snap from center. The guards would pull out to whichever side the play was called, with fullback Triplett leading the ball carrier around end. The end and tackle to the play side would double-team the defensive end, and the two guards would gang up on the outside linebacker.

Rather than run to a particular hole, Gifford or Webster would look for any opening. "Run to daylight" would become a Lombardi mantra. Long before Paul Hornung and Jim Taylor ran it to championships in Green Bay, Gifford and Webster became the league's premier backfield combo because of it in 1956. Factoring in fullback Mel Triplett, that trio gained 2,028 ground yards that season.

Moreover, it became the ultimate hallmark of a coach who demanded teamwork over individual talents. If Gifford got out ahead of his blockers, the Power Sweep would not work. If the guards didn't hustle enough, a linebacker could shake a one-on-one block and trip up the running back.

The Power Sweep combined the qualities of fellowship, camaraderie, and brain power Lombardi learned in his Seven Blocks days. He had taken two old-fashioned offenses to create one modern idea. Lombardi loved it. It was the embodiment of his life principles put onto the gridiron. You had to be selfless to run the Power Sweep, Lombardi reasoned. You had to think to make it work. And when it worked, it was a thing of beauty. Multiple holes for the halfback to run through, all created by the halfback's hesitation that allowed him to read the tight end's block on the linebacker and the pulling guards' blocks up front. But come across the line too fast and it all went up in smoke, the halfback either outrunning the guards, thereby encountering some angry defensive linemen, or working up too much momentum to allow for an inside cut if the defensive end makes a decisive move outside.

Gifford became a master of that hesitation or, as Lombardi termed it, the belly.

"I've been fortunate to coach a couple of great all-around backs who made the sweep their personal play, Paul Hornung and Frank Gifford," Lombardi said. "Though neither had that blinding speed, they both were quick, intelligent runners who could control their running so that they used their blockers and got every possible yard out of each play."

*   *   *

As if pre-ordered by mail, Landry's defense arrived at the same time. More accurately, the missing link showed up.

The 4-3 couldn't really work without a middle linebacker who not only went straight ahead into the hole, but who had the speed to pursue ball-carriers sideline to sideline, too. Ray Beck had done an acceptable job switching between middle guard and middle linebacker, but he got hurt in an exhibition game.

Luckily, Landry had noticed this baby-faced, third-round draft pick sitting over on the offensive line. Robert Lee "Sam" Huff had been a two-way lineman for West Virginia, and a pretty good one at that. Though he always was more comfortable on the defensive front, the Giants were trying to make the 235-pounder into an undersized guard, with only limited success.

"That was okay. I could play it," Huff said. "But they could run over you. I had to do everything I could to get the job done—clutch, hit a guy in the chinstrap, scratch."

Landry liked the kid's mobility and his mind. A coal miner's son trying to avoid life underground, Huff was physically and mentally tough, qualities that became apparent during a senior year matchup with Syracuse, when one Jim Brown ran over the defensive tackle and knocked him out. Huff woke up moments later to a broken nose and four shattered teeth, but that didn't stop him from re-entering the game.

Huff's mean streak also attracted Landry, but not as much as his excellence in following directions.

So they talked.

"Sam, have you ever thought about playing linebacker?" Landry asked.

"I could play wherever you want me."

"I'd like to see what you can do at linebacker."

"Fine. I'm a rookie. I'm trying to stay alive."

With that exchange, a sort of evolutionary moment happened that would change the Giants' defensive look forever. Huff crossed scrimmage and, like Cro-Magnon Man morphing into Homo Erectus, rose from his three-point stance and stood up behind the defensive line. The whole world opened before him.

Cue the heavenly chorus.

"So now, I can see everything," Huff remembered years later. "I have terrific peripheral vision, even to this day. So now I can see everything, and boy, I made tackle upon tackle. It was the best move for me in my life. This was so much easier because I was standing up and could see everything. I could see the whole field and react to it."

In an odd way, Lombardi could claim as much a part of Huff's defensive success as Landry, for it was the offensive assistant who kept Huff in camp in the first place. Frustrated by his difficulties with the pro game at guard and tired of the daily verbal goings-over Howell inflicted on him, Huff, along with fifth-round punter Don Chandler, had had enough two weeks into camp. One account indicated that Huff had overheard line coach Ed Kolman telling another assistant that Huff was "a step too slow for offensive guard" and, at 235 pounds, "too light to play defense." Part angry, part defeated, and part homesick, Huff and Chandler went to Howell's room one night, playbooks in hand. Howell was out, but his roommate, Lombardi, was there.

The ensuing discussion did not go well for either player.

"He called us every name in the book," Huff said. Hearing the commotion, Kolman came into the room and promised Huff he'd get Howell off his back, a promise he wound up keeping. But even that wasn't convincing enough. The two players eventually decided to head for the airport, only to have Lombardi head them off.

"Now hold on!" Lombardi screamed. "You may not make this club, Chandler, but you're sure as hell not quitting on me now! And neither are you, Huff, in case you've got any ideas of running out. We've got two weeks invested in you. Now get the hell back to St. Michael's and be at practice tomorrow morning!"

Lombardi did them both a favor. Chandler went on to play a decade and became Lombardi's star placekicker and punter with Green Bay's championship teams. And Huff? The move across the line would start him on a Hall of Fame career and cement his name among the most violent of middle linebackers ever to play the game. He would soon acquire a taste for quarterbacks that never left him. "You rap that quarterback every chance you get," Huff said in a 1959 cover story in *Time* magazine. "He's the brains of the outfit. If you knock him out clean and hard on the first play of the game, that's an accomplishment. For that matter, we try to hurt everybody. We hit each other as hard as we can. This is a man's game."

If Huff became Landry's violence, Andy Robustelli became his on-field conscience. Robustelli had already forged a career as a standout defensive end with the Rams when Wellington Mara traded a first-round pick for him on July 27, shortly after training camp began. Ironically, the Rams turned that pick into end Del Shofner, who would come to the Giants in 1961 and post three consecutive seasons of at least 1,100 receiving yards.

Robustelli had scored 6 touchdowns for the Rams from the time they drafted him in the nineteenth round out of tiny Arnold College (now the University of Bridgeport) in 1951. He had scored one by returning a blocked punt 51 yards against the Packers. But his most memorable may have been the interception off 49er and future Giants teammate Y. A. Tittle on November 6, 1955, because it put the Rams in the lead in an eventual 27–14 victory. Robustelli had broken in for a clear shot at Tittle, but then changed direction as he sniffed out a screen pass. He plucked it out of the air and returned it 10 yards for the touchdown.

Had Robustelli been any less than a devoutly religious family man, the Giants never would have had a shot at him in the first place. What team would willingly part with an economical—at $7,000 per year—All-Pro defensive end who regularly put quarterbacks on their rear end and caused a slew of fumbles and blocked punts? Apparently, the Rams would, all over a couple of lost days of training camp the experienced Robustelli didn't need anyway.

Robustelli's wife, Jeanne, was expecting the couple's fourth child in late July and Robustelli insisted on staying for the birth in Stamford, Connecticut, where his home and sporting goods business were located. He had called Rams coach Sid Gillman to ask if he could report after Jeanne returned from the hospital.

Gillman, who players never confused with Mr. Warmth, found the sentiment less than touching.

"I've got a team to worry about, not your family," Gillman said.

"Well," said Robustelli, "I've got some kids to worry about, and I've got to do what's right for me. And what the hell, it's only a couple of days."

"I don't care if it's a couple of days or not," Gillman said. "You get your ass out here."

Robustelli held his ground.

"Sid, I'll be out there as soon as my home situation is settled."

With that, Gillman slammed down the phone. Several days later, as he packed for Los Angeles, Robustelli's phone rang. It was Wellington Mara at the other end.

"I've been talking to the Rams about you and they're willing to trade you," Mara said. "I know you're 30 years old, but do you think you could play two or three more years? If so, we'd certainly love to have you play for us."

Robustelli was shaken at first, as he never had any qualms about playing in L.A. He liked his teammates, and aside from the recent issue, the organization had treated him well. But he soon realized that coming home to the East Coast would benefit everybody, especially a family that would eventually grow to nine children.

He told Mara to make the deal.

Mara preserved a Hall of Fame career in the making. Closer now to hearth and home, Robustelli stayed with the Giants for nine years until his retirement after the '64 season, playing in six championship games. For a player who wasn't particularly big at 6-1, 230, not particularly fast, and far from elegant on the field, Robustelli made the most of his physical abilities from day 1.

"When you analyze Andy Robustelli on a piecemeal basis, there's little about him that suggests a great defensive end," Landry said. "He seems lacking in size, speed, and other traits. But as soon as you put them together, you have the best there is."

Robustelli's intellect put him above the rest, a fact Landry quickly recognized. As Landry remained the only coach on the defensive side of the ball—Lombardi, Ken Kavanaugh, and Ed Kolman coached the overall offense, ends, and offensive line, respectively—he used Robustelli as an unofficial player-coach. Robustelli would work his defensive linemates during practice, as per Landry's instructions, while Landry busied himself with the linebackers and defensive backs.

Not that Robustelli took to Landry's system immediately. It was quite a change for him coming from the free-wheeling ways of the Rams.

"When I was with Los Angeles, the Rams used a very active type defense, one where they would just turn you loose," Robustelli said. "When I got to New York, I didn't know what was happening. Landry had this methodical defensive scheme in which you read the offense and used techniques. It was completely coordinated and everybody had a job.

"I didn't understand what was happening at first, but Tom would just say, 'Do it.' Do this or that in a certain situation.

Then I did understand the defense, and it was amazing. [I'd see the play] so far ahead of its time that it was incredible."

Robustelli also took charge of lighting the motivational fire under Grier and anyone else who appeared lax in preparation. He was fiercely proud of his unit and demanded it outshine the offense, be it in practice, scrimmages, or games.

Defensive tackle Dick Modzelewski came before Robustelli's arrival. On April 27, just four days after the Detroit Lions worked a trade with Pittsburgh for the bulky tackle, the Giants sent tackle Ray Krouse to Detroit for Modzelewski.

In Little Mo—not so little, actually, at 6 feet, 260 pounds—the Giants had a player in the middle who could not only occupy blockers to keep them off Huff, but also rush the passer. And he was tough.

"I remember a game in '56 when Mo got stepped on," Huff said. "Blood's shooting out of his hand and he comes up to me in the huddle and says, 'Call timeout! Call timeout!' And I said, 'I'm not calling timeout. The offense needs it. It's third down. Just run the play the best you can and we'll get you off the field.'

"I squeezed his four fingers together and he goes out there and makes the tackle and gets off the field. Tough guy."

Huff may have offered a sanitized version of the event, however.

"We're playing the Browns and my fingers split and blood's coming out between my fingers," Modzelewski said. "I get back to the huddle and say, 'Huff, look at my damned hand. It's bleeding like hell.' And he turned around and said, 'Here, stick it up my ass, then you'll play better.' We laughed like hell. At halftime, they stitched it up and away we'd go."

Former trainer John Johnson called Modzelewski "a tough son-of-a-gun" who you never had to wind up to get ready to play. "Guys like him never wanted surgery, either, because in those days it could end their careers."

For Modzelewski, coming to the Giants after a 4–8 year under Walt Kiesling in Pittsburgh was a blessing. Training camp under the Howell-Lombardi-Landry triumvirate was tough, but it wasn't inhuman. Considering where Modzelewski had just come from, he was just happy to get fresh water during breaks instead of the repulsive oats-and-water concoction the Steelers offered to dissuade their players from drinking.

And once the season started, the hitting stopped. Most of the Giants' in-season practices were conducted in baseball cap and sweats.

"I was happy because the situation at the Steelers was terrible," Modzelewski said. "We had a coach, Walt Kiesling—we scrimmaged how many days? Unbelievable. The guy killed us. We had a twelve-game schedule and we won the first four games and lost eight in a row. People cheered us for four games and booed us for eight, and it was terrible. He beat the hell out of us.

"Then, when I got traded to New York, and working at Yankee Stadium, my God, I thought I was in heaven. Absolutely heaven."

Katcavage completed Landry's list of newcomers, and the defensive coach could again thank Lombardi for the assist. Lombardi had scouted the 6-foot-3, 230-pound Katcavage at Dayton on the urgings of the Flyers' head coach Hugh Devore, who shortly thereafter left to take over the Eagles head coaching job. Lombardi took close note of the former basketball player over several games, and came back to Howell and Landry with rave reviews.

"Katcavage is real fast with good moves and the kind of defensive end that a quarterback hates to know is coming his way," Lombardi said.

The Giants drafted him in the fourth round of 1956, right between Huff and Chandler.

Others key components were already there. Em Tunnell, one of the greatest interceptors in history, had been working the Giants' defensive backfield since the undrafted Iowa star walked into Tim Mara's office in 1948 and asked for a tryout. The soft-spoken Tunnell, the Giants' first African American player, quietly endured the racism he encountered in cities like Baltimore, instead focusing his rage on the field. He would end his career with a team-record 74 interceptions (second-most in NFL history) and 257 punt returns. In 1952, he gained 923 yards on interceptions and returns, more than the NFL rushing leader Dan Towler gained that year.

Defensive backs Dick Nolan and Ed Hughes and linebackers Harland Svare, Bill Svoboda, and Cliff Livingston had all come by '56 to give Landry a tremendous cadre of talent that he molded in his own fast-developing image. His platoon complete, Landry's 4-3 inside-outside innovation was ready to take flight.

"I don't know who takes credit for the 4-3," Gifford said, "but it was Tom. He exploited it, coordinated it, made it work. Few people outside of football realized what a great coach he was, what a great innovator he was. Most coaches would have been worshipping at his feet."

In the summer of '56, though, the genius of Landry and the greatness of the individuals on defense were just starting to come together.

"We had a great defensive coach in Tom Landry," Katcavage remembered. "We were always working on new maneuvers. And you had to come up with new things back then because there were so many great offensive linemen, all bigger than us on the defensive line, and much bigger than the guys I played against when I was with Dayton."

"Our defense was the model for the whole league," Grier said. "Tom was a very sharp guy. We had automatic defenses. We had to go to that a lot of times. We'd come out of the huddle and somebody would yell out a color. Then the offense would go into a shift and all those things, and we used to laugh at them. They didn't know we had an automatic defense. And we'd come up with something they didn't know was gonna get them. And if they came up with something we didn't know, we blitzed them and wrecked whatever they were doing."

"We used a defensive system whose success depended upon every player carrying out his assignment—teamwork in the truest sense," Robustelli later wrote. "This defensive strategy did not allow for glory-seekers, prima donnas, or guys looking for great statistics. Everyone was the same on the field, on every play and every postgame film session."

*　　*　　*

The 1954 and '55 seasons were basically primers, but good ones, even as Landry split time between coaching and playing. Lombardi held the spotlight those first two seasons as the newspapers focused on an offense Lombardi made increasingly more complex. Quickly realizing the Split-T Option offense he ran at Army wouldn't work in the pros, Lombardi transitioned into a pro set—two halfbacks and a fullback behind a quarterback. Gone, much to Conerly's relief, was the running quarterback, replaced by a settled system that relied more on power than college-style finesse. The halfback option, with Gifford flying wide to either run around the end, cut it up inside, or throw it, became a staple of the early offense. The Power Sweep, for which Lombardi is most known, became an evolutionary element.

It worked right away, as the Giants scored 11 more points in the '54 regular season opener—a 41–10 blowout of the Chicago Cardinals—than they had in their first three decisions of 1953. No less than the *New York Times* invited Howell and Lombardi to "take a long, deep bow," for transforming Steve Owen's stagnant offense into a unit "designed for deadly striking power."

"This team can go!" cried *Times* beat reporter Louis Effrat.

They continued to go, too. A 51–21 plastering of George Preston Marshall's Washington Redskins on October 10 produced the Giants' biggest point total since 1950. The first evidence of the option series came in a 31–17 win over the Cardinals the following week, as Conerly faked a handoff and pitched out to Gifford, who completed halfback option passes to Bob Schnelker and Eddie Price.

Lombardi's running game, the staple of all his offenses, continued to command everyone's attention as the backfield took apart the Eagles' fabled "Suicide Seven" defensive front in a 27–14 victory in Week 8. That line had held opponents to an average of 2.4 yards per rush in its previous encounters, only to give up 4.3 yards per rush despite the fact that the Giants threw a whopping 42 passes, 16 of which were completed. Many of those were Conerly-engineered shovel passes. "The attack," the *Times* analyzed, "is more imaginative and daring. The 1954 Giants go in for multiple ball-handling and faking. Each week finds something new added."

Little attention was paid to the defense at that point, partly because it was transitioning to Landry's philosophies, partly because newspaper coverage skewed toward more easily understood offense (whose results were also easier to quantify), and partly because it was a young unit. Landry and Em Tunnell were the grand old men of the defense at that point, and Tunnell actually garnered more print for his electrifying skills as a punt returner.

The defense had to wait until 1955 to get its first glowing review, and even then it didn't come right away, as the Giants had gone 0–3 largely because of the unit's ineffective play. They had held halftime leads against the Eagles, Cardinals, and Steelers, only to fall in the second half. Finally, on November 20, the defense starred in a 31–7 pounding of the Eagles. Tunnell returned a punt 66 yards for a touchdown for his first score since 1951 and added two interceptions. "The defense was terrific!" read the *Journal-American* story. It had actually taken some time for the newspapers to catch on, however. That game came at the end of a 4–2 streak that saw the Giants shut out the Cardinals, hold three opponents to a single touchdown, and allow more than 19 points just once.

Landry's group stayed solid the remainder of the season. Even a 35–35 draw with the Browns brought a measure of satisfaction, as the tie was preserved when Ray Krouse, the player who was traded for Modzelewski the following offseason, charged through the line and blocked Lou Groza's go-ahead field goal attempt with twenty-five seconds left.

By the end of 1955, even Howell had seen the potential of Landry's defense.

"Tom took a green defense [in 1954] and transformed it into one of the best defenses in the league," Howell said. "We intercepted 33 passes, more than anyone else in the league. [In 1955], we had only two holdovers up front and still he's done a good job.

"I think the world of Tom. He's one of the finest men I've even known, and a great football player."

*　　*　　*

One other element loomed over the '56 camp, though its full effect wouldn't hit them until they opened their home schedule October 21 against Pittsburgh. Like the offense and defense, the franchise itself was on the move. The Giants had agreed in the offseason to transplant themselves from the splintery old Polo Grounds to a more dignified setting in Yankee Stadium.

Players would soon settle into the same lockers as Mickey Mantle, Yogi Berra, and Whitey Ford. The floors were clean and tiled. The showers had plenty of hot water, and the locker room staff did all the laundry.

It was even a better place to get one's legs taped.

"Oh, the Polo Grounds," Johnny Johnson said. "We trainers would have to throw a sheet over an old wooden table just to do our work. Yankee Stadium was nice."

Decades later, Wellington would proclaim, "I was happy in the Polo Grounds," as his son, John, tried to convince him of how happy he'd be in the yet-to-be-built New Meadowlands Stadium that would replace Giants Stadium, for which they abandoned Yankee Stadium and New York in 1976. But in 1956, it was certainly time to move on. The baseball Giants only had the lease on the Polo Grounds until 1962, at which time the city planned to tear it down and put up apartments, and there were rumblings that the baseball Giants might move out to Minnesota. Of course, they would go to San Francisco after 1957, but there was plenty of writing on the wall already in 1956.

Plus, commissioner Bert Bell had relayed an offer from two Texas oilmen to buy the football Giants for a then record $1 million and move them into Yankee Stadium. The Maras suspected it came from the Murchison brothers, who eventually started the Dallas franchise. They refused the offer, hardly imagining that in four years they'd give Clint Murchison an even bigger value in the Giants' defensive assistant.

Howell welcomed the move as a psychological aid, just sharing quarters with baseball's greatest team. Landry, the only Giant who had called Yankee Stadium home due to his prior career there with the AAFC's Yankees, was just as happy to leave the dilapidated Polo Grounds behind.

"It was good to get out of the Polo Grounds," Landry said. "Yankee Stadium had a great deal of tradition, and it was a great place to play, to be. Of course, it seated a lot more people, too, and we were going to draw crowds."

*　　*　　*

That was for the near future. The here and now was training camp, ironically on the same St. Michael's field where Robustelli played his final collegiate game in 1950. That contest had not ended happily. While having one of his best games ever—the Arnold College star caught 6 passes as an end, had made 12 tackles, and had blocked several punts—Robustelli wound up breaking his leg. Fordham line coach and former Giants guard Lou DeFilippo, bird-dogging for the Rams, suggested the organization draft Robustelli, anyway. The Rams took a shot on him in the nineteenth round.

Now he was back, and the new offensive and defensive teammates who surrounded him showed a surprising amount of enthusiasm for the rigors of training camp. It became clear that once in pads, the Giants were all business.

Off the field, the team was more like family, as players and their wives from both sides of the ball would gather for post-game cocktails at Charlie Conerly's apartment in the Concourse Plaza Hotel, where a third of the team lived during the season. But sequestered in their northern training camp with only themselves to hit, they got after it. And Lombardi and Landry, in their own ways, stoked the competitive boiler that heated such potentially mundane activities as intra-squad scrimmages.

"The intra-squad game last Sunday was rather unusual," Frank Blunk of the *Times* wrote of the first major go at St. Michael's. "If one hadn't known that this was one team split into two squads, he might have thought it a regular-season game between rivals battling for first place.

"The men were blocking and tackling hard. The quarterbacks were snapping signals for the plays with mid-season seriousness. The passing was excellent, the line plays were cleverly designed and run off with precision."

True to his tough-love method of education, Lombardi rode his offensive charges hard throughout camp. The fans, granted entry to the practices gratis, heard him even more than Howell. Bear in mind that Howell could get on players pretty good, too, regardless of positional orientation. But Lombardi put on the real show.

"What I remember, at least once a day when we'd have teams period, you never heard from Jim Lee Howell much, but it was Vince," said Ray "Whitey" Walsh Jr., who, as a fourteen-year-old, worked his first of eight camps as waterboy and general gofer. "He wanted things run right, and you had to run them again and again and again. He'd stop practice at least once a day and stand there like a military guy, feet together, hands on his hips, and so loud. 'We're gonna stay here all day! If you want to stay here 'til midnight, that's fine! I got nowhere to be!' Loud. I'm sure you could hear him out on the highway by the school. And he wasn't laughing and he wasn't looking at anybody in particular. He was just kind of yelling at everybody and nobody. He just wanted things to go right."

Webster always seemed to be under Lombardi's closest scrutiny, probably because of a somewhat lackadaisical attitude. More than once, fans heard the assistant impart some not-so-gentle reminders. "Damn it, Webster! I told you to hit that hole!" Lombardi would scream. "Now run that play over until you do it!"

"Vince would yell at me, and I must say, I was scared of him," Webster said. "I know I was lazy at times, and Lombardi knew what he was doing."

Landry, on the other hand, was quiet. The fans heard not a peep from him as he methodically, cerebrally instructed his group. But the message to his players was clear—those people on the other side of the ball are not to move.

"We hated the offense," Huff said.

One could never trace that hatred back to Huff's boss, however.

"Landry was too smart to turn the defense on the offense, but he'd do it quietly," former Giants public relations director Don Smith said. "He'd calmly say to them, 'There's nothing you have to worry about. We know that on this pitch play, we know what Alex Webster is going to do. We know where he's going to be, so get there and get him.'

"He had the defenses down so well that they knew if something happened with the football, they knew where to be. Landry didn't believe in that *mano-a-mano* stuff."

Lombardi did.

"There was a lot of intercamp rivalry," Smith said. "Lots of guys getting knocked off and hurt and guys screaming and yelling."

Within a very short time, it became apparent that the defense, not the offense, would be the hallmark of the '56 team. As the season progressed, Robustelli and Huff and other verbally expressive defenders would pass the offense as they changed units on the field and tell Gifford or Webster or Conerly, "Now, see if you guys can hold them for a while."

For a competitively ambitious coach like Lombardi, the rise of the defense was more unsettling than glorious.

"It all got to Lombardi," Smith said, "and he made no attempt to handle it. He'd stop a scrimmage play and call a guy down in front of the whole team. 'You dumb son of a bitch! Don't you know you're supposed to be here instead of there?' He'd curse like a sailor. He'd stalk the sidelines looking for victims. He wasn't bashful about insulting them in front of their friends. He could do and say things other coaches couldn't do."

That was especially true in the evenings. Now well into the era of the one-way player, Lombardi and Landry split their units into separate rooms for positional meetings, ushering in a practice that has become standard in today's NFL. But they also continued to hold the full-team meeting, where film of the previous game or Saturday's intrasquad scrimmage would be shown and critiqued.

Lombardi controlled the projector. He was the only one who spoke. And when things went wrong, he spoke loudly.

As rough as some of those sessions were on the players who incurred Lombardi's wrath, the effect they had on a fourteen-year-old camp kid who was just tending to some of their needs was even more profound.

"Of course, it's pitch black except for the screen and the light from the projector," Walsh recalled. "Every once in a while, he'd say, 'Oh, hell!' and shut the projector off. And now it's pitch black, and here is this guy shouting at the top of his lungs, 'That's not the way . . . we're supposed to run . . . this play!' And on and on and on.

"It was scary. I was fourteen years old, and here's this nice man who's always nice to me, and he's yelling at the top of his lungs, like from his abdomen. After a while, I didn't want to go down there because he'd shut the projector off."

Lombardi only softened up when somebody barked back. During one film session, he climbed all over Mel Triplett for missing a block. He rolled the play back and forth, three, four times, until Triplett had had his fill. "Get off my back," Triplett threatened, "or get yourself another fullback!" With that, Lombardi rolled past the play. As the players filed out, Lombardi whispered to offensive lineman Jack Stroud, "I wanted to make him mad, but I didn't mean to make him that mad."

Landry would never provoke such histrionics, even as expectations grew higher for his unit.

"Tom could be as boring as hell," Gifford said.

"Even then, the team was becoming famous as a defensive team, and Landry was the right coach for them," Don Smith said.

The Giants embarked on their usual preseason odyssey knowing full well something special was happening. By the time they finished a 4–2 preseason, their first winning exhibition schedule since 1953 and the only Eastern Conference team to finish above .500 in '56, everybody else knew it, too.

The legend of the defense grew from the very first exhibition, a 28–10 win over Baltimore in Boston. The Colts were touted as having the best ground game in the Western Conference, but the Giants' defensive front held them to just 20 yards. Modzelewski starred, recovering two fumbles. Along with the rookie Katcavage, the duo kept Johnny Unitas backpedaling the whole game. The Newark *Star-Ledger* game story of August 21 boomed the glad tidings in its lead. "The Giants, hurting for defensive help last year, aren't hurting anymore. New York's defense was brilliant."

The same newspaper led the next day's follow-up with a qualified ode to Landry's unit.

"The veterans are in line; the rookies have done fine; the title mold is cast; a defense at last!

"The Giants' chief demand last year was defense, and Monday night they showed [a] resistance alignment that put the old umbrella defense to shame, providing it was not a mirage."

The team broke camp after that and headed west for a five-game swing. A stumble came in a 17–13 loss at Green Bay. But the Giants rebounded with a 20–10 win over the Rams in Seattle, with both offense and defense shining. Don Heinrich, embroiled in a three-way battle with Conerly and Bob Clatterbuck for Lombardi's two-quarterback rotation, completed 17 passes for 110 yards. Modzelewski starred again for the defense by stealing a handoff from Skeets Quinlan, with Triplett eventually scoring from the 1. Heinrich threw to Ken MacAfee for the go-ahead score, and Don Chandler connected on two field goals, the last in the third quarter. The defense choked off the Rams' attack the rest of the way.

A 21–14 comeback win over San Francisco in Portland, Oregon, followed as Heinrich's 51-yard throw to MacAfee set up the first of two touchdowns in the fourth quarter. Alex Webster had scored a tying touchdown in the second quarter after the 49ers took an early lead in the first.

A 21–16 loss to the Bears in which George Blanda hit the defensive backfield for two touchdown passes preceded a preseason finale in which the Giants drubbed the Chicago Cardinals 42–7 in Memphis, Tennessee. By then, some were convinced that this team, which hadn't been to a championship game since 1946 and hadn't won one since 1938, was destined for glory. The players and coaches were confident the Giants had the stuff of champions.

It didn't hurt that outside influences had also affected the league. Landry, a student of Paul Brown's offense, no longer had to worry about the magical powers of the great quarterback Otto Graham, who retired after the '55 season. While still a good team, the perennial NFL champions would have to rebuild, and that left the door open for the rest of the league.

The Giants eventually stepped through that opening. As they did, Lombardi and Landry would solidify their reputations as geniuses while also learning valuable lessons they'd each harken back to in future challenges.

4

THE SEASON STARTS

NO ONE KNEW it in the preseason, but the regular season of 1956 would bring Vince Lombardi and Tom Landry into battles not only against the vaunted Cleveland Browns and Chicago Bears, but against some new-fangled technology that had nothing to do with shifting offensive formations and revolutionary defenses.

They'd win most of those varied encounters, and wrap it all up with their first championship trophy since they beat Green Bay 23–17 for the 1938 title. Frank Gifford would collect the league's Most Valuable Player Award after leading the league in yards from scrimmage with 1,422—and he wouldn't have to dress up to do it, either. "Picked it up at some guy's apartment," Gifford remembered. "It wasn't a real big deal back then."

The Giants were still a long way from becoming champs when they broke camp, however. And few outside the locker room seemed aware of what was brewing. About the only ones who knew the Giants' defense had truly arrived were the Giants, the San Francisco 49ers, and the 41,000 or so fans who came to Kezar Stadium for the regular season opener. The rest of the country, especially the New York area, was more concerned with the Dodgers' final-day win over the Milwaukee Braves that allowed the defending world champions to face the Yankees for a second straight time in the World Series.

For those who witnessed that 38–21 Giants victory, and for those who chose to dig a little deeper than the offense-oriented Associated Press stories the New York dailies buried under the baseball news, the game justified the growing enthusiasm of the preseason. The Giants had put it all together, on offense and defense.

Lombardi had started using a two-quarterback system, playing former University of Washington star Don Heinrich the first quarter or two, while constantly talking in the ear of the aging Conerly. Heinrich would conduct what amounted to probing operations, ferreting out a team's weaknesses as Lombardi and Conerly took copious mental notes on the sidelines. Then, Lombardi would bring in Conerly for the kill after halftime, a move that often opened the offensive assistant to a barrage of abuse from his starting play caller.

The first game indicated just how effectively the arrangement would work, however. The Giants, behind Heinrich, scored on their first three possessions, leaving San Francisco stunned, confused, and behind 17–0 before the 49ers had even tightened their chinstraps.

Heinrich first found Alex Webster on a 44-yard touchdown pass. Then, Gifford took a handoff 59 yards for a touchdown. And then Gifford booted a 17-yard field goal. The only reason Gifford was kicking that day was because the Giants' regular kicker, Ben Agajanian, absented himself as he weighed fulltime commitment to his garbage-hauling business in Southern California against continuing his NFL career. Agajanian would eventually return to the Giants, but at the start of the 1956 season, the placekicking job belonged to the multi-talented running back.

The Giants lead swelled to 24–0 in the second quarter when Mel Triplett and Heinrich hooked up on a 35-yard passing touchdown. Only Hugh McElhenny's 16-yard touchdown run around left end late in the quarter prevented the 49ers from hitting the intermission scoreless.

Newspaper reporters in that era had little inkling as to what a defense did, or if what they were doing was good or bad. But consider this. While the offense was piling up points, the defense had bottled up McElhenny and Joe Perry, two of that era's pre-eminent rushers, and had defended future Giants quarterback Y. A. Tittle to the point of frustration. Robustelli would later call McElhenny the best running back he ever faced besides Jim Brown.

Robustelli and the front four had gotten great penetration, even as they faced the 49ers' two Hall of Fame tackles in the gargantuan Bob St. Clair and iron man Leo Nomellini. And they chased Yelberton Abraham Tittle all over the place, an epic undertaking considering Tittle had become a master of the bootleg. Tittle's predecessor and new head coach Frankie Albert had turned that same tactic into an art form that terrorized AAFC and NFL opponents from 1946 to '52. To further strengthen the repertoire, Tittle added the screen pass. In fact, the majority of San Francisco's passing yards came off screens.

Landry knew plenty about Albert and his philosophies from their AAFC encounters. In fact, the two of them had engaged in one of football's most legendary punting duels on December 3, 1949, at Yankee Stadium. The 49ers eventually won that AAFC semifinal playoff against the New York Yankees 17–7. But the story was the punters, as Albert knocked a quick kick 66 yards, only to see Landry punt it back 73 yards when the Yankees couldn't do anything with their possession. Landry finished that day with a 55-yard punting average.

Triplett's 1-yard plunge in the third quarter put the game out of reach, though Tittle did bring the 49ers within 10 in the final minutes with a short touchdown pass. But Triplett's third touchdown of the game, coming on a 12-yard run up the middle, quelled any danger of a comeback.

The 49ers gained 107 yards rushing on 23 carries, but few of those runs were decisive. Tittle went 27-of-47 for 288 yards and three interceptions.

Of course, the only people who really knew how well the defense had played were at the game. Most of those reading the New York papers were treated only to a single line in the AP story about how linebacker Bill Svoboda "spent most of the afternoon hanging around Tittle's neck." But those reading the New York *Daily Mirror*, who actually sent Harold Weisman to the game, received a double-edged hurrah at the end of his story. Talking about several Giants injuries going into the Cardinals game next week, he said, 'They'll be ready. So will the tickets for the title game come December. This one has the goods."

The Giants seemed on their way. Enthusiasm was running high, and Landry's defense was getting mouthier by the minute.

Practices had changed. When the Giants headed back for a week at Lombardi's and Wellington Mara's alma mater, Fordham University—the Yankees were still conducting a bit of World Series business against Brooklyn at the Giants' new home—they hit the field in sweats and baseball caps.

"None of our practices in New York were hard," defensive tackle Dick Modzelewski said. "We never wore pads during practice during football season. Whenever we left training camp, you always made sure you had a baseball cap because that's what we wore. Training camp was different. We wore pads in the morning because you had to scrimmage. But once the season started, it was sweatpants and a baseball hat, and that was it. We never pounded the hell out of each other until we pounded the team we were gonna play against."

Unless, of course, Jim Lee Howell or one of his assistants sensed some complacency among the troops. Then, things might get a little bit uncomfortable, starting with the leather-lunged Howell's whistle.

"We'd practice for nickels," defensive tackle Rosey Grier said, "meaning you'd go full out and tackle. Other times it was not for nickels, so you didn't hit the back or the quarterback. You had interplay with the linemen, but you let the backs go.

"If you're playing for nickels, if you had a shot at them, you took it. Anybody. You'd even put the quarterback down. At least once or twice a week. It got to be that, when you played that way, you had to be careful you didn't hurt someone because they were your own teammates.

"You had to have hitting at least once or twice a week. You'd go with the linemen, but not the backs. But if you weren't running the plays right, the way the coach wanted you to run them, they'd change it. They'd say, 'This is a nickel!' because you weren't putting out."

Maintenance of conditioning in-season was fairly primitive, too. This was decades before football players would get into weight training to any great degree, so much of the Giants' conditioning after training camp came during practice itself. From Landry's end, it usually involved him ordering his entire defense to chase Gifford or Webster thirty yards or so during their practice reps.

Their week practicing on Edward's Parade, in front of Keating Hall's majestic, Gothic clock tower finished, the Giants took an eighteen-hour train ride to Chicago. There, in the White Sox' Comiskey Park, they would face the Chicago Cardinals, a tough but certainly beatable squad.

The Cardinals went into the game as 10-point underdogs despite a 9–7 upset of the Browns in their season opener. But that was only a partial reason the *Daily Mirror* cleverly proclaimed them "the hottest team in the NFL." That week, a fire at Comiskey Park had burned down the press box and caused $100,000 worth of damage.

It marked one of the few times in their history anyone would ever connect the Cardinals to a temperature metaphor stronger than "lukewarm." Though blessed with great talent in Hall of Fame running back Ollie Matson and Hall of Fame defensive back Dick "Night Train" Lane, the Cardinals were not an outstanding operation. Much like today's Arizona Cardinals under Bill Bidwill, their ancestors—owned by his father, Charles—were generally more interested in making a buck than producing championships. Actually, they weren't very good at either endeavor. The Bears, playing at Wrigley Field, dwarfed the Cardinals attendance-wise almost 2-to-1. And it actually took the league talent's collectively slow creep back from World War II to get them their first and only NFL Championship in 1947.

Even the smoothest of highways has its occasional pothole, however. And the first of the Giants' three bumps in the road in their 8–3–1 season came in this 35–27 loss.

The Cardinals, employing quarterback Lamar McHan in the option, flustered Landry's best-laid run defense and rushed for more than 100 yards. He threw all of 7 passes, but he completed 5 of them for 136 yards, including 2 touch-downs on the Cardinals' first two possessions of the second half. That put the Cardinals in front 28–13, a lead they never relinquished.

McHan, who eventually went on to play for Lombardi's Packers in 1959 and '60, also rushed for 2 touchdowns.

Unbeknownst to Lombardi, Landry, or Howell for that matter, the Giants had had their first brush with new-age technology. Cardinals coach Ray Richards had relayed the Cardinals' plays to McHan's helmet via the airwaves. The Giants found out about it long after the game ended, but they kept that knowledge in mind for their next opponent.

*   *   *

The world had begun to shrink around the Giants' organization as well as society at large. The transistor, which made electronics smaller and more portable—think of it as the early micro-chip—had come into the world in a big way in 1954, mostly in radios. Sound could now be sent and received through a box no bigger than the palm of one's hand. Bell Telephone had actually started using them in hearing aids.

The NFL had no rules against such things back then, so everything was on the up-and-up as far as Cleveland coach Paul Brown was concerned. A tactical genius alternately idolized and despised among the coaching brethren his teams routinely made look stupid, Brown always searched for that extra edge. And in 1956 he needed it, because his great quarterback, Otto Graham, had retired during the offseason. Bruising fullback Marion Motley was also gone, traded to the Steelers after 1953, as was tremendous defensive lineman Bill Willis and fast end Mac Speedie, who had jumped to Canada.

The Browns were really a shell of themselves and probably had little claim to the usual preseason championship predictions. But Brown, much like the Cardinals and Lions, who also joined in the experiment, thought science might fill the gap. He could use shortwave to make Graham's replacement, George Ratterman, an effective quarterback.

Brown didn't even try to hide that he was going to outfit the former Notre Dame standout with a wireless receiver. He'd put a shortwave specialist on staff. True to his meticulous nature, he even registered a frequency with the FCC.

"There was no secret to what the Browns were doing," Gifford said. "They'd talked about it openly."

But so had the receiver's inventor, George Sarles of Cleveland. Sarles told reporters that his shortwave transmissions were anything but secure. They could be jammed. Something as insignificant as an electric razor could create interference, and Sarles said he wouldn't be surprised if an entire opposing bench felt the sudden need for a close shave at key points in games. Even worse, the signals "could be swiped out of the air . . . and transmitted to a defensive captain or signal-caller."

Brown had actually tried the system against the Bears in the preseason, but the connection broke down early and he reverted to messenger guards—Brown's own innovation—to shuttle in Ratterman's marching orders. No loss. Ratterman was not a huge radio fan, anyway. Or of the way defenses tried to neutralize it.

"Please don't think you can put this radio out of commission by pounding me on the head," Ratterman told the International Press Service. "The radio won't break; my head might."

Those little blips tended not to dissuade Brown, however. And when the Giants came to town for Game 3, Ratterman was wired for sound.

Most of the world expected the favored Browns to beat the Giants for a seventh straight time since 1953. But it was evident early on that the Giants' coaching triumvirate had gotten the jump on everybody, and in a relatively simple manner. A few bucks bought them their own radio, and a brief call to the FCC gave them Brown's frequency, which was a matter of public record.

"I can't imagine nobody thought to do it before," Gifford said. "It's not a big step to say 'what frequency are they using?'"

With that, the Giants had a direct pipeline into Paul Brown's head. All they needed was the relay.

Lombardi took Bob Topp, a fringe end who saw limited action in 1954, did not play in '55, and would not see a single play in '56, and put him on the receiver. Kickoff returner Gene Filipski, a recent pickup who knew the Browns' playbook after spending the preseason with them, sat next to Topp and translated his raw data into Giants terminology. Filipski then called out the play to Robustelli, who clued in the rest of the defense.

It took seconds.

Only days later the Giants became one of the first teams to wirelessly connect coaches in the press box to the bench, thereby freeing the assistants from hard-wired phones and permitting them to roam the sidelines. But on October 15, it was purely a defensive measure.

The Browns may have had an inkling the Giants were up to something, because they warned the Giants of a $10,000 FCC fine for jamming licensed wavelengths. No fine was ever levied, however.

Instead, the Giants won 21–9. They were on to just about everything the Browns tried in the first half. At one point, Brown called for a pitchout, and the ball carrier was dropped for a two-yard loss.

As for Ratterman's published plea to defenders . . .

"We'd heard the quarterback had something in his ear, so we said whenever you're near the quarterback, make sure you bang him in the head," Modzelewski said. "Tom Landry would never say that. I think we did that among ourselves."

The Browns gained almost nothing on the ground in the first half. And Ratterman? Led by Robustelli and left end Walt Yowarsky, the pass rush put him on his backside a dozen times, with Robustelli getting to him six times.

Robustelli simply took over the game in the fourth quarter when the Browns put together one of their few real drives. After moving the ball to the Giants' 12, they never took another step forward as Robustelli blew through the line on three straight plays and dropped Ratterman for 42 yards in losses.

At another point, the Browns advanced to the Giants 1, where the defense stiffened and stopped three straight plunges up the middle. On fourth down, Dick Modzelewski's fullback older brother Ed—"Big Mo" to Dick's "Little Mo"—tried to hit the left side where Dick policed. Dick knifed in and brought Ed down for a two-yard loss.

When Dick appeared a bit too pleased with himself, Ed turned around and threw the football at him, hitting him squarely in the head.

"I think their guard slipped and I managed to get in there," Dick Modzelewski said. "We still laugh like hell about that."

Actually, Landry's system of defense, where everyone had strict assignments, made the play possible.

"Sometimes you'd try to pull these overaggressive guys," Ed Modzelewski said. "The lineman would pull the other way and [the defense] would take off on that and pull the other way. But Dick didn't buy that."

As for the pop on Dick's helmet . . . "I think he gave me a little extra because we were brothers," Ed said.

Most of blows fell on Ratterman, however. The Giants always aimed themselves at the quarterback. Landry's system may have forced players to hesitate and read to prevent any unwarranted surprises, but once a pass became obvious, the front had one duty, and one duty only: get the quarterback.

Those who did reaped rewards. Five bucks a shot. Whether Howell or Landry doled out the dough is unclear. What is crystal clear is that nobody saw much of the small fortune Robustelli and a few of his brethren made that day in Cleveland, including Robustelli. A religious man as well as a strong, convincing team leader, Robustelli would grab the bounties almost as quickly as they were paid out and send them to a priest in China.

"I remember Katcavage or I tackled [then Philadelphia quarterback] Sonny Jurgensen at the same time one game, and we were arguing about whose five dollars it was gonna be," Modzelewski recalled. "And Sonny said, 'I don't give a damned whose it is, just get the hell off of me!' It was all for a good cause, though. Rice in China, I think. Andy would grab the money first."

The Browns, one-point favorites, wound up with just 40 rushing yards on the day, with Big Mo supplying 28 and his team's only touchdown. Accounts vary as to when the Browns abandoned their radio experiment. Some say it ended just a couple of plays into the game, while others say it was well into the second half. Either way, Paul Brown eventually dumped it and reverted to messenger guards.

But if the former is correct, it only illustrates just how monstrous Landry's 4-3 defense had truly become.

And just how far it could take them.

"This was the day the Giants were to learn if this was their year," the *Daily Mirror* crowed. "It is."

The offense had its day, too. Alex Webster scored all 3 touchdowns, two after Ed Modzelewski's TD run sent the teams into halftime tied 7–7. Webster, Triplett, and Gifford rushed for 94, 91, and 73 yards, respectively, while Gifford also caught four passes for 42 yards.

The electronics issue became a moot point four days later, when commissioner Bert Bell deemed it illegal. It would take another half-century before the NFL embraced wireless communication with its quarterbacks. On this Sunday, however, outsiders cheered the group that buried the scientists along with the Browns.

"The Giants made hamburger of the Browns 21–9 at Cleveland despite transmitter and the like," Milton Gross of the *New York Post* glowed. "But with a defensive end named Robustelli virtually playing in Ratterman's lap all afternoon, the Giants likely set science back uncounted years."

*   *   *

Perhaps even more significant than the dominance of Landry's Legions was the overlooked fact that the Sam Huff era had begun at middle linebacker. Ray Beck was still struggling with an ankle sprain incurred during training camp. Moving outside backer Harland Svare into the middle against the Cardinals the previous week didn't work at all. Beck started the Cleveland game, but aggravated the ankle early on. So Landry, somewhat reluctantly, inserted Huff early in the game. With Paul Brown zeroing in on the rookie with Ed Modzelewski, Huff battered the 217-pound fullback up the middle and flew all over the field. Huff later called it the finest game he'd ever played.

He never sat on the bench when healthy again.

Beck, originally drafted as an offensive guard, eventually switched back there and played through 1957. But as far as seeing time with Landry's unit, he was Wally Pipp. It never really angered Beck, one of the many who saw firsthand how Huff had made the new position his own at Winooski Park.

"I just grew into the position," Huff said. "It was just such a wonderful time to have Andy Robustelli at one defensive end, Jim Katcavage at the other, Modzelewski at one tackle, Roosevelt Grier at the other tackle, and I'm standing up and here comes the ball carrier. And he's my man. There's nothing like that."

*　　*　　*

The 2–1 Giants were on their way. Mel Triplett had scored six touchdowns in three games. Frank Gifford's 8.7 yard-per-rush average led the league. Lombardi's Split-T was working wonderfully. And, to top it off, the Giants were finally going home.

Not just to any home, mind you. The next week's assignment against the Steelers marked their first game in Yankee Stadium after three decades in the Polo Grounds. The last contest the grand green cathedral had seen was Don Larsen's perfect game a week earlier. But now, the Giants would make it their office, at least until the beginning of next season when the annual preseason odyssey would start all over again. For the time being, they were football nomads no more.

It didn't hurt that they had moved to such a vaunted arena. The first thing Frank Gifford did was walk out to the centerfield monuments of Babe Ruth, Miller Huggins, and Lou Gehrig to soak in the history of the place. He had come there with USC to play Army in '51, but now this was his home. The feeling that came with it was much different than what he had had in the Polo Grounds.

"We always thought we were the poor prodigal son," Gifford said. "The Yankees were huge, what with Yankee Stadium, and the Giants hadn't moved yet. We were kind of second-class citizens and hadn't won anything to speak of in ages."

Now, the poor relatives shared the lockers of baseball royalty like Mickey Mantle, Yogi Berra, and Whitey Ford. They walked the same paths of Ruth, Gehrig, and DiMaggio. Their pregame personalities reflected the appropriate reverence and determination evoked by the hallowed surroundings. The last thing they wanted to do was screw it up.

"The Yankees laugh and joke and engage in horseplay," legendary *Times* columnist Arthur Daley wrote in his column from that October 21 game. "The Giants look like men who are heading for a mass execution without any hope of a reprieve from the Governor."

Pittsburgh had other plans, of course. Though Bert Bell had outlawed radio-to-quarterback transmissions, his ruling left the Giants free to wire the coaching staff. The Steelers threatened through public relations head Ed Kiley to pick off the signals. That prompted Howell into a jovial caution that Kiley should "freshen up on his Japanese."

In truth, the whole quarterback wiring experience was a mess. Transistor technology just had not advanced far enough in the mid-50s. The Steelers had actually used it for three plays against the

Eagles the same week the Giants swiped the Browns' signals. Steelers quarterback Ted Marchibroda had tested out receiving points on the field before the game using a walkie-talkie and exclaimed, "I just got Italy on this thing!" Cabbies outside the stadiums said they'd heard the coaches on their own dispatch radios.

What happened in front of 48,108 fans, the largest crowd to date for a Giants home opener, had little to do with electronics. The Giants rolled over the Steelers 38–10 in such a dominant defensive display that the newspapers barely knew whom to hug first.

"The defense today was superlative," the *Star-Ledger* wrote while giving a short nod to Charlie Conerly's 3 touchdown passes. Defensive tackles Grier and Modzelewski, linebackers Harland Svare and Bill Svoboda, and defensive backs Herb Rich and Emlen Tunnell were defined as "outstanding" in holding the Steelers to 91 yards rushing and 77 yards passing.

The offensive onslaught had started when a fumble recovered by Svoboda on the Steelers' 29 kicked into overdrive a flurry that started shortly after Conerly replaced Heinrich late in the first quarter, down 3–0. Conerly had just hit Ken MacAfee with a scoring pass, going 5-for-8 on the series, when Grier and Robustelli swarmed over Marchibroda to cause the fumble. Conerly then hit Webster in the end zone for his second touchdown in a minute and twenty seconds. The Giants scored 31 unanswered points before Marchibroda threw a touchdown pass midway through the fourth quarter.

Landry's defense was quickly coming of age, piece by piece. Huff, the most brilliant of Landry's moves, was flying all over the place and rapidly becoming a fan favorite. Right defensive end Robustelli, already well established when he arrived, was creating his usual disruption. Grier and Modzelewski were becoming forces in the middle. A defensive backfield chart that featured Em Tunnell, Jimmy Patton, Dick Nolan, Ed Hughes, and Herb Rich was providing the Giants with unheard of depth against pass-oriented opponents.

Robustelli's bookend hadn't quite settled in, though. Draft pick Jim Katcavage was doing well, but still splitting time with Walt Yowarsky. That probably had as much to do with Howell's legendary (but hardly unique) distrust of rookies. He already had one starting at middle linebacker. Two in the same lineup might have been too much for him to handle.

History would show Landry was of a like mind. As head coach in Dallas, he was loath to put rookies in his starting lineup.

There were exceptions, though. Katcavage became one the following week, the second home game against Philadelphia, when he became the Giants' fulltime left defensive end. He made life miserable for Eagles quarterbacks Adrian Burk and Bobby Thomason. Nor could the Eagles run.

"With ferocious consistency, ends Katcavage and Robustelli caught any attempts by halfback Skippy Giancanelli and Ken Keller to run wide," the *Star-Ledger* reported.

The offense played poorly, committing 4 turnovers (2 fumbles and 2 interceptions) in that 20–3 victory. In fact, turnovers created the Eagles' deepest penetrations of the game. That came as little surprise, actually, since the man now commanding the Eagles' defense was none other than the Giants' old coach, Steve Owen. Using a confusing 6-1-4 alignment, Owen's unit limited the Giants' rushing effectiveness, even though Gifford, Webster, and Triplett did combine to gain 159 total yards on the ground.

It was the defense, now described in some quarters as big and burly, that won it. The Eagles never crossed midfield in the final three quarters. That undoubtedly irked Lombardi. But the grandstand faithful was growing more intelligent, and they began pushing the offense to the background. The defensive bandwagon had plenty of seats, and the fans started boarding in droves.

They went wild as Tunnell picked off Burk in the first quarter to set up a tying field goal. They grew even crazier as Harland Svare blocked Burk's third-quarter punt that led to Charlie Conerly's touchdown pass to Gifford, a final touchdown that came off a double-fake handoff to Triplett and Webster as Gifford streaked down the sideline.

The media helped greatly in publicizing the defense, giving liberal credit to the interior of Grier, Modzelewski, Huff, and Yowarsky for their time frequenting the Philadelphia backfield.

"The fans became very sophisticated," Gifford said. "They had every right to be vocal. It was a first in football. The defense became so prominent. There were some pretty spectacular guys playing out there. You're talking about Modzelewski, Grier, and I don't want to leave out Sam Huff. He'll be down to fight me.

"We both respected each other, put it that way. Sam was a loudmouth. He knows it."

The relationship between defense and offense was growing strained, to say the least. Offense and defense had always maintained a quiet separation inside the locker room. But now, with the defense's newfound prominence, Conerly, Gifford, and Webster periodically would get an earful from Landry's group after a failed drive. "We loved doing that," Grier said. "Would you guys hold them for a few minutes so we can catch our breath?"

The Giants were now 4–1 and tied for first in the Eastern Conference with the Cardinals.

A trip to Pittsburgh produced a 17–14 win November 4 in a sloppy game in which each team turned the ball over twice and punted eight times. But the Steelers' turnovers were more costly, as linebacker Bill Svoboda ended one deep penetration with an end zone interception. The defense stopped another drive at the Giants' 6.

As is common with many defensive struggles, there was nothing pretty about it. But it did mark the Giants' fifth win in six games, and kept them tied with the Cardinals heading into a Yankee Stadium collision the following week.

*   *   *

By the time the Cardinals and Giants met on Nov. 11, virtually all of New York had started to believe that this could be the Giants' year. Even during the practice week, the coaches were upbeat and expectant, none more so than Lombardi. At some point around this time, Gifford remembered, Lombardi called the offense into the middle of the field, frost from the cold fall day steaming from his mouth, head rocking back and forth as he grinned a toothy grin, his large feet tapping the ground. "Gentlemen, I can smell something," Lombardi said. "Oh, I can smell something!"

As it turned out, so could the fans. The first two games at home had already evidenced how raucous an enthusiastic New York crowd could be. But in this 23–10 victory, the Giants' fifth straight that put them alone in first place, something quite interesting happened in the stands.

They started cheering specifically for the defense. That defensive bandwagon they were so quickly populating got noisy, and Yankee Stadium would never be the same again. Landry's defense, which by the end of the game had given up just four touchdowns in the winning streak, would finally, permanently become stars.

It started with a few hundred fans in the centerfield bleachers and grew from there. "Dee-fense! Dee-fense!" they shouted as the Cardinals drew to the Giants' 10-yard line in the fourth quarter. The cheer had never been heard anywhere before. But it would be heard time and time again after that. Soon, the never-varied tradition of introducing the offense first would vanish into the past as the defense got its share of the pre-game nods the remainder of the season. With that came the locomotive-like chants of "Huff-Huff-Huff-Huff," another bit of unprecedented notoriety for a defensive player.

Even the least knowledgeable of fans could see Robert Lee Huff was Landry's chief tackler, so he became the most recognized of the group. A *Time* magazine cover lay three years in the future. But for now, the outgoing Huff contented himself by playing to the TV camera.

"It didn't take long for Sam to realize a couple of things," Gifford said. "The guy who gets up last from the pile, the TV people are gonna recognize that he made the tackle. I used to kid him about it."

On Huff's part, he knew he didn't accomplish things on his own.

"I know I got credit for a lot of the tackles," he said, "but quite often one or more of the guys up front would have slowed down the runner, and it was easy for me to put him away. Here I was, a rookie who for a while thought I might not even make the team, and I was playing behind one of the best front fours of all time. Maybe even the best one ever."

If Huff ever forgot that, guys like Robustelli were there to remind him that the system made Huff's popularity possible.

"The fact that Sam Huff got so much of the public glory is simply the result of the work of Jim Katcavage, Dick Modzelewski, Rosey Grier, Swede Svare," Robustelli said.

In this game against the Cardinals, the defense held Ollie Matson to just 43 yards, and held their other standout back, Johnny Olszewski, to 46 yards. A blocked punt by Robustelli created the first score of the game, a safety in the opening quarter.

Despite the fans' verbal epiphany, this one was not all about the defense. Lombardi showed a bit of ingenuity with a trick play that produced their first touchdown and a 9–0 lead. With the ball at the Cardinals' 6, eight plays into the second quarter, Triplett and Webster lined up in a Split-T formation. Upon the snap to Don Heinrich, Triplett made like he was going to block for a Webster plunge on the left side. As the defensive front and linebackers reacted to the fake plunge, Heinrich rolled right, protected by pulling right guard Jack Stroud, as end Ken MacAfee cut over the middle. MacAfee drew two defensive backs, as planned. He split them and reeled in Heinrich's picture-perfect throw in the end zone.

"We didn't even send Kyle Rote out as a decoy receiver," Lombardi said afterward. "He moved to block to add to the picture of a buck over tackle on the left side."

That wasn't the only bit of chutzpah out of Lombardi on this day, either. When Ray Beck and a Cardinals player got into a scuffle, Lombardi leaped right in to help. Suddenly, Lombardi felt someone yank on his arm, and the coach, turning, ducked just in time to avoid a haymaker. As Lombardi cocked his arm for a return salvo, he realized his assailant was a fan. "A civilian!" he snorted. Lombardi pulled the guy's hat down around his ears and walked away.

Webster finished with 76 yards rushing, Gifford with 68. The Giants were in first place alone and the players were riding the celebrity wave, as big as anybody in New York. The crowds at Toots Shor's and Mike Manuche's and all the favorite watering holes made with the backslaps and hurrahs.

But tempers, especially Lombardi's, would flare soon enough to bring them right back to earth.

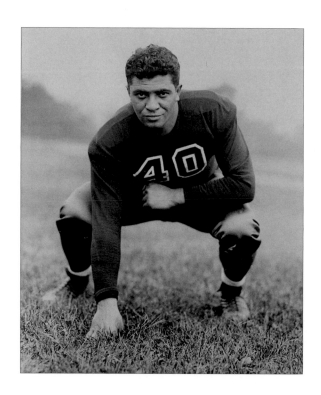

Before they were coaches, Lombardi and Landry were players. Here's Vince Lombardi as a member of Fordham's Seven Blocks of Granite, and Tom Landry in his New York Giants uniform. *Courtesy of AP Images*

Landry both punted and played defensive back for Steve Owen's
Giants teams of the early 1950s. *Courtesy of AP Images*

When Jim Lee Howell took over as the Giants head coach, he made Landry a player-coach. Here, Howell goes over some strategy with Landry (in uniform) and Lombardi, his top offensive assistant. *Courtesy of AP Images*

The 1957 New York Giants coaching staff. Standing (L to R): Tom
Landry, Jim Lee Howell, and Ken Kavanaugh. Kneeling (L to R):
Vince Lombardi and John Dell Isola. *Courtesy of AP Images*

Coach Jim Lee Howell gives some words of instruction to co-captains Kyle Rote (left) and Ray Krouse (right) at Fordham Field, October 1954. *Courtesy of AP Images*

Tom Landry holds ball as New York Giants defense huddles during a workout at Yankee Stadium, November 1958. Kneeling (L to R): Harland Svare, Sam Huff, and Cliff Livingston. Standing (L to R): Carl Karilivacz, Jim Patton, Emlen Tunnell, Bill Svoboda, and Lindon Crow. *Courtesy of AP Images*

Giants quarterback Charlie Conerly lets the ball fly during passing drill at Yankee Stadium, November 1958. Watching from left to right are Vince Lombardi, Mel Triplett, Phil King, and Alex Webster. *Courtesy of AP Images*

(L to R) Muddied defensive linemen Andy Robustelli, Dick Modzelewski, Jim Katcavage, and Rosey Grier walk towards the sideline during the third quarter of a game against the Philadelphia Eagles at Yankee Stadium, November 18, 1962. *Courtesy of Getty Images*

Vince Lombardi (left) and Frank Gifford watch from the muddy
sidelines, Yankee Stadium, 1956. *Courtesy of Getty Images*

The additions of offensive tackle Roosevelt Brown (top) in 1953 and middle linebacker Sam Huff (bottom) in 1956 helped form the Giants into a championship-caliber club. *Brown photo courtesy of AP Images. Huff photo courtesy of Getty Images*

Film stills from the Giants sideline, NFL Championship Game, December 30, 1956. (Top) Vince Lombardi confers with quarterback Charlie Conerly. (Middle) Frank Gifford (#16) runs Lombardi's famed Power Sweep. (Bottom) Landry confers with defensive end Andy Robustelli. *Courtesy of the New York Giants*

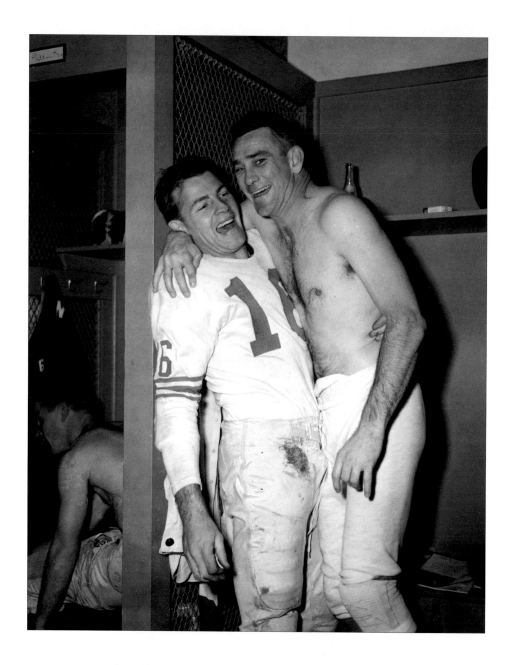

Frank Gifford (left) and Charlie Conerly celebrate the Giants
47–7 victory over the Chicago Bears in the NFL Championship
Game, December 30, 1956. *Courtesy of AP Images*

DAILY ⬥ NEWS
NEW YORK'S PICTURE NEWSPAPER ®

The Net Paid Circulation
For November Exceeded
Daily—2,075,000
Sunday–3,600,000
Over Twice the Circulation of
Any Other Paper in America

32   New York 17, N.Y., Monday, December 31, 1956   4¢ IN CITY LIMITS | 5¢ OUTSIDE CITY LIMITS

GIANTS THRASH BEARS, 47-7,
BEFORE 56,836 FOR TITLE

Story on page 28

...Losing to the Br-r-r-rs

Confounding the experts, Giants yesterday clawed Chicago Bears, 47-7, to win their first pro football title in 18 years. On the other hand, 56,836 fans were confounded by the weatherman who beat them black-and-blue (mostly blue) with sub-freezing temperatures.

"Rooting Ben" Agajanian, whose educated toe was not particularly bright earlier this year, puts boot to 43-yard field goal in first period to make score, 13-0.   —**Story on page 28**

Giants' Webster waits for diving Bear to fall on kisser before threading through line for four yards in 2d quarter at Yankee Stadium. Invaders, installed as 3-point choices, were never in game.

The front page of the New York *Daily News*, December 31, 1956. Inset:
The Giants 1956 championship ring.

Cleveland's great Jim Brown breaks loose for a 65-yard touchdown run on the Browns' first play from scrimmage in a pivotal late-season game at Yankee Stadium, December 14, 1958. *Courtesy of AP Images*

Frank Gifford takes a handoff from quarterback Don Heinrich and heads off right tackle in this same game against the Browns. Gifford's 8-yard touchdown pass to end Bob Schnelker tied the score at 10 late in the fourth quarter. *Courtesy of AP Images*

Placekicker Pat Summerall attempts a 49-yard field goal through swirl-
ing wind and snow to win this game against Cleveland and propel the
Giants into the 1958 postseason. The field goal today ranks among the
most historic in NFL history. *Courtesy of AP Images*

Vince Lombardi
clutches a play
chart behind his
back during a
game at Yankee
Stadium. *Courtesy
of AP Images*

Vince Lombardi and his longtime friend (and former employer),
Giants owner Wellington Mara, share a moment in Rome, Italy,
February 2, 1962. *Courtesy of AP Images*

5

BLIPS AND BAUBLES

UNHOLY hell.

Through the first two years and seven games they played under them, the Giants players had pretty much learned what to expect from their two assistant coaches when fortunes dipped. From Vinny Lombardi, it was silence and brooding, then flashes of anger, then back to tough-love teaching. From Tom Landry, it was a calm return to the blackboard, more teaching, and more low-toned preaching of adherence to what he believed was a near-foolproof system. But the aftermath of their 33–7 loss in Washington on November 18 was so brutal, and the coaches' reaction so extreme, that it rocked the players to their core.

Not that they couldn't have used a wakeup call at the time. They had won five straight games and, at 6–1 and alone in first place, were the hottest team in the NFL. And maybe a bit too full of themselves. They went into the game against the Redskins, winners of three straight, as a touchdown favorite. Better yet, backup quarterback Al Dorow would have to start because of an injury to little Eddie LeBaron, the Redskins' 5-foot-7, 165-pound successor to the great Sammy Baugh. With arm strength belying his tiny stature, LeBaron had built himself into one of the NFL's top passers since assuming the quarterbacking duties in 1952.

But LeBaron was down and Dorow, destined for the AFL as the New York Titans' first quarterback, was up. As so often happens when a lightly regarded entity faces a behemoth, Dorow took his slingshot and slew the great Giants. Actually, he tore Landry's defense to pieces. And Lombardi's offense didn't bail them out, either. His unit floundered just as badly. It was over by halftime, as the Giants hit the locker room down 24–0.

The tackling, always a point of emphasis with Landry, was disastrous during the Redskins' 231-yard rushing performance. The Giants, meanwhile, gained all of 74 yards on the ground, with Frank Gifford gaining 61 of them. Mel Triplett and Alex Webster combined for just 13 yards, with Triplett fumbling in the first quarter to set up Washington's second touchdown.

The way Dorow worked in a 10-of-18, 160-yard outing, one would never know he threw three interceptions that day. But neither Don Heinrich nor Charlie Conerly could capitalize, and the end result was the second-most lopsided loss of the entire Lombardi-Landry era in New York.

It was a physically brutal game, too. Gifford, guard Bill Austin, and Jim Katcavage all wound up on the injured list. Linebacker Bill Svoboda absorbed the cruelest blows as doctors needed nineteen stitches to close gashes on his face and left eye. The Giants limped out of Washington's Griffith Stadium bloodied both literally and figuratively.

Lombardi said not a word as he spent the five-hour train ride back to Penn Station reading the newspapers and descending deep into his usual sulk following a bad performance. But this had been much worse than a bad day. This was a disaster, and old Mr. High-Low was as low as the tide ever got at Coney Island. And while he was quiet on the train, he had plenty to say during the film breakdown the following day. As Landry and Jim Lee Howell sat mostly silent amid the plethora of failed blocks and missed tackles that flickered on the screen, Lombardi bellowed several times. "Jesus Christ! Hold onto the god-damned ball," he yelled as the projector showed Triplett's fumble. "Can't anybody out there block?" he screamed at another point as two Redskins threw Alex Webster for a seven-yard loss.

If that coaches-only session wasn't fun, the mood got worse when they presented the carnage in its grand totality to the players that Tuesday. Howell took the lead in that meeting, blasting just about everyone. He had even taken a shot at Lombardi and Landry (as well as himself) in interviews. "We did it up real good last Sunday," Slim Jim said. "No one, on the offense or defense, played a good game, and that includes the coaches." And then the whole lot of them put the team through a grueling practice where Lombardi delivered an ear-pounding from start to finish.

Perhaps even more startling than Lombardi's stepped up verbal abuse was Landry's role in the aftermath. Never one to get excited before, Landry let his entire defense have it in true minimalist style. "You can do better," he told his unit, "if for no other reason than you can hardly do worse."

For the silent man from Mission, Texas, that was like throwing a chair through a window.

Few took any comfort in the Cardinals' loss to the Steelers that week, even though it kept the Giants in first place in the Eastern Conference by one game. Some tough battles lay ahead in a stretch that would turn the end of the season into a do-or-die affair.

*   *   *

Landry continued to harangue his unit through the rest of the week that preceded Sunday's home game against the Chicago Bears. Paddy Driscoll's team came to town with just one loss, but were locked in a real struggle in the Western Conference with Buddy Parker's Detroit Lions. At least they didn't have to worry about the perennial Western strong boy, Los Angeles, because the 1955 conference champs were on their way to a 4–8, last-place finish.

The Bears hadn't visited the Giants since 1949, but the Giants knew exactly who they were. Bears-Giants went back to the very beginnings of the NFL. The newspapers of the week preceding that November 25 contest were filled with columns spewing yarns of long-ago epics. There was the first one, in 1925, where more than 70,000 fans jammed into the Polo Grounds to watch college great Red Grange in a game that saved Tim Mara's fledgling club financially. There was also the "Sneakers Game" that decided the 1934 NFL championship, a frigid scene that ironically would be re-enacted in the final game of the 1956 season. They talked about the 1927 blood-and-mud battle that left both teams exhausted wrecks.

These Bears sported a 7–1 record and a one-game lead over the Lions, thanks to the Packers' 24–20 upset of Detroit on Thanksgiving Day. Their defense, featuring ferocious middle guard Bill George, was just as powerful as the Giants', and their lead-leading offense averaged 36 points per game. They had the NFL's leading touchdown man and rusher, Rick Casares, and a strong passing attack headed by quarterback Ed Brown and fleet-footed end Harlon Hill. "The best team in football," Howell called them.

The Giants? Aside from an emotionally trying week, they weren't in such bad shape. Gifford and Austin recovered from their wounds nicely and would play. Even Svoboda made it back, his unhealed gashes guarded by a special mask.

They felt even better once the game kicked off at frigid Yankee Stadium. The Giants dominated, shooting out to a 17–0 lead on a Ben Agajanian field goal, Don Heinrich's 17-yard touchdown pass to Kyle Rote, and Alex Webster's two-yard touchdown run that Dick Modzelewski set up by forcing a third-quarter fumble at the Bears' 18. It should well have been the end of a brief downturn, but two things happened late in the game.

First, the Bears caught fire. And Lombardi, possibly for the first time in his coaching career—but certainly for the last— played it way too cautious at the end.

Lombardi's mistake lay not in his decision to replace the successful Heinrich with Charlie Conerly in the fourth quarter. That was simply the system he'd employed all season, though Conerly was usually inserted into the game earlier. If neither man ever grew enamored of the arrangement—Heinrich's "You guinea sonofabitch!" rebukes to Lombardi supplied ample evidence of that—they at least tolerated it. Conerly never did see the sense in it, but he never complained, either. Griping wasn't in his nature. The two quarterbacks grew close personally, and the system generally benefited their on-field work.

No, the system wasn't Lombardi's mistake. Instead it was what Lombardi told Conerly as he inserted him after George Blanda's field goal made the score 17–3 in the fourth quarter.

"Be cautious out there," Lombardi advised the quarterback he called "the Pro." Conerly was, if nothing else, the ultimate professional.

He had basically told his quarterback to keep the ball on the ground and sit on the lead. Conerly did, as best he could. But the careful drives, which served only to let a vulnerable Bears defense off the hook, opened the door just enough for the Goose Special and the Up and Out to leave Lombardi kicking himself.

With 8:09 left on the clock, end Bill "Goose" McColl lined up as a back and took a handoff from Brown and darted off to his right. Suddenly, just as Harlon Hill was outrunning safeties Emlen Tunnell and Jimmy Patton 50 yards down the right sideline, McColl uncorked an monster throw that found Hill in the clear. The 6-foot-3 end gathered it in and sprinted the final 29 yards untouched for a 79-yard touchdown play. The Goose Special.

Unable to run out the clock on their ensuing possession, the Giants left the Bears one last shot with just over a minute to play. Hill went down the middle and cut it up to the right—Up and Out—getting past Jimmy Patton. Brown let fly with a 56-yard pass and Hill, tipping the ball at the 5, and again at the 4 as Patton hit him, gathered it in spectacularly as he hit the ground in the end zone.

Blanda's extra point tied the score at 17, as miraculous a result for the Bears as it was a devastating one for the Giants. Even worse, some of the fans serenaded the Giants to their postgame locker room with the first boos heard all season.

The players, still a half-game ahead of Washington and the Cardinals for the Eastern Conference lead at 6–2–1, were well aware they were 0–1–1 over their last two games. And considering this was a game in which both coaches and players let a sure knockout victim off the ropes, it hurt that much more.

"The Giants reacted afterward as if they'd just lost a game, everyone being in the bluest state of mind," the *Times'* Arthur Daley wrote the next day.

Lombardi swore he would never again let up on an opponent. The concept of sitting on a lead immediately became a foreign concept to him in light of the events of November 25, 1956. "From then on, no matter what the score was, I coached as if it was nothing-nothing," Lombardi said years later.

*   *   *

As one might imagine, the post-mortem of a second Giants disaster was hardly a happy affair, what with critical home games against Washington and Cleveland and the season finale in Philadelphia remaining. If there was a small bright spot, it was that Landry's defense could be partially exonerated. The secondary did make plenty of mistakes against the Bears, but Tom Landry also pointed out that Harlon Hill had made a couple of exceptional catches. His routes and execution had been perfect, especially on the last one. Patton had been in excellent position and had delivered a jarring shot that would have dislodged the ball from any other pass catcher. Defensive end Andy Robustelli and linebacker Sam Huff would tell future authors it was one of the greatest catches they'd ever seen.

Lombardi wasn't nearly as charitable with his group. He blasted them for scoring one touchdown over the last twenty-five minutes and warned that performances like that would not do if they expected to win the conference. Really, his laments were misdirected, and nothing short of hypocritical. He was the one who had told Conerly to play it close to the vest over the final quarter. He was the one who refused to let Conerly test a tired defense when a mere additional field goal would have put the game out of reach. He was the one who sat on the lead.

But that's football, then and now. As in the Army, shit rolls downhill.

As was always the case with Lombardi, however, his bombast had a purpose. The Redskins were coming and that 33–7 pounding lay only two games in the past, so he wanted to make sure the latest horrors with Chicago didn't blot out that first disaster. "You guys better wake up for Washington next Sunday, or it's going to be over," he said. "You all know what they did to us last time."

This time, the Giants were ready. Their Yankee Stadium locker room was nearly silent in the hours leading up to kickoff, totally absent of the good-natured give-and-take of happier times. Some things didn't change, though. Jim Katcavage, called Mr. First by his teammates because of his obsession with being first into the locker room, onto the bus, or on the practice field, was already there when the others filed in. Cliff Livingston was well into his tradition of meditating on the couch, closed eyes aimed at the ceiling, open playbook on lap.

The Giants then went out and tore the Redskins apart, 28–14. Gifford, destined to earn that year's MVP award, had what Lombardi called his best game as a Giant. He figured in all four touchdowns, running for two, catching one, and passing for one. His 18 points tied what was then the club single-game scoring record. And the108 yards he gained on 19 carries (an average of 5.7 yards per rush) marked the first time a Giants runner had eclipsed the 100-yard mark in a game that season. Gifford also caught 6 passes for 53 yards.

The Giants hit the Redskins for two touchdowns in the first quarter, and then added others in the third and fourth quarters.

The most impressive aspect of the offense's game plan was, again, Lombardi's willingness to adjust. The winding and rewinding of film from that first encounter might have been excruciating for the staff to watch, but it revealed hidden treasures. One of them showed the reason a particular sweep right to Gifford—the Belly 26 Reverse—failed to work. "After seeing pictures of the move, we decided on the new angle at the end of the play," Lombardi said.

Lombardi turned it into an option pass, and it produced a 29-yard scoring throw to Ken MacAfee for the Giants' first touchdown. Don Heinrich's double-fake to Triplett up the middle and to Webster coming left across the backfield set the whole thing up. Gifford, the right halfback, eventually took the real handoff, and proceeded as if on a sweep with right guard Jack Stroud leading the interference. Meanwhile, right end MacAfee headed out for a pass, as opposed to his decoy status on the left side in the original sweep play. At the point Gifford ordinarily would turn upfield, he stopped and threw, finding a wide open MacAfee as the defensive backs abandoned him to stop the run.

The defense, urged on in the now traditional chant of "Dee-fense! Dee-fense!" picked off Al Dorow four times. Sam Huff accounted for two of them and Jimmy Patton added another, but the most important one came at the hands of interceptor extraordinaire, Emlen Tunnell, who picked one off in the end zone when it was still a game in the second quarter.

Now, many outside the locker room were thinking the Giants had the stuff of champions. And with one win over the last two games, the Giants would have their chance to prove it on the field.

A rematch with the Browns was up next on the schedule. This time around, the Giants couldn't help themselves with any electronic monkey business, since commissioner Bert Bell had outlawed such things in the days after the Browns' failed Game 2 experiment. This one would be pure football, which was probably better for Paul Brown, whose rebuilding team had floundered to 4–6. Still, his Browns had won three of their last five games, and had gotten healthier since their first meeting with the Giants. They also had a decent quarterback in Tommy O'Connell, who had replaced injured George Ratterman and Babe Parilli four games earlier.

The Giants entered as 10 ½-point favorites, but the Browns were ready for them. With Lou Groza making up for the punishment Andy Robustelli inflicted on him the first time around, the Browns tore at the Giants' defense with a series of traps and draws, utterly befuddling Landry's group. Robustelli was unable to use his patented spin move because of Groza's aggressiveness, and guard Herschel Forester kept Dick Modzelewski in place. That allowed other blockers to handle Huff.

Triplett's fumble on the Giants' 19, undoubtedly an event that sent Lombardi's rocket-like emotions into full-scale take-off, created the Browns' first touchdown in the opening quarter. Conerly found Gifford in the end zone at the end of an 85-yard drive in the second quarter to tie the game, but the Giants didn't score again on the cold, muddy December afternoon. "Against the Browns' energetic and spirited aggregation, the New Yorkers were a do-nothing, go-nowhere outfit," lamented the *Times* the next day. "They seemed sluggish on defense and immobile on offense."

Cleveland backs Fred Morrison and Preston Carpenter were the chief beneficiaries of Brown's trapping game plan. Indicative of the damage inflicted was the 74-yard drive that produced the Browns' second touchdown and a 17–7 lead in the second quarter. The Browns ripped off 13 plays, and O'Connell's 6-yard touchdown pass to Morrison was the only throw of the series.

"We couldn't stop them," Howell said. "We just weren't sharp. We took too long getting the ball, and then when we did, we did nothing with it."

The Browns went on to beat the Giants 24–7, and the Yankee Stadium crowd booed both the previously-beloved defense and Conerly, who finished a weak 10-of-24 for 103 yards. The defense? They allowed Morrison 116 rushing yards, eight more than the Giants totaled. Gifford had just 16 yards rushing but did manage to gain 56 yards on six catches, setting a then-franchise record for receptions in a season.

The game was the home finale. Little did the small crowd of 27,707 know that the units they booed off the field would, in three weeks, afford them the champagne taste of a championship season. But first they had to dispatch Philadelphia.

It was actually a do-or-die game at Connie Mack Stadium the following week. The Giants needed either a win or tie that Saturday to lock up the Eastern Conference crown.

It was easier than they expected. The Eagles, 1–6 over their last seven games, had been destroyed by injuries. It took the Giants just two failed series to throw their offense into gear, and Webster, Triplett, and Gifford did the rest. The Giants did a masterful job with Lombardi's run-heavy game-plan, amassing 291 yards on the ground. Meanwhile, the defensive front held the Eagles to 71 just rushing yards. Writers dubbed them "the Fearsome Foursome," making Andy Robustelli, Rosey Grier, Dick Modzelewski, and Jim Katcavage the nominal ancestors of a future Rams Fearsome Foursome that, not ironically, would feature Grier teamed with Deacon Jones, Merlin Olsen, and Lamar Lundy.

Don Heinrich went the whole way for the first time as the coaches decided kept the thirty-five-year-old Conerly on the bench for safe keeping. Heinrich threw just 11 passes, completing four of them for 41 yards and also throwing an interception towards the end of the first half.

Gifford threw an option pass to Kyle Rote for the first touchdown, and then ran in from the 10 for a second score. In the third quarter, Em Tunnell picked off Adrian Burk deep in Eagles territory to set up Alex Webster's touchdown run. The Eagles offense didn't cross the 50 until the fourth quarter.

Whether they had in their minds the fickleness of the football gods or the fact that they simply didn't know who they would play for the championship, the players rejoiced little in the post-game locker room. Aside from Jim Lee Howell going around the room glad-handing his players for the franchise's ninth conference title in history—its first in a decade —the mood was almost businesslike.

That was appropriate. Since they last won a title in 1938, the Giants had gone to four championship games and had lost by a cumulative score of 102–30. They had lost each of those games by a touchdown or more, and the Packers and Bears had routed them, 27–0 and 37–9 in' 39 and' 41, respectively. The players and coaches knew there was much work to be done.

*　*　*

Tom Landry and Kyle Rote saw first-hand who they'd have to beat for the trophy. Howell sent them to Wrigley Field to scout the Lions-Bears game for the Western title the next day, Sunday. They came back that night armed not only with a full scouting report, but a warning: Protect yourselves.

The 38–21 Bears victory was nothing short of a bloodbath. And that was to say nothing of the 444 yards of total offense the

Bears rolled up, or the 190 rushing yards Rick Casares totaled all by himself. Plus, there was real blood that spilled onto the Wrigley Field grass.

The effusion started with the opening kickoff and proceeded throughout the game in six separate brawls. The dustups, however, were simply sidelights to what happened seventeen minutes after the kickoff. That's when Bears defensive end Ed Meadows knocked out Detroit's free-wheeling and hard-living quarterback, Bobby Layne, with a concussion. In the days that followed, Lions coach Buddy Parker alleged to the NFL that Meadows had cranked up a roundhouse punch to level Layne, and threatened to resign if Meadows went unpunished. But a subsequent investigation exonerated the defensive end and drew an apology from Parker.

In the final three minutes, the crowd ringing the Wrigley Field sidelines swarmed the field and caused a near riot as team officials and cops spent several minutes breaking it up. Parker had his own opinions about that, too, noting that profit-monger George Halas was the only owner in the league who sold standing room spots on the field, and that fans at Wrigley had disrupted games two straight weeks.

Jim Lee Howell, perhaps in an effort to deny the Bears any bulletin board material, took a diplomatic approach to the grizzly events when asked about them by reporters. He said the general play around the NFL had been the cleanest in years, and could not condemn the Bears for the tactics they used in that tough, 17–17 tie at Yankee Stadium. "That was a hard-fought game, too, but [there was] no extreme rough stuff that I can remember," Howell said. "I know I won't stand for any dirty stuff from my players. I'd rather get rid of them first, no matter how good they might be."

Interesting words coming from a coach who knew first-hand
how ruthless the Chicago Bears could be. He was on the field,
playing defensive end, when the Giants got a taste of football,
Bears style, in the 24–14 championship game loss of 1946. In
that one, the vicious middle guard Ed Sprinkle was George
Halas's hitman. He was known to many as "the meanest man in
football" and nicknamed "the Claw." Indeed, that day he lived
up to both names, as Sprinkle had a direct hand in sending two
Giants to the hospital. Running back Frank Reagan suffered a
broken nose and a concussion thanks to a Sprinkle hit and quarterback Frankie Filchock was taken away with a broken nose
after Sprinkle nailed him with a left hook.

Coach Steve Owen was so livid afterward that he called them
a dirty team.

So when Meadows did his dastardly deeds against the Lions,
Howell was far from ignorant about the potential for cheap
hits. But perhaps that's because he knew his players, like many
others around the league, always had the "bootsie" in their back
pocket.

The bootsie essentially was a player's form of old-fashioned
vigilantism. Should an opponent depart from the unwritten
rules of football etiquette, a huddle call for retaliation could
come from the offended unit to knock said miscreant out of the
game. It might cost a team 15 yards on a personal foul call, but
it was all in the name of justice.

According to the players, the coaches wouldn't teach it. Especially Landry, who never wanted to give an opponent advanta-
geous field position through penalty.

"You don't play dirty," said Sam Huff, who undoubtedly
participated in his share of bootsies. "I've been accused of that,

but I never played dirty. You wouldn't do it. We weren't taught that. Landry would never teach that."

But the players always knew somehow that retaliation for a cheap shot was just a signal call away.

"There were some games, they were like games of war," Rosey Grier said. "There were some teams that did things to our teammates. We had a bootsie play to get that one particular guy. A guy on the next play would tackle him and the rest of the guys would put him out. That was a 15-yard penalty. So we had a way of protecting a ballplayer if we thought [a guy] was playing outside the rules. If you're outside the rules, you have no right being in the game.

"It's not after the whistle. In the game itself, a guy would deliberately tackle him and the rest of the guys would pummel him. That's a 15-yard penalty."

The bootsie could be run on any unit, but it would be used in only the severest of cases. Ill-feelings could escalate after a bootsie.

"Then they'd run a bootsie on us," Grier said. "And then you'd see a series of ballplayers being carried off the field."

Bootsies were only run with great discretion, and might even be called off if the teams had to meet again. That's what happened in one game where Em Tunnell, as good a kick returner as an interceptor, was targeted and eventually knocked unconscious on special teams. Charlie Conerly brought the offensive huddle together and called for a bootsie, but after lingering a bit so he wouldn't tip it off by breaking the huddle too quickly, Conerly had a change of heart. He called off the bootsie. The only thing was that Gifford, a flanker on that play, had already headed out to his position and never heard the change.

Upon the snap, Gifford rammed the offending defender to the ground, standing over him, wondering where everybody else went to. The defender remained sufficiently shocked and motionless long enough for an official to get over there and step between the two, quite possibly saving Gifford from another serving of justice.

Others, like Grier, never really had the stomach for the bootsie. That Grier eschewed it is no surprise, considering he became a minister after his playing days. But he never forgot the chaos the great San Francisco and Pittsburgh running back John Henry Johnson caused.

"They'd say if you go after him and don't get him, he got you," Grier said. "I remember one time we were playing against them with the Steelers, he laid out one of our guys and we went after him but we got another guy. Somehow, I ended up against John Henry Johnson legitimately, and he grabbed me by my helmet and he was trying to twist my neck off. I told him, 'Hey, John. I know you have to protect your guy, but I don't shoot at a ballplayer. So if I come at you, I'm gonna get you, but I don't play that way.' He apologized for twisting my head around.

"It was a rough time."

*   *   *

Landry imparted all the warnings and caveats in his characteristically understated manner during his scouting report. But he also informed the players of two other key bits of information. The first was that Ed Meadows may be the Bears' hired gun, but their other defensive end, Jack Hoffman, was the better player. He said the best Bear on defense that game was, in fact, Hoffman, even though he didn't cripple anybody.

The other was that Paddy Driscoll used the lightning-fast J. C. Caroline on both offense and defense. Caroline was strictly a defensive back when the Giants first played them, but against the Lions he saw action as a halfback, too. Thus, he became a stunning change-of-pace back to the tough Rick Casares, the NFL's rushing king of 1956 and author of a 68-yard touchdown run in the Lions game.

For the next two weeks, the Giants trained hard, thanks to the stepped up practice schedule Howell instituted. And Lombardi and Landry had them studying film, which had to be a laborious, tedious process since the Bears-Lions film the Bears sent was shot from the end zone, so distant that few numbers and even fewer details could be discerned.

Sam Huff got his assignment early—follow Casares. One-on-one.

*   *   *

Sunday, December 30, was a lovely winter's day—if one were a polar bear. For the 56,836 fans, many of whom streamed into Yankee Stadium well before the 2 p.m. kickoff, it was one of the coldest days of their lives. A strong wind was blowing in from the centerfield bleachers through the outfield goal posts, contributing to the minus-20-degree wind-chill factor. The cold bit so hard that the cops eventually had to step in when some of the frozen bleacherites built a trash can fire in a futile attempt to stay warm.

For Lombardi and Landry, the day started in nervous fashion. Each of them knew the Giants' fate in championship games had not been good, and by now they were all well aware of the havoc the Bears could create. Besides seeing visions of their players hauled off the field on stretchers—an ever more distinct possibility now that serious postseason money was on the line—they knew well the Bears' explosive potential on offense. Chicago's 363 points, just over 30 points per game, led the league and stood 99 points better than the Giants, scoring leaders of the Eastern Conference. But they also knew that the Giants had the better defense. It had allowed just 16.4 points per game, third-lowest in the NFL.

So it was a somber trip to Yankee Stadium for both assistants. Lombardi, in fact, didn't say a word to Vince Jr. on the ride from their Oradell, New Jersey, home. "During the regular season, he might critique my play in a high school game he'd seen me play the day before," the son said. "But as I recall, he didn't say anything on the way to the championship game."

For most of the players, though, the morning was pretty routine. Andy Robustelli kept to his ritual of attending early Mass with his wife, Jeanne, and then sitting down to his usual game day breakfast of steak, toast, and tea before heading off about 10 a.m. But even before Sunday came, he had already made a significant contribution to the Giants' efforts. Remembering how well sneakers had worked for the Giants in 1934 on a frozen championship game field—the fabled "Sneakers Game" against the Bears—Howell had asked Robustelli to procure another shipment for what were sure to be adverse conditions this time around. Robustelli, the owner of a sporting goods store in Greenwich, had his partner, Ed Clark, pick up four dozen pairs of U.S. Rubber's new Big League sneakers and deliver them to the locker room.

Whether two weeks of preparation had made them confident, or whether it was just their personality, the players were loose and joking in the locker room, much to the consternation of their tightly wound coaches. But Howell didn't intercede. He had other, more important things on his mind, like figuring out whether those new shoes would come in handy or not.

An hour before game time, he sent rookie halfback Gene Filipski out on the frozen field wearing the sneakers, while defensive back Ed Hughes ran around in metal cleats. After watching Filipski cut flawlessly while Hughes stumbled on his first change of direction, Howell declared, "Sneakers all around!"

Filipski, the twenty-five-year-old rookie messenger boy of the radio hijinks in Cleveland in Game 2, had great reason to smile. He would get the first touch of the game, as he had become the Giants' kickoff returner. The thick-soled sneakers, he figured, would allow him to pick up extra yardage.

He had other reasons to be thankful that frigid day, however, and they involved Vince Lombardi. Filipski had played on Lombardi's unit at West Point until he was dismissed in 1951, along with eighty-two other cadets, in the Honor Code scandal that destroyed the varsity roster. Lombardi, who helped many of the expelled boys find other colleges, pointed Filipski to Villanova, where he performed well enough to prompt the Browns to draft him in the third round. He wasn't going to make it there, but Lombardi persuaded the Giants to send a seventh-round pick for him.

Without Lombardi, the 5-foot-10, 180-pound Filipski would not have had a career in pro football. Today, he was going to reward the offensive assistant for everything he'd done for him.

The opening kickoff came to Filipski at the Giants' 7-yard line. He headed up field and broke one tackle at the 25, and another at the 40. As his teammates set up some solid blocking for him, Filipski crossed midfield with only three Bears left to beat. But bruising, 255-pound rookie John Mellekas brought him down on the concrete-hard turf at the Bears 39, 54 yards from where Filipski began his journey.

"We were on our way when Gene Filipski returned the opening kickoff (54) yards," Lombardi said. "That good criss-cross blocking for the runner who went straight up the field showed the team was out for a 33-man effort."

The offense took it from there. Given the field conditions, Howell followed Lombardi's pregame advice to "keep it simple." So the passing game took a distant back seat to the running game throughout. And early on, that mean some heavy use for bullish fullback Mel Triplett.

Gifford set things up when he wrestled a pass away from J. C. Caroline at the 17. Then, Lombardi sent in Triplett's favorite play, "Run-99." Triplett, No. 33, would take the handoff and run directly behind the up-the-middle power blocking of No. 66, guard Jack Stroud. Add the 33 and 66, and you have the name of the play.

Triplett indeed followed Stroud, but also got a terrific block from left tackle Rosie Brown as the fullback barreled through. Triplett carried two Bears up the middle for a touchdown and flattened umpire Sam Wilson in the process.

Robustelli recovered a Casares fumble on the Bears' second play from scrimmage, and Ben Agajanian converted that into a 17-yard field goal soon after for a 10–0 Giants lead. On the Bears' next possession, Jimmy Patton nabbed an interception as Robustelli interrupted Ed Brown's throw with a shot to the knees. Agajanian's 43-yard field goal, his season long, made the score 13–0.

The Bears never did get started. When they attempted a Caroline run on fourth-and-1 near the end of the first quarter, linebacker Bill Svoboda and defensive back Em Tunnell beat the speedster to the hole and dropped him for a loss.

Lombardi kept the offense basic in the frigid conditions, calling safe passes and lots of runs. By the time Agajanian hit his long field goal, Conerly had replaced starter Heinrich. He'd come out wearing gloves, an idea he picked up from an old Mississippi friend, Jackie Parker, who had played in Canada for the Edmonton Eskimos. But a fumbled exchange on that field goal drive had Lombardi in his ear. The coach quickly convinced him that the gloves were a handicap. "I thought I could pass better with them," Conerly later explained. "I still think I might have, but I fumbled the pass from center once and I agreed to take them off."

Not that he had to look downfield much after that. Alex Webster started the next possession with a 6-yard sweep to the right, and Gifford went up the middle to the Bears' 26. On third-and-6, Conerly faked a throw to the left and dumped it off to Webster, who took it 22 yards to the Bears' 4. Webster went off left guard on the next play for a touchdown and a 20–0 Giants lead.

The Giants were actually responsible for the Bears' only score, too. Tunnell fumbled the next Bears punt at the Giants' 25. Despite Harland Svare sniffing out a deep reverse to Caroline at the 9, Casares broke through for a touchdown halfway through the second period.

A Conerly flip to Webster went for 50 yards as receiver Pete MacAfee led the downfield blocking. Triplett banged up the middle to the 3, and Webster's touchdown dive off right guard put the Giants up 27–7. The Bears bobbled the ensuing kickoff at the 7, after which Brown barely escaped a safety as Grier, part of an all-out pass rush, brought the quarterback down at the 1. Showcasing another of his many skills, Robustelli then blocked a punt which Henry Moore fell on in the end zone for a 34–7 halftime lead.

With the game well in hand, many of the frostbitten spectators headed for the exits. They had no worries. The Giants had just put up their biggest offensive first half of the season, and had scored 14 more points than the Bears' defense had yielded on average over the entire schedule.

Casares and his blockers were never really able to get going on the frozen field, while the Giants moved flawlessly. There remains a common misconception that the Bears fell victim to their metal cleats as they had in 1934, but they in fact wore sneakers, too. It was just that the ones that came out of Robustelli's stock room were better.

"I don't know where they got theirs," Driscoll said, "but those sneakers were better than ours. The soles were thicker than the soles of our shoes, and I think that helped their footing greatly."

The Giants' dominance on both offense and defense continued in the third quarter as Lombardi, in fedora and tan coat with white wool trim around the neck, and Landry in black topcoat and what would become his trademark snap-brim fedora, prowled the sidelines. Aside from the combatants, however, few eyewitnesses remained.

The Bears actually made it to the Giants' 3-yard line early in the quarter, but Tunnell and Ed Hughes broke up a third down Brown pass to Bill McColl in the end zone. On fourth down, Dick Nolan and Patton combined to break up Brown's throw to Hill, with Patton stripping it out.

There would be no miracle comebacks against Landry's well-prepared and hungry defense on this day.

But there would be more scoring. Conerly found Kyle Rote between the goalposts for a 40–7 lead and capped the scoring with a touchdown pass to Gifford before exiting the game to raucous applause for third-stringer Bob Clatterbuck. Conerly, much maligned during the down years, earned the skimpy, but standing, ovation after his 7-for-10, 195-yard, 2-touchdown performance.

Gifford added some elegant acrobatics to the proceedings, half-pirouetting and then ducking under penetrating defensive end Dick Klawitter, then breaking a linebacker's tackle for a 16-yard gain on a blown run-pass option. "Big play, 48-pitchout," Gifford said. "Get the ball from the quarterback and head outside."

The final score was 47–7. Not only had Lombardi's offense torn up the vaunted Chicago defense, but Tom Landry's defense had shut down the league's highest-scoring team. Sam Huff brutalized Casares (43 yards on 14 carries) all afternoon. And big Rosey Grier became such a major part of the effort that famed *New York Post* columnist Jimmy Cannon anointed him, along with the rest of Landry's unit, as a Giants' savior. "But it was the Giants' defense, moving with a ramming agility, that decided the ballgame and Roosevelt Grier, massing and quick, was thrilling as he smashed at the Chicago offense, waving his arms to distract passers, tipping off blockers, and dragging down the runners with a controlled brutality," Cannon wrote.

The postgame locker room was far different than the one after the conference clinching. Glad hands all around. Even Conerly, a man of precious few words, could not contain himself. "Yippee!" he exulted. "Champions of the world! Yippee! 47–7! Can you imagine? Yippee!" And his amazement continued into the evening, as he asked everyone in sight, "Do you realize we're champions of the whole wide world? That covers a lot of territory." To which one wise-acre or another would answer, "Hey, Charlie! Don't forget Afghanistan, or Outer Mongolia, or Dutch Guiana!"

Howell gave Robustelli a game ball. Robustelli turned around and said, "This doesn't belong to me," and gave the ball to Landry. Robustelli told the press that it was simply because the

Giants had the Bears well-scouted that victory was possible, a nod toward Landry's meticulous study habits.

Howell summed it up. "The way our defense and offense played was a great tribute to two men," he said. "Vince Lombardi and Tom Landry."

* * *

The championship brought to an end the first season of nationally televised football. The NFL was catching on with the public. The Giants had caught on in New York, especially at popular establishments of the day like Toots Shor's, Mike Manuche's, and anywhere else Giants players congregated.

"We became like the toast of the town," Rosey Grier said. "We could go out and park my car down in Harlem and no one would touch it."

And Jim Lee Howell's assistants had begun to grab the attention of front offices around the league.

For Vince Lombardi, the rewards of 1956 made the road to a head coaching job that much shorter.

6

FINALLY, AN OFFER

THE GIANTS DEFENSE may have taken center stage for good, but it was Vince Lombardi who became a star. The points explosion that blew away the Bears in the 1956 championship game had given the offensive coach league-wide exposure. Anyone who knew anything about what made the Giants tick understood it wasn't just the thick-soled sneakers that did in the Bears' mighty defense—it was Lombardi's offensive game plan.

Even an up, down, and finally out 1957 season that saw the balance of Eastern power shift back to the Browns would not dilute Lombardi's reputation among the NFL's more astute minds. By late January 1958, those observations reached the ears of Eagles general manager Vince McNally, and McNally was certainly in a listening mood. Hugh Devore had guided the Eagles to last and next-to-last place finishes in the two years since he arrived from Dayton. But despite having to pay Devore's in the last remaining year of his contract, the Eagles hierarchy was bent on replacing the upstanding man critics characterized as "a nice guy who finished last."

Weeks of media speculation ended when they fired Devore January 11. A month-long coaching search ensued as the Eagles threw twenty candidates into the pot.

Tops on the list were two names—Buck Shaw, the man who beat out Lombardi for the Air Force job in 1955, and Lombardi. Were it not for Wellington Mara, the offensive mastermind might well have spent his next summer leading a detested enemy's training camp.

And coming to hate the job.

Lombardi and his reputation had come too far for that. In the end, he decided to wait for another, better opportunity.

*   *   *

Nineteen fifty-seven was a year of irony for both Vince Lombardi and Tom Landry, but also a year of achievement. Through the first nine games, their units appeared poised to fulfill the pundits' predictions of a championship game repeat. They had compiled a 7–2 record and were neck and neck with the Cleveland Browns, who that year had drafted a running back that basically turned tough fullback Ed Modzelewski's career upside down.

"This kid from Syracuse came along, Jim something, and that was it for me," Modzelewski said, laughing.

By the time James Nathaniel "Jim" Brown finished abusing would-be tacklers in 1965, he would hold every significant career rushing record in the league. To this day, many regard him as the greatest running back who ever lived. But back in 1957, the legend was just starting, as was Brown's unforgettable personal rivalry with Sam Huff.

Brown singlehandedly brought Cleveland out of its one-year, 5–7 slumber with a running style that befitted his 6-2, 232-pound, V-shaped torso. Huge, with a broad chest that tapered into a nothing waist, only to flare out again in a set of massive legs, he could run over people and leave them not only beaten, but mangled as well. Fast, he could outrun the quickest linebackers. Wily, he changed gears frequently, slowing to let a cornerback draw a bead on him, and then accelerating to leave said DB spinning and grasping at air. Devious, he rarely let on whether he was hurt or not as a slow, labored rise from the turf always gave the impression of injury.

And then the next snap would come.

Huff knew the drill well. The two had met during Huff's career at West Virginia, with Brown leaving him with four smashed teeth after he trampled the All-America middle guard. Huff likened tackling Brown to hitting a tree. But in their encounters through the years, Huff and his teammates made like lumberjacks and felled that tree many a time. Nobody handled Brown better than the Giants, and nobody on the Giants handled him better than Huff. Though the great running back might get frustrated at times, he was never dirty. A good, hard tackle might well be answered with a pat on the shoulder pads, a smile, and a "Nice tackle, big Sam."

Brown's pro debut against the Giants was not particularly auspicious by supernatural standards, though certainly above average by most mortal measurements. The Giants, with Landry keeping his group in his normal 4-3 alignment, "held" the rookie to 89 yards on 21 carries, with no touchdowns. The Browns won the defensive battle, 6–3, on Lou Groza's 47-yard field goal with just twenty-one seconds remaining.

Howell basically cost the Giants a tie when he took Ben Agajanian's field goal that would have put the Giants up 6–0 off the board to accept a drive-prolonging offside penalty. Agajanian then missed a 14-yard chip shot.

Landry later changed his tactics when it came to defending Brown, making the fullback Huff's sole responsibility. But the fact that the defense handled Brown in the opener not only foreshadowed how well the Giants would defend him, but that they would survive—at least for a while—the absence of their huge space-eating defensive tackle.

Rosey Grier had gone into the Army.

A lot of the Giants joked that before Grier struck fear into the hearts of his country's enemies, Uncle Sam would first have to find a uniform that fit him. But all laughs aside, it took some juggling to make up for his 300-pound presence. Landry moved Jim Katcavage inside from end, making him a fulltime starter. The rest of the line, with Robustelli at end, Dick Modzelewski at tackle, and Walt Yowarsky at the other end, remained solid. And linebackers Harland Svare and Bill Svoboda continued as strong complements to Huff in the middle.

The defense pitched shutouts against Pittsburgh and Philadelphia in a 7–1 run after that Opening Day loss. A goal line stand and defensive touchdowns by Huff and Em Tunnell beat the Packers 31–17 a week after their second loss.

Lombardi's bunch wasn't doing too badly, either. By now, they were a veteran group that had played as an intact unit since 1955. In fact, the only rookie out of the twenty-seven players the Giants drafted in 1957 to make the squad was an end from Texas Southern named Don Maynard. He would spend most of his two years with the Giants as a kick returner before forging a Hall of Fame career with the Jets.

Aside from Maynard, whose greatness lay well in the future, the Giants came up empty in one of the most transformative drafts in history. Besides Jim Brown, that draft sent Stanford quarterback John Brodie to the 49ers, Notre Dame back Paul Hornung to Green Bay, Oklahoma end Tommy McDonald and Duke quarterback Sonny Jurgensen to Philadelphia, and massive but agile Ohio State tackle Jim Parker to Baltimore, among others. These players led the way to a more refined game of precision passing, moving pockets, and vertical play-making.

For now, though, the Giants and their veteran-based power game sufficed in getting past most opponents. Frank Gifford was still the smart runner, aided by an offensive line whose wisdom overrode advancing age in some spots. Alex Webster could still pound. And Kyle Rote remained one of the most electric receivers in the league, whether it was Don Heinrich or Charlie Conerly doing the throwing.

As usual, they were far from a scoring machine. But they were steady, helped by a steadfast commitment to Lombardi's game plans.

A helpful adjunct came from the upper deck, where Wellington Mara snapped pictures of opposing defenses and flung them down to Lombardi in a weighted sock, there to be analyzed by the coach and fed to Conerly on the bench while the Giants' defense did its work.

The Giants had as far back as 1955 become the professional forerunners of the photographic system all teams currently use, only they had no fancy binders to keep the mountain of pictures the camera crews send today with the press of a button. It was primitive, as most revolutionary ideas are at the start. But the combination of Lombardi's vision and Mara's willingness to do anything to help his team changed the way coaches talked to their quarterbacks between series.

The idea hadn't sprung full-blown from Lombardi's mind, however. Former Army coaching colleague Murray Warmath had put him on to it after the 1954 season. Warmath, then heading into his second year as head coach of the University of Minnesota, had heard that Florida coach Bob Woodruff was using a photo system and passed the thought along to his friend.

Lombardi didn't have to do big sell job on Mara, who was always open to any idea that would help the team win. A self-styled handyman, he didn't mind getting his hands dirty, either, whether it was shooting pictures or shagging punts at practice. He embraced the concept as enthusiastically as he did his other self-assigned duties, and headed right out to buy a Speed Graphic, the iconic bellowed camera that was standard issue for all newspaper photographers from the 1920s until well into the 1960s. Then he began experimenting. Mara jerry-rigged a Polaroid magazine to the bottom of the camera and a developing tank to the back to speed up the process.

The system needed some work. At first, the pictures were poor, almost indecipherable, sort of like Madam Curie's first X-rays. The figures on defense were so small that Lombardi could hardly make out who was who.

Eventually, Mara found that a 15-inch telescopic lens provided adequate zoom. He also learned that a thirty-second development period, as opposed to the prescribed sixty seconds, proved sufficient to get a grainy but distinguishable picture to the field in enough time for it to be useful. "We're not after any Oscar for photographic excellence," Mara said. "We're just after information."

With ends coach Ken Kavanaugh sitting next to Mara, the two formed a veritable spy ring in the sky. When they spotted an unexpected defensive formation, Kavanaugh would phone down to Lombardi and let him know a picture of a "hot situation" was coming. A sideline aide, a key go-between in the operation, would receive the sock and run it over to Lombardi.

The coach swore by the system.

"It's a tremendous help to us," Lombardi said. "I have great faith in its value.

"The visual aid to the quarterback is a lot more convincing than the old-fashioned word of mouth. He sees what we've spotted and is more apt to remember it and call for the proper play when he goes back out on the field and runs into a similar situation."

Lombardi saved the two dozen pictures Mara shot each game for future reference.

Mara and Lombardi had refined the system enough by 1957 that it was directly responsible for winning at least one game. In the team's third contest, one photo showed a Redskins linebacker shadowing the halfback who remained in position rather than the halfback Lombardi split wide, as per the coach's usual application of the T-formation. So Lombardi adjusted and went to a fullback-based attack.

Bobby Epps, starting for the injured Mel Triplett, gained 115 yards on just 13 carries in the Giants 24–20 victory.

Even the abundance of photographic artwork that flew from the upper deck weren't enough to sustain the good times, however. With the Giants at 7–2 and just a half game behind the

7–1–1 Browns, injuries took their toll on both Lombardi's and Landry's units. Svoboda was dinged up and lacked the speed he had earlier to catch fast halfbacks that now ran around him. The defensive line suffered injuries. Guard Bill Austin's age caught up with him, and he would retire after the season. Quarterback Don Heinrich missed eight games.

The Giants lost their last three games. San Francisco came first, and then a loss to Pittsburgh on a field so muddy that the description on the front page of the official score sheet read "quagmire." The Giants called it "a disgrace." A $13,200 tarp, untested before its use during the previous day's rain, had leaked at the seams, creating treacherous footing. The setback officially eliminated them from the playoff race, making the finale against the newly-crowned Eastern Conference champ Cleveland meaningless.

Landry's defense had enough left to handle Brown, holding him to 78 yards. But the defenders held down little else as Lew Carpenter went for 117. The 34–28 loss put the Giants at 7–5 and mattered little. But it did signal the true beginning of the Huff-Brown rivalry.

It was in this game that Landry made his great linebacker Brown's new best friend. Not that he keyed on Brown every play. If he had, Paul Brown would have picked up on it quickly, and he would have turned Brown into a decoy to take Huff out of the play. But the coach left no doubt that if Brown touched the ball, it was Huff's responsibility to bring him down. No ands, ifs, or buts about it.

"You didn't make excuses with Tom," Huff said.

Huff's teammates were always welcome to help, too.

"I always tell people I had both shoulders operated on, and I got knee operations and a bad ankle—all from trying to tackle Jim Brown," Dick Modzelewski said.

Landry's tactics not only produced a tremendous personal rivalry. They worked, too. Over the next two seasons, the Giants beat Cleveland five straight times, including once in the 1958 Eastern Conference playoff. Nobody in the league handled Brown, and by extension the Browns, better than the Giants during that period. The Browns managed just 40 points over those five games (an 8.0 average), and the Giants hung only one of two shutouts on them since the 1950 game where the defensive back Landry worked Steve Owen's Umbrella Defense to perfection.

The Giants did outstanding work against Jim Brown. In three seasons against Landry and Huff, Brown played in seven games, the last five of which were losses. He carried 119 times for 472 yards and three touchdowns. He never saw the end zone in the final three matchups during the Landry era.

A look at how Brown terrorized the rest of the league during that period shows just how well the Giants handled him. His seven-game, per-rush average against the Giants came in at 4.0 yards. Against the rest of the league from 1957–59, he rushed 630 times for 3,326 yards, or 5.3 yards per carry. Over that same period, he scored 37 touchdowns against anyone not wearing the Giants' red, white, and blue.

The season ended with Jim Lee Howell proclaiming that as disappointing as the 0–3 finish was, there would be no major house-cleaning for 1958. The team would instead look for some pieces—a guard to replace Austin, a bulkier cornerback, and a fast end to complement Rote.

While Howell thought about that, Lombardi pumped up his hopes for a head coaching job.

*　*　*

The phone call Lombardi had waited for all his life came to his house in late January. The Eagles were looking for a head coach, and general manager Vince McNally had heard good things about Lombardi.

Actually, Lombardi was the Eagles' third choice. Negotiations with the man who eventually took the job, Buck Shaw, had stalled because Shaw insisted on being free to return to some business interests he held in San Francisco until training camp opened in late July. Basically, he'd coach the Eagles for five months, and live in California for seven.

The Eagles were more interested in a fulltime coach, if they could get one. Hampton Poole, the former Rams coach who at the time was leading the Toronto Argonauts in Canada, might have been that choice. But the day after they fired Devore, Poole turned down the Eagles' offer and chose to stay north of the border.

Whether Lombardi was aware of the events surrounding the phone call is unknown, and unimportant. He greeted McNally's call with the enthusiasm of a little kid, and quickly arranged for a meeting at a Philadelphia train depot. The whole thing took on a cloak-and-dagger mystique, since Eagles president Frank McNamee urged McNally to contact Lombardi directly instead of going the traditional way first of asking Giants ownership for permission to talk to him. It's unlikely that route would have worked. Handing a division rival one of their prized assistants was the last thing Wellington and Jack Mara would have entertained.

Lombardi came away from that meeting with his first head coaching offer: $22,500 per year, for one or two years. That offered no security for someone charged with turning around a losing program, but McNally and McNamee were in no position to go longer. The Eagles' stockholders were upset that they were still on the hook for Devore's third year and insisted on seeing quantifiable improvement before they kept anybody past two years. An extension would be worked out if Lombardi won.

It wasn't a great deal, but considering Lombardi had already lost out on jobs at Air Force (to Shaw), Washington (to Darrel Royal), and Penn (to Steve Sebo), he wasn't about to quibble. Besides, the Eagles did have some talent.

In addition to the rookies Jurgensen and McDonald, they had just traded for the Rams' do-it-all quarterback Norm Van Brocklin. Young talent in receiver Pete Retzlaff and running back Clarence Peaks added to the attraction on offense. Lombardi certainly could have success with that group. The defense contained such names as Chuck Bednarik, a hard-hitting linebacker who nearly decapitated Frank Gifford with a devastating hit in 1960, defensive back Tom Brookshier, and linebacker Tom Scott. All would make the Pro Bowl, and Bednarik would find his way to Canton along with Van Brocklin and McDonald. The nucleus of that team would also beat Lombardi's Packers in the 1960 NFL championship game, the Eagles' last title.

The Eagles' change of venue made things even more attractive. They had just signed an agreement to move from the Phillies' tiny Connie Mack Stadium to Penn's Franklin Field, whose 67,000 seats made for the league's fourth-largest stadium behind

L.A.'s Memorial Coliseum, Cleveland's Municipal Stadium, and Yankee Stadium.

One major negative factor eventually caused Lombardi to reject the offer. The Eagles were up for sale. A syndicate headed by former Villanova athletic director Bud Dudley had made an offer of $700,000. As with current sales and mergers, any change in ownership creates instability and uncertainty down the line.

Wellington Mara brought all that up to Lombardi as soon as he caught wind of the Eagles' offer. It was a bad situation, Mara hammered home in repeated phone conversations. Lombardi could never call his own shots, even if there was no sale, because the meddlesome and unwieldy ownership group would never allow it. The Giants also had the stronger roster. Even Wellington's wife, Ann, got into it, urging Marie Lombardi to talk her husband out of it.

Lombardi was torn as the phone calls from both sides kept coming. Finally, Marie told him to go to church. Lombardi went there every day as a matter of course, imploring his god for patience and guidance. But this time, Marie didn't want him to pray.

"Just think," she said.

He did exactly that, for several hours. The next morning, he called Mara and told him he would stay.

He wanted a pro head coaching job more than anything, but the Eagles were not the right situation for him. It had to be the right job, the kind that would allow Lombardi to do things the way he wanted.

So he would wait.

Mara did make his decision easier with a significant pay bump to match the $22,500 the Eagles offered. That made him the highest paid assistant in the league, and was nearly double what his hard-working cohort Landry made.

The unsuccessful wooing of Lombardi may have been the best-kept secret in the media, though few observers outside the walls of NFL offices would have given his name a second thought. The New York newspapers made little mention of the coaching search and no mention of Lombardi as a candidate. The *Philadelphia Inquirer* threw out names like former Green Bay coach Lisle Blackbourn, Browns assistant Dick Gallagher, Steelers line coach Nick Skorich, and former Cardinals coach Ray Richards. Even the Cardinals' great running back, Charlie Trippi, came up for speculation, but Lombardi drew not a mention.

The Eagles finally hired the sixty-year-old Shaw on February 14. Lombardi, forty-four and growing ever impatient, would wait one more eventful year for his shot.

He would not let the next offer go by.

7

BEATING THE BROWNS

VINCE LOMBARDI RECEIVED his bump in pay, but Tom Landry received the biggest gift of the 1958 offseason, quite by accident.

He got Pat Summerall.

By season's end, Summerall would produce the greatest kick in one of the greatest plays in Giants and, arguably, NFL history. Without his long, improbable, and believed-to-be-impossible field goal that won the snow-swept regular-season finale against the Browns, there would have been no Eastern Conference playoff that year. Without the playoff, the Colts-Giants overtime championship game that rocketed pro football up the nation's popularity chart never would have happened.

In training camp at Oregon's Willamette College, however, Summerall was received simply as an established foot that would allow Landry, also the special teams coach, to settle on one man for his placekicking needs. He had Don Chandler for punts, but Babe was still four years away from beginning a legendary placekicking career with Allie Sherman's Giants and Lombardi's

Packers. And Ben Agajanian's injuries and flirtations with retirement had forced Landry to go with Frank Gifford on occasion.

When, in 1957, Agajanian finally hung up the massive square-toed boot that covered a right foot short four toes lost in a work accident in college, Wellington Mara went out and got Summerall from the Chicago Cardinals as a throw-in to the same trade that brought cornerback Lindon Crow. It cost the Giants steady defensive back Dick Nolan, who Mara would get back the following season, and fifth-round rookie halfback Bobby Joe Conrad.

So began a four-year stretch where Summerall led the Giants in scoring each year and missed just two out of 138 extra points. His 20-of-29 (69 percent) performance on field goals in 1959 led the league in all three categories.

But his greatest impact came in 1958. Besides the legendary field goal, he also beat the Colts in a regular-season game with a late kick, and then provided a cushioning field goal in the conference playoff against the Browns. They could easily have hung a Reggie Jackson-style nickname on him—perhaps Mr. Fourth Quarter—for nobody in the 1950s had more game-deciding field goals than the four Summerall recorded. Besides the two in '58, he beat the Rams on a kick inside two minutes in 1959, and Pittsburgh on a fourth-quarter kick in 1960.

In 1958, though, some players called him the offense, as Summerall produced 64 of the Giants' 246 points, roughly a quarter of their production, on field goals and extra points. It was no surprise that the defense remained its crusty self in relation to the offense.

"We didn't think we were doing our part, and the defense let us know about it," Summerall said. "One of the defensive players [Cliff Livingston] said to me, 'How does it feel to be our whole offense?' I didn't know how to answer that."

Summerall didn't come by his heroics by coincidence. Landry had as much to do with it as the kicker did. He was a different type of special teams coach—a guy who could actually make a kicker better because he made it his business to understand the art of kicking and the rhythm of what is called "the operation." In center Ray Wietecha, holder Charlie Conerly, and kicker Summerall, Landry had the best operation in the league, and he drilled it not only on Saturdays, the traditional day back then for special teams work, but ten to fifteen minutes every day as well.

Summerall had done well with the Cardinals during an era where most coaches left kickers to figure things out on their own. He ranked as one of the top kickers in the league while also serving as a defensive end and backup offensive end, all for a salary that topped out at $7,500 over his five seasons there. His leg strength was right up there with Lou "The Toe" Groza's, the league's pre-eminent kicker, and Summerall had already put a 50-yard field goal on his résumé. That came October 17, 1954, against the Giants. The year before, he had kicked a 49-yarder against the Giants.

In his years in Chicago, he hit 41 of 100 field goal attempts. Those numbers would, of course, buy him a one-way ticket out of any team's training camp roster today. But back then, the fact the coaches even allowed him to try that many attested to his skills. Only Groza, with 114 tries, and the Bears' George Blanda, with 90, kicked with that kind of frequency between 1953 and '57. Only the Browns, Lions, Rams, and Bears attempted more field goals than the Cardinals did in Summerall's time there.

Groza was that period's most accurate kicker, hitting 76 of those 114 tries for a .667 success rate. That, too, would be insufficient to land a job in today's NFL, which demands 85 percent.

Lombardi and Landry

For all of Summerall's success, he played for an outfit that was, and would remain for decades, decidedly second-class. The equipment dated back to the Cardinals' "glory days," when they won their only championship in 1947 and appeared in the title game in 1948. They practiced on the University of Chicago field, where between tar-paper–covered bleachers rose smokestacks, artifacts from the subterranean facility under the field where scientists ushered in the atomic age with the first controlled, self-sustaining nuclear chain reaction.

The players hung their uniforms on nails in a shabby locker room, and lived in an equally shabby hotel. Coach Joe Stydahar, a winner with the Rams, was less than inspiring strategically and emotionally in his final coaching stop.

Then Summerall came to the Giants, and his whole world changed. In one training camp, he learned more football than he had in five years in Chicago. As a backup defensive end, he sat in on Landry's defensive meetings. As a reserve offensive end, he was required to attend Lombardi's offensive meetings. Thus, he became the only Giant to be simultaneously coached in all three phases by both Lombardi and Landry.

It was nothing short a doctoral program in football. Tutored by two masterminds, Summerall gained a store of mechanical, strategic, motivational, and life-altering knowledge that carried him through the remainder of his playing days and into a distinguished broadcasting career.

And to think, he had no idea who Lombardi was as he waited for his first offensive meeting in training camp to start. Much chatter filled the air as an assistant tried to bring the room to order, with no luck. But when the bespectacled offensive coach entered and simply cleared his throat, all fell silent.

Summerall leaned over to Don Heinrich and asked, "Who the hell is that?"

"That's Lombardi," Heinrich replied, "and you'll know soon enough."

"And I did know soon enough," Summerall said.

Summerall would grow to accept all of Lombardi's criticisms, and Landry's too. His only gripe was that he never quite knew what Landry thought of him. He treated Summerall no differently than any of his defensive players—he was stoic, businesslike, and impersonal to them all.

"Landry never put his arm around me and told me 'good job,'" Summerall said. "In fact, later when I was broadcasting Cowboys games, I asked him about Harvey Martin. The worst thing he could say about anybody was 'He's working.' I asked him how Harvey Martin was playing, and he said, 'He's working.' And that was as derogatory or as complimentary as he'd get about anybody.

"It was nice to have recognition from Lombardi, to have him call you out in a team meeting and say you did a good job. But Landry wouldn't. I wouldn't say Lombardi did that often, but he did it as the year passed. [He was] a lot more vocal than Landry."

After Summerall's historic kick against the Browns sailed through the uprights that snowy, late December afternoon in Yankee Stadium, he'd get enough pats from teammates to make him forget Landry's chilliness.

*   *   *

The events of 1957 made one thing fairly obvious to the Giants and everyone else who played in the Eastern Conference—the road to the 1958 NFL championship game ran through Cleveland. Even in their worst years, like 1956, the Browns proved worthy opponents for the Giants. Jim Lee Howell's squad had never beat them more than once in any season, even as the Browns finished 5–7 while the Giants trekked their way to the 1956 title. And now that the genius Paul Brown had Jim Brown at fullback, the thought of anyone beating them three times in a season seemed unfathomable.

"Winston-Salem cigarettes had a saying: 'They said it couldn't be done,'" Dick Modzelewski said. "We picked up on that, 'We said it couldn't be done, and beat the Cleveland Browns three times in one year.' We wound up beating them."

Creativeness on both sides of the ball made it possible.

Landry's adjustment of the previous season—putting Huff in sole charge of containing Brown—continued. And with Rosey Grier back from the Army, Jim Katcavage moved back out to defensive end to reunite one of the NFL's most historically fearsome front fours.

Still, Brown stood as the most awe-inspiring player in the league, and in 1958 he got off to the most jaw-dropping start in history. Over the first five games, he compiled 815 rushing yards, 14 rushing touchdowns, and a nearly seven-yard-per-carry average while touching the ball on more than 50 percent of the Browns' offensive plays.

With an athlete like that, Paul Brown's great offensive mind seemed almost superfluous. When in doubt, all he had to do was put the ball in Jim Brown's hands. Simple.

The Giants alternated wins and losses over their first five games and went into their first meeting with Cleveland November 2 at 3–2. The Giants won 21–17 in a comeback in front of a raucous Municipal Stadium crowd of 78,404, the largest crowd to ever witness a Giants game so far. Huff and his cohorts held Brown to "minimal" damage: 113 yards and a touchdown on 13 carries. Actually, the defense did an even better job than that, as 58 of Brown's yards came on the touchdown run, a third-and-inches call where the big fullback banged up the middle and broke three tackles to rumble into the open field.

Quarterback Milt Plum, never to be mistaken for the Browns' long-retired great Otto Graham, was battered, sacked twice, and held to 4-of-14 passing for 26 yards. Jimmy Patton intercepted him twice.

Meanwhile, Charlie Conerly went 12-of-23 for 194 yards and three touchdowns while hearing the loudest boos since an atrocious home loss to the Cardinals two weeks before. At least he was in an enemy stadium this time, where booing was expected. Conerly and his receivers had to do most of the work, as torn knee ligaments incurred against the Cardinals turned Frank Gifford into a sideline spectator.

The Giants had to come back from a 17–7 halftime deficit after Groza's first-quarter field goal and second-quarter touchdowns by Brown and defensive back Kenny Konz, who scored on a 46-yard interception return. But Conerly was up to the challenge. He hit Alex Webster for two touchdowns, one of which Webster pulled from Konz's grasp, and the Giants pulled ahead. If Summerall hadn't missed a field goal, the Giants would have won as comfortably as anyone could expect against any Paul Brown-coached club.

Meanwhile, Landry's defense stuffed Brown and held Cleveland scoreless in the second half for the first of three times, an unthinkable feat. The Browns never moved the ball out of their own territory in the second half, gaining just 27 yards and three first downs.

The Giants finished with a distinct statistical advantage, outgaining Cleveland 337 to 201. For all of Conerly's aerial heroics, there were some achievements on the ground, too. Mel Triplett actually outran Brown, picking up 116 yards to Brown's 113. The Giants' fullback had a little extra fuel for the game, thanks to Landry's uncharacteristic taunt at Triplett during the practice week about Brown's statistical dominance over him.

"Brown owns you, doesn't he?" Landry said.

Triplett took it as a direct and very personal affront. Rightly or wrongly, Triplett always believed himself Brown's equal, and for at least one afternoon he dedicated himself to showing the calculating Landry exactly that.

The Giants followed up their victory with a 24–21 win over Western strongboy Baltimore. Summerall won it with a 28-yard field goal in the fourth quarter. But the game was just as notable because Colts backup and future Giant George Shaw quarterbacked the team while John Unitas sat while recovering from injured ribs.

The Yankee Stadium record crowd of 71,163 didn't seem to mind the substitution. While the fans had little idea that this game would preview the teams' transformational matchup at season's end, most knew the quality the Giants faced that November 9 afternoon. So did the players. The 6–0 Colts came in fresh off a 56–0 win over Green Bay. They'd also hung 51 on the Bears in the second game of the season. But great defense, one of Lombardi's old standby plays, and one of his trick plays pulled the Giants through.

A 13-yard option pass from the just-healthy Gifford to Bob Schnelker set up the Giants' first touchdown. Lombardi called that one because he noticed a hole in the Colts' defense during his film study that week. Gifford also scored a touchdown on a 13-yard run behind a Conerly block that left the old quarter-back with a cut nose and cleat marks on his chin.

Shaw, one of the first true running quarterbacks of the modern era, had a good day, though, and the teams went into the fourth quarter tied at 21. Shaw nearly pulled out the win, too. But as he marched his team deep into Giants territory, Huff intercepted a pass at the Giants' 12 to preserve the tie. Summerall kicked the eventual game-winner a few minutes later.

Also prominent in the win was a blocked field goal by Landry's defense, and Lombardi's call of a fake second-quarter punt that Chandler ran for a first down. Lombardi knew his call was a long shot, and marked one of the few true gambles he took that year. "The odds against making a first down from punt or field goal formation are 10 to 1," Lombardi told the press amid the joyous mayhem in the Giants' postgame locker room.

For Summerall, his kick served as an early morale booster.

"I knew I was going to have a good year and I remember the confidence building as success continued," Summerall said. "I remember it was going to be a good year."

The Browns' loss to Detroit that week put the teams into a first-place tie at 5–2. But the Giants gave the lead right back the next week in a 31–10 pratfall in Pittsburgh. Still, the Giants regrouped after a week of tough fundamentals-heavy prac-tices—the standard operating procedure after any loss—and continued to hang off Cleveland's rather broad shoulders until their second meeting, the regular-season finale.

Little changed in the meeting rooms. Landry continued teaching in his understated style. Lombardi, bombastic as ever, continued to pat his boys on the back for good plays and call them out over bad, running and rewinding the projector, running and rewinding until the player, and his teammates, got the message.

Lombardi could at times get a tad too emphatic with his teaching style. As Triplett had demonstrated a couple of seasons earlier with his walkout threat, everyone has a line that shouldn't be crossed. This time, Lombardi ventured across his Pro Bowl running back Webster's boundary.

Webster, a tough brawler out of Kearney, New Jersey, actually held a special place in Lombardi's heart. The two had become personal friends in the years since Webster arrived from Canada in 1955, often going to dinner together in the offseason. But Lombardi always made it a point to put that friendship aside the day training camp opened. Webster was just another player during the season, susceptible to the same criticism and accountability as everyone else.

Except, one day, Lombardi got on him a little too hard over a substandard outing.

"Vinny, go fuck yourself," came Webster's voice from the darkness.

Off went the projector. On came the lights.

"I'll meet you at home plate in a half hour," Lombardi said. "Nobody talks to me like that."

Lombardi kept the appointment. Luckily for him, Webster's teammates talked the tough Jersey kid out of it. An altercation probably would have derailed Webster's career and certainly put Lombardi in the hospital.

The dust quickly settled, and a business-as-usual—and winning—atmosphere returned. It's a good thing, because the Giants needed every one of those three wins to keep pace with a Browns team that was rolling through the Eastern Conference.

The Giants had to escape a close call in Detroit the week before the finale, winning 19–17 as Detroit coach George Wilson all but handed them the game with one of the most ridiculous late fourth-quarter calls in history. Up five and facing a fourth-and-21 at the Lions' 44, Wilson called for a fake punt. Yale Lary, a Hall of Fame defensive back who also won three punting crowns, dutifully took off for the right corner. But he didn't fool Cliff Livingston a bit, and the linebacker tackled Lary after a 1-yard gain.

Wilson was pilloried for making such a silly call. His defense was that the same play had worked three times in the last four years. Had the right end made the proper block on Livingston, it would have worked.

Instead, the Giants got the ball on Detroit's 45, and Conerly made his biggest play of the year shortly after that, hitting Schnelker for 34 yards on fourth-and-10. Gifford took it in from the 2 on another fourth down to give the Giants a 19–17 lead. But they didn't lock down the victory until linebacker Harland Svare and Andy Robustelli ran a stunt that freed Svare to block Jim Martin's 25-yard field goal attempt with 1:13 to go.

The Giants were both relieved and elated. They would not be strangers to those emotions in the weeks that followed, one of the most amazing two-game sequences in franchise history.

* * *

The hours before the 2 p.m. kickoff December 14 were typically cold, but the field was in decent enough shape. The Yankee Stadium turf was free of snow, but muddy, which was usual during the late season. Snow fell, but not blindingly. At least not at first. But conditions would deteriorate rapidly into a full-blown blizzard as the game progressed.

In the locker room, though, the Giants' biggest worries were the Browns themselves and Pat Summerall's physical status.

The Browns, 9–2 and a game up on the Giants, had scored at least 20 points in all but two of their games, and one was the 21–17 loss to the Giants. A win or a tie would earn them a berth in the NFL championship game against the Baltimore Colts.

Jim Brown was about to wrap up his first 1,000-yard rushing season with a then NFL record 1,527 yards, a 5.9-yard-per-rush average, and a then league record 17 rushing touchdowns. Those numbers might lead the league even now, but in the days of the 12-game schedule they were nothing short of supernatural. Even today, Sam Huff considers Jim Brown as "the best—the greatest running back, bar none."

As a further complication, Paul Brown had started using tough Lew Carpenter in the same backfield with Brown to increase the team's power running potential. And Paul Brown had thrown in a quarterback sweep for the mobile but weak-armed Plum.

As for Summerall, a severe charley horse in his right leg nearly relegated him to the sideline. Hit while covering his kickoff in Detroit the previous week, he could barely practice. The pain grew so bad that Summerall warned Chandler to stay warm, for he might have to do the placekicking despite having just a handful of professional extra points and some college field goals on his résumé.

Summerall continued warming up, though, and the leg eventually loosened enough that he could report for duty.

The Giants soon learned just how valuable he would be in this 13–10 heart-stopper. They fell behind almost immediately, as

Brown rumbled 65 yards for a touchdown on the Browns' first play from scrimmage. Huff, biting on Plum's fake to Carpenter, came inside with his first step. But Plum handed it to the fullback, who cut it up over right guard. Jim Katcavage, penetrating too deeply on the trap play, never had a shot at him. Nor did Rosey Grier. Huff, fighting through traffic, came within inches of touching him, but the linebacker's main assignment flew safely out of his reach. He blew past Svare and safety Carl Karilivacz downfield, running the final 15 yards unchallenged, for a 7–0 Browns lead.

As soon as the defense came off the field, Landry huddled his group on the sidelines. In his usual calm manner, he told them to settle themselves, stick to the game plan, and do what they'd been taught during the week.

"I remember what happened because I played next to Katcavage, and they ran a trap play on Katcavage," Dick Modzelewski said. "We come out of the ballgame and we were all shook up, and Tom Landry met us right there on the sideline. And he said, 'Men, don't worry about it.' And he said to Katcavage, 'Jim, that was a trap, and it won't happen to you again.' And Kat said, 'You're damned right it won't.'"

The chat, not uncommon for Landry after something bad happened, did its job, and the Giants did not allow another touchdown after that.

"We went in and we shut 'em down," Modzelewski said. "That was Tom. He never yelled, never screamed. Gently, he just said it. You knew talking to Tom he meant everything he said."

With Huff homed in on Brown, the defense held the fullback to 83 more yards on 25 carries (a 3.3-yard average), ultimately making his 26-carry, 148-yard total for the game seem inflated.

All might have been well, too, had the offense been able to move the football in the first half. But they could only muster one Summerall field goal—a 46-yarder—in the second quarter. Groza matched that with a 23-yarder of his own, and the Giants went into halftime trailing 10–3.

It was significant that Summerall actually missed a 46-yard attempt shortly before his make. Howell had enough faith in Summerall that he had little problem calling for long field goals from a kicker with a gimpy right leg on a cold, windy, and snowy day. And the last time Howell shouted out his name, Summerall would reward the coach's faith from even farther out, though not without protest from a trusted assistant.

Much had to happen before that, however. The heavens, as they had throughout the Giants' fortunate stretch leading into this game, smiled on them again by providing a coaching misstep. This time it came from Paul Brown, who elected to eschew his usual calculated thinking in the third quarter and forgo an easy 20-yard field goal try with the accurate (for that era) Groza. Instead, he called a fake field goal.

It was yet another case of a coach, in this case a recognized genius, thinking too much for his own good. As holder Bobby Freeman rose and headed off toward left end with the snap, Harland Svare zoomed in untouched and made the tackle.

The field goal would have put the Browns up by 10, a sufficient number to achieve the tie, as it turned out. But, Brown later explained, he wanted the touchdown to go up 17–3 so that even an unlikely pair of touchdowns by the Giants would leave them only tied, with Cleveland going to the title game.

Instead, it blew up in Brown's face. "Your thinking in retrospect was better than mine was at the time of the play," Brown later told reporters. All the momentum Cleveland had maintained through that seven-minute Jim Brown-led drive evaporated with Svare's tackle. And both offense and defense took advantage.

After Andy Robustelli recovered a Plum fumble at the Cleveland 45, the Giants tied the score in the fourth quarter on two Frank Gifford option passes. The first was a 39-yard, cross-field throw to Kyle Rote as Gifford rolled right. Rote, seeing that he could split the defensive halfback and safety, had suggested it early in the game, and Conerly kept it in the back of his mind until just the right time.

Three plays later, Conerly called 48-Green Option. Gifford took the pitch, turned up as if he about to run, and threw the ball just past Kenny Konz's outstretched fingertips, finding Schnelker in the back of the end zone for the game-tying touchdown with just over ten minutes to play.

"I remember I just sneaked back into the back of the end zone and just stood there," Schnelker said. "Frank threw it and I sort of leaped up to make sure I caught it. There wasn't anyone around me. Frank read it perfectly."

The defense stopped Cleveland on three plays, and the offense drove to the Cleveland 31 on its next possession. However, Summerall missed from 38 yards with four and a half minutes left. Dejected, he headed back to the bench to hear his teammates assure him that his day was not yet over.

Again, the Browns went three-and-out.

Darkness had fallen over Yankee Stadium. The temperature, cold to begin with, had grown bitter. The light snow of early afternoon had turned into a blizzard, and the accumulation obscured the yard lines. The swirls of heavy flakes backlit by the lights gave the whole thing a surreal feeling.

Fittingly, and against that backdrop, the football gods took, and then gave.

A shanked punt had put the Giants in business at the Browns' 44 with time enough to maneuver for a short field goal or a touchdown. After Conerly threw an incomplete pass on first down, they nearly got their touchdown. Webster had been lobbying Conerly to throw it to him, convinced he could beat the cornerback down the left side.

Conerly called the play.

Webster beat his man, as promised.

The Old Pro launched as beautiful a 40-yard pass as he'd ever tossed, as needed.

And Webster dropped it. Plain, flat out dropped it.

"I just dropped the damned thing. It was the most humiliating thing I can remember," Webster said. "It wasn't the snow. I just misjudged it. I felt so bad about that."

Webster would have needed only to take a few steps on a defender-less path to the end zone. Instead, the Giants still had work to do, and they needed a stroke of good luck to get it done. That came on the next play. Conerly hit Gifford at the Giants' 35, but as Gifford turned for his first step, linebacker Galen Fiss slammed him and the wet ball popped loose. Walt Michaels, later the coach of the Jets, recovered for Cleveland, only to have head linesman Charley Berry rule the pass incomplete after some hesitation.

"That was the big play of the game," said Paul Brown, who criticized that call for the remainder of his life.

Now came the decision that changed history. Would Howell let Conerly call a fourth pass to keep the drive going? Punt and pin the Browns back inside their territory? Or do the totally unexpected?

The unexpected it was. Lombardi argued lustily for a pass play, but instead Howell called on Summerall. Lombardi stepped back, the loser in a battle he swore he'd never have again. As a head coach, he'd be the guy making the decisions, not the one debating.

"Yeah, I was standing right there," Summerall said. "Always was. Lombardi didn't think we'd be successful and he argued and fought against it. He tried his best to get Jim Lee Howell not to try a field goal."

Why go for an impossible kick on a slippery field swept by wind and snow, Lombardi thought. He folded his arms and stepped back, seething. There was just over two minutes to go, this was probably the Giants' last chance, and a tie would do them no good.

A lot of the players couldn't understand the call, either. The two most surprised ones, though, were Summerall and Conerly, his holder.

"I was surprised Jim was going to try a field goal under those conditions, but I thought I was going to make it," Summerall said. "You can't go on the field thinking you're not going to make it."

The quarterback probably thought differently.

"Conerly said in the huddle, 'What the fuck are you doing in here?'" Summerall recounted. "And I said, 'They sent me in to try a field goal.'"

Conerly cleared a spot in the snow. He told Summerall to keep his head down, the same advice Conerly always gave him before a field goal try. All the mechanical tricks Landry had taught him in those short but effective daily sessions came into play now. Set up a step and a half back of the ball. Get it over the line. Kick it hard, in the middle, straight on. Keep the head down. Follow through.

Summerall hit the ball dead center. *Thump!* Up it went. Through the surreal glare that was the floodlit Yankee Stadium night, Summerall could see his kick knuckle through the uprights.

It went down as a 49-yarder officially, but Rote said he judged it at 52 from his spot on the sideline. Others have said it was from right at midfield.

It didn't matter. It had enough length to be good from 60. All the rest was bookkeeping.

Pandemonium broke out on the Giants sideline. As Summerall arrived, Lombardi, in his trademark camelhair coat, was the first to greet him.

"You son of a bitch," Lombardi said through an ever-widening gap-toothed grin. "You know you can't kick a ball that far, don't you?"

Landry never said a word. Injury and bad weather aside, Summerall had simply done what was expected of him.

The media searched frantically for parallels and finally settled for calling it a Bobby Thomson moment, recalling another New York Giant in another sport whose "Shot Heard Round the World" in 1951 won a pennant. Even though Summerall's kick won nothing but another crack at the Browns in a conference playoff, the comparison held. No chase in NFL history had ended in such dramatic, unlikely fashion.

Through the years, Webster was never shy about reminding Summerall about his own part in the drama.

"Alex always says, 'If I hadn't dropped that pass, nobody would have ever heard of you,'" Summerall said.

Apparently, Giants owner Tim Mara hadn't caught complete wind of his hero kicker. Jubilant in a rare locker room visit moments after Groza's last-ditch, 55-yard field goal try fell short—his third miss of the day—Mara exclaimed, "How about that Summerville? But what the hell. I'm paying him good money and he doesn't even play. All he has to do is kick. That was the least he could do to earn his money."

Well-earned and well-fortuned, the Giants were off to a playoff game against the same Browns.

*   *   *

If Tom Landry had learned anything from studying Paul Brown, he understood the Browns' coach stood intractable in his fundamental approach to the game. It's something the two men had in common, and each stuck to that quality to both benefit and detriment throughout their careers.

So Landry knew that, even with a conference title on the line, Brown was not going to stray too far from his usual game plan. The keys he gave his defense for the regular season games still held. A week of preparation would give Brown little wiggle room to install new concepts, not that it was in his nature, anyway.

"Landry told us straight out, 'Paul Brown is not going to change,'" Sam Huff said. "'Just do what we've been taught and we'll be all right. Paul Brown is not going to change.'"

Vince Lombardi could at times be as stubborn as Brown about his offensive system. But he did have a certain disciplined flexibility about him that produced the occasional surprise. The halfback option pass was always one of those plays that provided a shock to a defense keying on the power running game, a play the very threat of a sweep made possible. But for the Eastern Conference playoff, Lombardi did himself one better. He reached way back to 1954, to his early days in his first training camp, when

Frank Gifford and Charlie Conerly chafed at his college-type playbook.

The instincts of both assistants proved correct. The defense, once again with Huff targeting Jim Brown, not only swarmed him under to limit him to eight yards on seven carries, but at one point actually sent the tough-as-nails fullback to the sideline dazed from a monster hit. Lombardi's gadget produced the only touchdown in the 10–0 shutout, the Browns' first in 114 games.

Landry's group began the bitterly cold but clear December 21 afternoon dominantly. Whereas Jim Brown broke the first play from scrimmage in the last game for a huge touchdown run, this time he fumbled his first touch thanks to Jim Katcavage's read on Milt Plum's swing pass. His thunderous hit on Brown knocked the ball loose, and Rosey Grier recovered at the Giants' 38.

Even though Cleveland's defense stiffened that series, it wasn't long before the Giants got on the scoreboard. And they did it through Gifford's razzle-dazzle lateral to none other than Conerly, the old quarterback who all but refused to run the quarterback option Lombardi brought from Army for fear of getting his old body annihilated.

Working from the Cleveland 18, Conerly handed off to Alex Webster, who took it five yards toward left end before handing a reverse to Gifford. The halfback sprinted off right tackle and might even have scored himself had he made a move on linebacker Galen Fiss. Instead, he proceeded straight to the 10. Just as Fiss lined him up for a hit, Gifford flicked the ball to Conerly, trailing the play near the sideline. Conerly fell into the end zone as safety Junior Wren drilled him.

Lombardi had installed the play during the week, but Gifford kept the ball whenever they practiced it. His decision to pitch it off came as quite a shock to the taciturn quarterback from Clarksdale, Mississippi.

"Well, I was supposed to be there," Conerly explained. "The lateral was an option Vinny set up that way. I was supposed to be there if Gifford needed me. I don't know how long it's been since I scored a touchdown, but it was great for an old guy like me to run it in."

Conerly was somewhat blunter in his comments to Gifford after he scored only his second rushing touchdown since 1954, his first since 1957.

"The next time I give you the ball, you fuckin' keep it," Conerly said.

Lombardi's keen eye saw the play's potential early in the week. While breaking down film, he noticed that the all-out pursuit of the defensive tackles left big gaps across the right side. "We just put that play in to exploit the shift," he said. Jim Lee Howell never saw the end of the play coming. "We just added that lateral at the end as a little something extra," Howell said. "I didn't really think they'd use that flip."

Summerall's 26-yard field goal in the second quarter put the Giants up 10–0. That's all they needed because the defense had the game well in hand. The chanting Yankee Stadium crowd of 61,174 was delighted as Jim Brown was thrown six times for 12 yards in losses, twice on blitzes by Em Tunnell. His biggest gain went for 20 yards to the Giants' 4 in the third period, giving the fans temporary pause. But when Andy Robustelli threw Plum for a 12-yard loss as a receiver stood open in the end zone, and when Huff picked off his cross-field throw near the goal line, all exhaled.

Robustelli and the pass rush kept Plum and rookie backup Jim Ninowski running for their lives all afternoon.

No one took a bigger beating that day than Brown, however. One tackle, with Huff hitting him high and Modzelewski hitting him low, put a wobbled Brown temporarily on the sidelines.

"We hurt him pretty bad," Modzelewski said. "And Mel Triplett got hurt. I always heard Paul Brown told Jim Brown to go back in the ballgame.

"Nobody was worried that much about concussions, but Jim and Mel Triplett both might have had concussions. I don't know. All I remember is Brown ran the ball and three or four guys laid into him. To hurt Jim Brown was itself great. He'd just run over people. To me, to this day, he's the greatest runner God ever made. I don't care who he is. The only time he'd run out of bounds is when he needed the time. Otherwise, he'd just knock everybody over."

The game left the Giants bruised. Grier came out of it with a knee injury that would eventually drive him from the NFL championship game. Summerall was aching. Gifford was cut up from the frozen turf.

But little of that mattered to a team who now had a chance to gain their second championship in three years. The defense, of course, took the lion's share of the accolades—from both sides.

"Tom Landry is the best coach in football," Howell said in the winner's clubhouse.

"There's only one man who could have done this to us," a disconsolate Groza said in the loser's locker room. "Tom Landry. Nobody else."

8

THE NOT-SO-GREATEST GAME

IT SEEMED ALMOST unfair that the Giants had to play a juggernaut like the Baltimore Colts after beating Paul Brown's terrifying Browns twice in two weeks to reach the championship game.

What's more, a strike by New York newspaper deliverers, ongoing since December 9, had created a huge information blackout across the area. People didn't know when or where tickets would go on sale, nor if there were any to be had. As a result, thousands of seats opened up and were eventually taken on the eventually sold-out afternoon of December 28 by an estimated 20,000 Baltimore fans who had sojourned north on the generosity of Carroll Rosenbloom, the Colts owner, who had offered to pay half the train fare for anyone willing to make the trip.

So, before a single snap had even occurred, the Giants lost one advantage as enemy loyalists sat in nearly a third of the 64,185 occupied seats at Yankee Stadium. The loud 125-member Colts band and cheerleaders had also accompanied the team, creating an endless noise stream to create an incongruous home-field edge for the visitors.

Then there were the 9–3 Colts themselves, a luminous collection of offensive and defensive talent that had blown through the Western Conference with an NFL-high 381 points while giving up just 203, second-fewest in the league to the Giants' 183. Johnny Unitas, Alan Ameche, Raymond Berry, Jim Parker, Lenny Moore, Art Donovan, Gino Marchetti, Bill Pellington, Big Daddy Liscomb; the whole NFL knew them just as well as Charlie Conerly, Frank Gifford, Alex Webster, Kyle Rote, Sam Huff, Andy Robustelli, and Rosey Grier by that time. And feared them just as much, too.

As if the usual trappings of such a game didn't challenge the Giants enough, the two locker rooms presented a diametrical contrast in mood. The Colts were jacked, spurred on by an uncharacteristically emotional speech by the otherwise dispassionate Weeb Ewbank. One by one, the coach went down his roster, noting how all his great players were unwanted before the Colts picked them up.

Unitas? His hometown Steelers had cut him out of training camp, forcing the soft-spoken University of Louisville thrower to prove himself in the semi-pro ranks for only slightly more remuneration than wampum. "Pittsburgh didn't want you," Ewbank said. "We got you for a 75-cent phone call."

Liscomb? "The Rams were glad to get rid of you. We got you for a hundred bucks."

Marchetti? "They said you weren't going to get any better, but you did. See if you can show up today."

Berry? "One leg shorter than the other, with bad eyesight to boot."

The Giants? Suffice to say they were hardly a galvanized team when they hit the field for warmups less than an hour before kickoff. Up to that point, they had been sequestered in a players-only meeting called to divvy up the playoff shares. Jim Lee Howell, in the few command decisions he'd make outside of the game itself, would always have the final word on the list of full and partial shares, and if it wasn't to his liking, he'd gruffly throw it back and order the players to "do it again!" But on this day, as the Giants tried to allocate shares the Associated Press reported to be worth $4,718.77 per winner and $3,111.33 per loser, Gifford and Huff nearly came to blows over the share for $450-a-month backup quarterback Jack Kemp.

Kemp was still years away from becoming an expert in mediating political squabbles as a nine-term congressman from Western New York. Too bad. The two stars could have used somebody to step in as Gifford lobbied for Kemp to get a full share and Huff, his long-held antagonism for the offense again bubbling to the surface, lobbied for a minimal payout. Things got personal, and when Dick Modzelewski finally yelled at Gifford to "Shut your mouth!" Gifford stood down before somebody belted him.

Kemp wound up getting a full share, but the blowup was hardly an inspiring way to preface an NFL Championship game.

The locker room fell into an uncomfortable calm after warmups. Vince Lombardi, not knowing that his offensive plan for this game would be his final one as a Giant, went around the locker room encouraging players and quietly going over with Gifford a special pass play they had worked on during the week. Landry met with Huff and Robustelli in the trainers room to go over some last-minute details. Third-and-long was of particular concern. As it turned out, Landry should have saved his breath on that subject.

*   *   *

"I didn't have a good game at all," Gifford said, his comment a gross understatement even from the distance of 52 years.

Although their bleakness was applicable to most of those Giants, Gifford's words were especially poignant in relation to his own performance. He basically lived a nightmare that afternoon, fumbling twice and, through little fault of his own, falling inches short on a key third down run late in the game.

He wasn't alone, though. Huff would become confused in pass coverage and wouldn't even be in the frame when Alan Ameche barreled over from the 1 for the historic winning score in overtime. Andy Robustelli would get to Unitas only once as left tackle "Big Jim" Parker decisively won that matchup of Hall of Famers. Charlie Conerly would be left so exhausted by the intense end to regulation that he could barely drag out his thirty-seven-year-old body for the extra period.

But all would have been well if the Giants could have held off Unitas in the final two minutes of regulation.

In Robustelli's book, *Once a Giant, Always . . .,* the defensive end remarked how people came to regard this one as the greatest game ever played because of how it drove football to the forefront of the national conscience. "I don't," Robustelli wrote. "Not by any stretch of the imagination, because we lost a game we should have won. I never felt worse. We had let the world championship slip away from us 23–17, and we did it in the first overtime game ever played."

Lombardi called it the most disappointing moment of his years with the Giants.

"We had it won, and we gave it away," he remembered. "We had the world championship in our hands and we couldn't hold it. I know it must have been a thrilling, exciting game to watch, but I didn't watch it that way.

"I knew we were the better team. I knew we were going to win. When we didn't, I couldn't accept it. I suppose it is my personality. I'm not well-adjusted enough to accept a defeat."

For such a historic game, it didn't start out well for the Yankee Stadium crowd and the estimated 45 million watching it on TV. The teams played a sloppy first half, with the Colts turning it over twice on a Unitas fumble and a Carl Karilivacz interception. Those sandwiched Gino Marchetti's recovery of a botched handoff by Giants starting quarterback Don Heinrich.

By this point in the season, Lombardi had reverted to his old two-quarterback system, leaving Conerly on the bench to absorb the photos of the Baltimore defense Wellington Mara threw down from the press box. It was all part of his educational philosophy: Teach, repeat, simplify, and when possible, show.

It went right along with another Lombardi innovation, the wide-angle camera view for game films that allowed coaches and players to see the entire play unfold, not just the key portion of it. The wide angle soon became a staple in every team's meeting rooms.

He was also not shy about getting out there and demonstrating how a play should be run. He wasn't afraid to take a few lumps as he made his point, either. Once, while attempting to demonstrate the proper way for the quarterback to fake a handoff to the fullback on an option play, he told the bulky Mel Triplett to run at him. Lombardi assumed Triplett would take that to mean an angled approach, where the coach would then stick the ball in his stomach and pull it out again as he headed out on the option. Instead, Triplett ran right at him—and over him. The trampled Lombardi, his neck and cheek bearing the cleat marks of a 230-pound fullback, popped up and yelled, "That is not how you run that play!"

The first quarter continued in fits and starts, though it appeared the Colts had gained the upper hand when Unitas connected with fast Lenny Moore on a 50-yard throw, Moore beating defensive back Lindon Crow by half a step. But the defense held. Steve Myhra, a backup linebacker and one of the most inconsistent placekickers in the league, missed a 31-yard attempt, but got a second chance as the Giants jumped offside. Huff bailed his team out on Myhra's mulligan when he charged untouched up the middle for the block.

Conerly was in the game now, and in the huddle on third-and-1 the taciturn Mississippian drawled out Lombardi's signature play, "48-sweep" for Gifford. With Rosie Brown leading the way, the halfback took it 38 yards for the Giants' first big play in a game of big plays. But they eventually settled for a 3–0 lead on a Summerall field goal with under three minutes to go in the quarter.

Gifford called it "the worst first quarter in the annals of championship football, before or since," and he said it only half-sarcastically. But at least the Giants held the lead and, for a time, the momentum.

A very short time, as it turned out. As the second quarter began, Gifford took a Conerly throw on the left side. Brown blocked defensive end Don Joyce; stood him up, even. But he failed to hold the block and Joyce broke free and grabbed Gifford. As Gifford tried to spin out of the tackle, the arm carrying the ball flew away from his body. Defensive tackle Big Daddy Liscomb, all 306 pounds of him, had first gone after Conerly, but changed direction with the most athletic of moves and came crashing in to Gifford, knocking the ball loose. Ray Krouse, the defensive lineman the Giants had sent to Detroit for Dick Modzelewski two years earlier, jumped on it at the Giants' 20.

It took five plays and a big-gainer by Moore to the 1 for Alan Ameche to put the Colts up 7–3.

The worst part about the short drive was that mammoth defensive tackle Rosey Grier had aggravated a knee injury he suffered the week before. Early on one of the Browns linemen had cut him from behind as he chased quarterback Milt Plum, and the pain had grown just about unbearable by the second quarter. It didn't help that he was being mauled by Colts guard Art Spinney.

Grier could go no longer, and he pulled himself out of the game. With today's roster, he would have had at least one real backup. But with the 1958 rosters set at thirty-six, up from thirty-three, bodies still came at a premium. Consider, too, that Wellington Mara was really an offensive man, and he tended to encourage his coaches to load up on that side of the ball while making their final cuts. Tom Landry was the lone coach on defense, and he only had about fifteen players to coach. The other twenty-one belonged to Lombardi. So when Grier went down, there was no one to turn to except for a big second-round offensive tackle named Frank Youso. Howell liked his size, and he decided large replacing large was the best way to go in such desperate times.

Youso was lost, even as Huff directed him from behind—a pat on the right cheek meant Youso would go right; if Huff patted the left cheek, he'd go left. No pat meant they were coming straight at him, so buckle up.

To make matters worse, even the healthier among Landry's Legions were no match for the Colts' pass protection. Aside from an early sack, Unitas stood virtually untouched. And offensively, the Giants had done next to nothing. In fact, Gifford had fumbled yet again. After Brown recovered a fumbled punt at the Colts' 10, Gifford went off on a sweep. Colts defensive back Milt Davis flew in behind the line of scrimmage and knocked the ball free, with Joyce recovering at the 14.

A second fumble by the Giants' great ground gainer. A scared, confused rookie offensive tackle playing defense against one of the most high-powered offenses in history. Against that backdrop, Unitas engineered his first great drive of the game.

Youso would have just as soon deciphered a quantum physics equation as one of Landry's defensive keys, but it wasn't long before Unitas fed him all the information about how his day would go. He came right at Youso, now the weakest part of the defense. Unitas called four straight runs over him early in a 15-play, 86-yard touchdown drive, leaving the rookie not only dazed, but bleeding from two fingers that were torn and crushed when a lineman stepped on them.

It wasn't just Youso, though. The entire defense was in a quandary. Unitas, a mobile quarterback, scrambled for 16 yards to the Giants' 30. A few plays later, he suckered the entire defense on a play-fake to Ameche and hit Raymond Berry with a 15-yard throw between Jimmy Patton and Em Tunnell for a 14–3 halftime lead.

The only successful halftime adjustments were made by Lombardi. Seeing that Gifford was being contained, anyway, he ordered Conerly to throw more. Aside from telling the defense to continue to double-team Moore, Landry stuck to his 4-3 guns and made only minimal adjustments to the pass rush. In truth, neither Lombardi nor Landry were big on in-game modifications. They believed in their preparation. They believed in their philosophies. And they believed that if their players executed what their coaches taught them during the week, they could overcome anything.

Of the two, Lombardi had the firmer grasp of the obvious.

"Frank," he told Gifford, "you've got to hang on to the ball."

Landry simply urged his defense to stay the course.

"If you keep doing what I'm telling you to do, we'll be all right," Landry told his unit. "Now it's up to you."

Landry's words, as non-threatening as they were, hit home. The defense rose up in a third-quarter goal line stand that kept the Colts from blowing the game wide open. On fourth-and-goal from the 1, Cliff Livingston threw Ameche for a 4-yard loss as the fullback, failing to pick up Unitas's signal for an option pass, ran instead of throwing it to the open Jim Mutscheller in the end zone.

The defensive stand revitalized the offense and Conerly, with a little bit of luck, took advantage. On third-and-2 from his own 12, he fired a 30-yard strike to Rote, who took off across midfield. As he reached the Baltimore 25, safety Andy Nelson stripped him, and the ball bounced forward several yards before Alex Webster scooped it up and ran it to the 1. Carl Taseff knocked him out of bounds there, but it's just as good a bet that Webster, an avid smoker on the sidelines, might have fallen there from exhaustion. Webster was a great short-yardage runner, and a decent pass catcher. But when it came to running 87 yards on one play, all bets were off.

"I was happy to get out of bounds," Webster said. "I was out of gas completely."

Triplett banged in two plays later, and the Giants were down 14–10.

Momentum was firmly in the Giants' favor now. Conerly led a fourth quarter drive that included passes of 17 and 46 yards to Bob Schnelker, and ended with a 15-yard touchdown toss to Gifford and a 17–14 Giants lead.

The defense held the Colts until just over two minutes remained in the game.

That's when the gods, so benevolent to the Giants during the home stretch, turned vengeful and changed football history forever.

On third-and-4 at their 40, needing just one first down to run out the clock, Gifford took a handoff and cut inside. Marchetti and Donovan grabbed the running back and dragged him down. As Gifford sank to the ground, Liscomb leaped on top of the pile, breaking Marchetti's ankle.

Instead of spotting the ball immediately, referee Ron Gibbs picked it up and held it as the trainers carted Marchetti off on a stretcher. Only then did he put it down—near his back foot instead of his front foot—about five inches short of a first down. He had spotted it incorrectly, a fact Gifford tried to relay to the ref, to no avail.

"There's no question in my mind I made it," Gifford said.

Lombardi urged Howell to go for it on fourth down. Landry wanted to go for it, too.

Howell called for a punt.

The wisdom of that move would be debated for years. But the fact was it seemed a safe bet at the time that the Giants' defense would continue to pitch its second-half shutout. Besides, Chandler's punt wound up at the 14, which meant Unitas had a long way to go for a tying field goal with 2:22 remaining.

What happened next opened Wellington Mara's—and the nation's—eyes to the wonders of Johnny Unitas, then just twenty-five years old.

"I realized that we were at the hands of the master," Mara said.

Landry had ordered his defense into a "prevent" mode, which meant the secondary and linebackers closed off all avenues to the clock-stopping sideline. So Unitas took what the defense gave him—the middle of the field—in orchestrating one of the great two-minute drills of all time.

Calling two plays at a time, Unitas first hit Moore for 11 yards to move the Colts out from the shadow of their own goal posts. Then came the real nightmare. Landry sensed that the ball would be going to Berry, so he ordered the double-team off Moore and onto Berry.

It didn't matter. Unitas found his short, slow, contact-lens-wearing receiver for 25 yards to midfield, with Berry snaring the throw in front of Harland Svare. Then he got between Patton and Huff for a leaping catch at the Giants' 35. And finally, Unitas called an audible to Berry and found him with a throw just off the grass, which Berry corralled at the 20 and ran to the 13.

Three straight throws to Berry, for 25, 15, and 22 yards.

"I go to bed every night hearing, 'Unitas-to-Berry. Unitas-to-Berry. Unitas-to-Berry,'" Sam Huff said. "I got tired of hearing the announcer say it. You couldn't stop him."

Myhra took the field at the 20 with backup quarterback and holder George Shaw and kicked the teams into football's first overtime contest with a mere seven seconds to spare.

*   *   *

As great a physical toll Unitas's no-huddle drive took on the defense, it paled in comparison to what the stress and physical exertion of the Giants' three-game stretch had done to Charlie Conerly. Sam

Huff and his battered, exhausted group might have been content to settle for a tie, as they would have in a regular season game. But at least they still had some amount of energy to continue playing after the three-minute break before overtime.

Conerly's old tank had gone empty, though. As he sat trying to catch his breath with Gifford as Unitas maneuvered to the tying field goal, the old quarterback looked at his best friend and proclaimed, "I just can't go on anymore," to which Gifford responded, "Boy, you're going to have to go some more."

"I just can't," Conerly said.

A lot of the Giants were mentally spent by that time. The Colts? They were as fresh as today's catch, ready for anything after an early conference title clinch and a week off.

"They were a hell of a football team," Gifford remembered. "And our team was so beat up. They had that cruise to the title, and then they had a week to sit back and watch while we had to beat Cleveland twice in a row to get there. A lot of little things that people forget."

Conerly had certainly put in an honest day's work. He would finish 10-of-14 for 187 yards and a touchdown. The sportswriters up in the press box had voted him the game's MVP award, symbolized by a brand-new Corvette. More pickup than sports car, Conerly probably wouldn't have minded losing the wheels, anyway. But Mrs. Perian Conerly certainly would have driven it. Instead, Mrs. Dorothy Unitas wound up in the driver's seat after her husband forced a revote with yet another brilliant drive.

"For months afterward, I had nightmares about Dorothy Unitas driving gaily around Baltimore in 'my' Corvette," Perian Conerly wrote in her beguiling ode to pro football and her husband, *Backseat Quarterback.*

Cars were the last thing on the Giants' mind at the time. Just wrapping their heads around the very concept of playing extra time was a challenge. There was some confusion on the sidelines. Huff thought they'd deem it a tie, and had decided that getting the average of the two shares was better than just getting the loser's. Pat Summerall and Kyle Rote had no clue what came next until the officials called Rote to midfield for the coin toss.

That Rote would be confused at all came as a bit of a mystery, however, for the Giants actually had played an overtime game before. This was just the first official journey into OT. On August 28, 1955, the Giants and L.A. Rams played an overtime preseason game at Multnomah Stadium in Portland, Oregon. The game's promoter, Harry Glickman, had petitioned for and received the NFL's permission to invoke a rule written in 1946 that provided for sudden-death overtime in playoff games. Although Glickman simply saw it as a publicity stunt to help sell tickets, commissioner Bert Bell was dead serious about the rule, and had in the recent past urged the owners to adopt sudden-death for all games. Bell was long dead by the time the owners finally embraced the concept in 1974.

Bell had also reminded the public in 1957 of the rule's existence when he declared that sudden-death would be invoked if the Western Conference playoff between the Lions and 49ers ended in a tie. The Lions won 31–27 in regulation.

As Glickman's luck would have it, the first sixty minutes of his game ended in a 17–17 tie. After some confusion, referee Ross Bowen consulted with Wellington Mara and Rams owner Dan Reeves (who shared a name, but no blood, with the future Dallas running back), and the three agreed a sudden-death period would be played. It lasted three minutes and twenty-eight seconds as Norm Van Brocklin led an eight-play, 70-yard drive off the kickoff that ended with Tank Younger plunging in from the 2 for a touchdown. Interestingly, Rams coach Sid Gillman later criticized the setup as being unfair to the team that lost the coin toss, an argument that still rages today.

Though Conerly, Gifford, Rote, and Robustelli (then with the Rams) had played in that game, most of the others on the roster had not. Thus, the confusion.

Lombardi and Landry did not hold any impromptu meetings on the sideline.

The reality of the situation became clear soon enough as Rote, linebacker Bill Svoboda, and Unitas gathered with referee Ron Gibbs for a coin toss. The quarterback lost the toss.

The Giants had an overtime period to play, but no energy left to play it. The temperature had grown bitter as the sun disappeared. The Giants took the kickoff not only cold of body, but also weary of mind from two emotional wins over Cleveland and the letdown of a squandered championship game lead.

The offense went out quietly. A 4-yard sweep for Gifford, an incomplete pass to Bob Schnelker, and a 5-yard scramble by the spent Conerly left the Giants a yard short of a first down at the Giants' 29.

Don Chandler banged a 62-yard punt that Carl Taseff returned a yard to the Colts' 20.

Unitas needed to cover 80 yards against the best defense in the NFL. It should have been a near-impossible task. Problem was, for the Giants at least, he had all the time in the world now. If he could move 73 yards for a tying field goal in just over two minutes, why would it surprise anyone to see him go 80 unfettered by a dwindling clock?

Unitas went right to work, combining the physical with the mental. Reading the defense all the way, he threw when the Giants thought he'd run, and ran when the defense thought he'd throw.

For the next six minutes and fifteen seconds, he caught Landry's defense cheating red-handed all over the field, and he exacted a gunslinger's price for it.

Jim Lee Howell's genius had ordered Huff out of the middle to help Carl Karilivacz cover Raymond Berry on the right side. With the middle open, Unitas handed off to L. G. Dupre who gained 11 yards up the gut and the Colts' first first down of the overtime period. On the ensuing third-and-8, Unitas saw that both Svare and Huff had dropped into coverage early on Berry, so he found Ameche on a flare pass for another first down.

Dick Modzelewski finally got through the Colts' protective wall on second down for a sack that brought up third-and-14. So Unitas went to his afternoon's favorite target, Berry—he finished with a then-record 12 catches for 178 yards and a touchdown—for 21 yards on a quick sideline hook as Karilivacz slipped on a piece of iced-over turf.

Convinced Unitas would throw again, Huff cheated back a step. Unitas saw him and instead called an audible, a draw to Ameche. As Modzelewski came roaring in for the sack, Unitas handed it off. Little Mo flew past the runner, and Ameche went up the vacated middle for 23 yards before Patton dragged him down at the Giants' 20. Some of the players still regard that play as Unitas's greatest call of the game.

The Colts could have tried a field goal right there, but Weeb Ewbank had no faith in either Myhra or his other kicker, Bert

Rechichar. Likewise, Unitas had been thinking touchdown from the first huddle of the drive.

And now, here they were, poised to take their city's first championship in any sport since Wee Willie Keeler's old Baltimore Orioles of 1895 and 1896.

Landry's vaunted unit was on its heels, thoroughly confused by Unitas' unpredictable play-calling. Even after they guessed right, stopping Dupre for no gain, Berry got free the next play for a 12-yard slant to the 8.

"He put that ball by my ear," Huff said, reliving Unitas's needle-threading accuracy. "Put it between my hand and my helmet. You can't stop the perfect play."

Ameche ran for one yard on the next play. And then Unitas made his most daring decision of the game.

Just a short, safe run would bring in Myhra for a field goal even he couldn't miss. A bobbled snap would simply force another try on fourth down. Unless something went horribly wrong, the game would be over.

The book said run. Ewbank said run. Indeed, the Giants' defense figured run.

Unitas threw.

Unpressured by pass rushers, Unitas faded back and froze Lindon Crow with a pump-fake to Moore. Then he looked to the other side where linebacker Cliff Livingston had checked tight end Jim Mutscheller before he started back toward Unitas. Unitas lofted a soft toss to the wide-open Mutscheller, and the tight end gathered it in as he fell out of bounds at the 1 while Ewbank turned white on the sidelines.

Had Unitas not gotten enough height or distance on the ball, Livingston was in perfect position to intercept it and return it for a touchdown. But the pass cleared Livingston easily. Unitas later shrugged off all those who called it a gamble.

"Why shouldn't I have passed then?" Unitas asked reporters. "After all, you don't have to risk anything when you know where you're passing."

Third-and-goal from the 1.

Landry stacked the front, thinking run. He guessed right. It didn't matter. Ameche took the handoff and got blocks from tackle George Preas on Huff and Moore on Tunnell. Mutscheller's seal block on Livingston drove the linebacker into Jim Katcavage, creating a hole so big that Ameche could have strolled through it smoking a victory cigar. He lowered his shoulders and broke the plane of the end zone untouched.

Huff, who might have made a play had he lined up as a linebacker, wasn't even in the frame. The great Landry had been anything but infallible on December 28, 1958.

"Landry put me down in a short-yardage situation in a three-point stance as a defensive lineman," Huff said. "We called it a Gap-8. And Unitas knew what the hell we were in.

"I didn't understand what the defense was and I'm saying, how in the hell did Ameche score, he's my man. Well, I looked at the film and I was down in a three-point stance, shifted to the strong side, and Unitas read the play and handed it to Ameche and he went outside our defensive ends and scored from the 1-yard line. If I'd been playing the regular Red Left formation from the middle linebacker's spot, I could have tackled him. But I was in a three-point stance in the short-yardage defense."

But Huff never blamed Landry.

"I don't know if it was a mistake because they might have scored, anyway," Huff said.

Though Lombardi later remembered the loss as the greatest disappointment of his career, he seemed almost glib at dinner that night, saying that his only two complaints were that "it was a couple of inches too short and seven seconds too long."

Gifford sat at his locker almost inconsolable over the fumbles that had cost the Giants the game. In one of his last acts as a member of the Giants' coaching staff, Lombardi sidled up to him and offered comfort.

"Don't worry about it, Frank," Lombardi said. "If it wasn't for you, we wouldn't even be here."

By the end of January, Gifford and Lombardi would have one more talk, at Al Schacht's Steakhouse on Fifty-second Street.

That night, Lombardi said good-bye to the player he called "my halfback."

9

LOMBARDI MOVES ON

AL SCHACHT'S WAS one of those gems of the Manhattan night scene, not unlike Toots Shor's or Mike Manuche's. Good food. Good drink. Laughs. Schacht, a former-baseball-pitcher-turned-entertainer, occasionally would offer some comedic stylings from the stage. The menus were round like baseballs, the prices moderate. Comfortable surroundings frequented by enough celebrities that their presence was commonplace. Nobody bothered anybody.

One of Vince Lombardi's favorite spots, it seemed the ideal place to break some hard news to his favorite player.

Lombardi was headed to Green Bay.

"Told me he was gonna go," Frank Gifford said. "We were both sad. I actually didn't think he was gonna do it. It wasn't that big a deal with me at the time. I was thinking myself whether I should play anymore."

The 1958 championship game had left both men at a crossroads. The guilt Gifford felt over his two fumbles and missed first down had left him thinking about retirement. Young, handsome, with dough rolling in from endorsements and movie roles, Gifford made far more money off the gridiron than on it. He knew well that a guy didn't have to take a physical beating on a Hollywood sound stage. He also knew that Jim Lee Howell was far less appreciative of his competitiveness than Lombardi or his teammates were. Barely tolerant of the head coach before, he lost all respect for him in 1957 when, a season after Gifford was named MVP of the league, Howell chewed him out as "one of those Hollywood characters" when a commercial he was shooting caused him to arrive late for a meeting.

Lombardi had thought about getting out of the game, too. Maybe head into the banking racket, where he had made some headway over several off-seasons. At forty-five, and not growing a day younger, he wondered if he'd ever get his shot to run things. Lombardi had lost out on jobs at Penn, Washington, Air Force, and Wake Forest. His best chance came crashing down when his alma mater, Fordham, dropped football in 1954.

There was that offer the year before from the Eagles, but it wasn't a good situation for him. He could stay with the Giants until Howell left, but that might be a long wait for an assistant who already sat way behind on the age curve.

But just as today, things turn around quickly in the NFL. The last three seasons had engraved Lombardi's name in the minds of some of the league's more influential people. Paul Brown knew all about him. Rams coach Sid Gillman was a fan, as was Commissioner Bert Bell. So when the Packers forced friendly, easy-going rookie coach Scooter McLean to resign after a 1–10–1 disaster, a ripened Lombardi was sitting right there. And people were ready to speak for him.

Problem was, those who headed the Packers had no clue about him. Other more high-profile candidates wound up in the conversation: former Browns quarterbacking great Otto Graham, former Browns assistant and current Kentucky coach Blanton Collier, Jim Trimble of the Canada's Hamilton Tiger-Cats, and University of Iowa coach Forrest Evashevski, whose squad won the Rose Bowl that year. The Packers' original coach, Earl "Curly" Lambeau, was also briefly considered.

The *Green Bay Press-Gazette* actually ran a premature, and ultimately incorrect, story that had Trimble ready to take the job. But Evashevski was regarded as the early favorite until he pulled himself out of the running hours after a late-January visit.

They didn't know it at the time, but the man the Packers would eventually pick fit the publicly owned team's new coaching model perfectly. The board of directors didn't want a pure coach, anyway. They wanted a coach-businessman, someone to take on the dual role of coach and general manager. One board member described the ideal candidate as "a Paul Brown of Green Bay." Coaches like Brown were a rarity at that time, however. He was the only coach in the league to wear both the coach and general manager's hats. Bears owner/president/coach George Halas was the only other coach to perform more than one job.

As it happened, Lombardi could not have been more right, or more prepared, for the job. That his mind was a bottomless well of football knowledge was undeniable to anyone who had ever heard him speak at a clinic. And those who knew about his offseason work in the insurance and banking industries understood that he had solid business acumen. Lombardi, in fact, had just taken a job as a public relations executive with the Federation Bank and Trust Company in Manhattan, where many of the Giants had their accounts. He had even considered giving up football to take a bank vice president's job. Some of his former supervisors marveled at how he would master his job, and then out of sheer curiosity, learn other areas of the business. One found him behind the teller's counter one day, trying to figure out the intricacies of that role.

Just like in football, Lombardi was determined to understand the whole play, not just his part in it. Here was the kind of man Packers president Dominic Olejniczak needed.

"At no time did I ever think of Vince as a coach alone," Olejniczak said in later years, "but only on a combined deal where he'd be the boss. We needed a boss."

Olejniczak didn't approach Lombardi until the league convened January 22 at Philadelphia's Warwick Hotel for the final 26 rounds of the draft. Actually, another board member, a friend of Gillman, had asked the Rams coach if he could recommend a candidate. Gillman suggested Lombardi, and the board member relayed the recommendation to Packers personnel manager Jack Vainisi. Conducting his own private search as he attempted to head off another hiring fiasco, he made an unauthorized call to Lombardi to gauge the backfield coach's interest.

Lombardi jumped at the chance.

Vainisi received endorsements from all over the league, none more important than Paul Brown's. The Cleveland coach mentioned both Lombardi and Collier, but the more he talked up Lombardi, "the more interested they became," Brown said. "I became interested, too, and pushed full tilt for Vince because I really believed he'd make a good coach."

After Vainisi heard Lombardi's old Army boss Red Blaik offered a glowing assessment, he let Olejniczak in on the secret.

Olejniczak made his move at the draft. He sidled up to Lombardi, seated at the Giants' table, and tapped him on the shoulder. The two adjourned to Olejniczak's room where Lombardi proceeded to entrance both the president and board member Tony Canadeo, the great Gray Ghost whose rushing helped lead the 1944 Packers to the last of Lambeau's six league titles. A flood of football knowledge, all wrapped neatly in his plan for resurrecting the Pack to its former greatness, poured over the two Green Bay honchos.

"He grabbed our attention from the first minute," Canadeo said. "He knew where he was going. In football terminology, he knew his game plan."

Only fate and the tandem of Wellington and Jack Mara put Lombardi in a position to even speak to the Packers. There was a possibility, at least in Lombardi's mind, that he could have succeeded Col. Red Blaik at Army. Blaik retired after the 1958 season, and Lombardi probably would have run back to Army and the academy's free staff housing. But that dream ended when the athletic committee refused to break with a tradition that restricted head coaching candidates to West Point graduates.

The devastating rejection came the day after Lombardi's draft meeting with Olejniczak and Canadeo. He was stung, not just from West Point's adherence to the old ways, but in what he perceived as Blaik's betrayal. Lombardi believed that merely a good word from the old coach might have softened the committee's hidebound stance. Instead, Blaik backed eventual successor Dale Hall. Later speculation held that Blaik felt Lombardi's temper made him too much of a risk for a college hire. Indeed, Blaik lectured his emotional assistant several times in his early years at Army about the verbal thunderstorms he rained down on the cadets.

Lombardi suspected, as he usually did when faced with rejection, that his Italian heritage had done him in again.

The pros were the best place for Lombardi, anyway. He may have loved his collegians and his high school players. He may have loved the teaching. But deep down, he always wanted to work with the best. It's why he took the Giants' offer back in '54 in the first place.

"I decided to go with the pros because I felt I could come closer to finding the perfect football player," Lombardi once said. "College students are great to work with, especially the sort you find at military academies. But many are just not equipped to become outstanding athletes. Professionals are, or they should be, at any rate.

"The lure was fascinating. I would be working with more mature, more gifted football players. I don't think that I had any other choice, being the kind of man I am."

The other obstacle had been removed some time before. Because there were still two years left on his Giants contract, the Packers first had to get the Maras' permission to speak with him. At first, Wellington Mara was reluctant, and suggested that the Packers might be more interested in his other genius assistant, Tom Landry. Olejniczak pressed him on Lombardi. Perhaps feeling a sense of responsibility for talking his man off the Philadelphia job the previous year, Mara relented. But he did so on the condition that he could have Lombardi back whenever Howell stepped aside. Olejniczak agreed. But when that time came two years later, the Packers president would renege.

West Point was really the only hedge Lombardi had against taking a job in a place he had called "God forsaken." But with Army disqualifying him, he went after Green Bay wholeheartedly. He even talked contract numbers with Olejniczak, right out of the box.

The Monday after the draft, Ole flew him out to Green Bay. As soon as the plane stopped moving, the president escorted his prospect to the H. C. Prange Department Store for a meeting with Packers director (and Prange chairman) Jerry Atkinson and vice president Dick Bourguignon.

The directors grilled him about his administrative abilities. Well satisfied, Atkinson proceeded to sell Lombardi on the merits of coming to Green Bay. The Packers, he said, could offer him more money, total control, affordable living, a good school system for Vincent Jr. and Susan, a young and talented roster, and league-wide prestige if he turned the program around.

It soon became apparent that the Packers were a unique situation. After eleven straight non-winning years, all those Midwesterners wanted to give one of the most faithful fan bases in the league was a winning team. That they were about to hire an Italian fellow from Brooklyn whose last name ended in a vowel made no difference at all.

They made him an offer—$36,000 per year for five years, with bonuses on a sliding scale for first-, second-, and third-place finishes. Lombardi countered, asking that the third-place incentive of $5,000 also be attached to the first-place figure.

The board members agreed.

The deal wasn't done yet, however. The search committee had to sell it to the entire board of directors, and Lombardi had to bring the deal back to the Maras. And he had to convince Marie—like her husband a creature of the big city—that heading to the heart of Wisconsin dairy country lock, stock, and barrel was the right move.

The household discussion remained basically a one-way affair between the coach and his wife. It never did hit the dinner table.

"It was a done deal by the time we were made aware of it," Vince Jr. said. "I was a junior in high school and I knew enough about football to understand it was a great opportunity. Having said that, this was the late fifties, and people in the East thought Wisconsin was still cowboys and Indians. But it was a great opportunity, and we understood that."

Make that almost everybody. Daughter Susan was reluctant to leave the comfort zone of her friends, school, and neighborhood.

"My father comes home with a map and says, 'This is a map of Wisconsin,'" Susan recalled. "And he's looking. 'Where's Green Bay?' It's not even on the map. And I'm going, 'I'm not moving anyplace that's not on the map.' And he said, 'When I am done, it'll be on the map and you'll know exactly, Susan, where you live.'"

The discussion with Wellington Mara was somewhat more extensive, though no less emotional for Lombardi. Deep down, he had hoped someone on the Giants would talk him out of it. He never could see himself in a small town, especially one where players were heard to issue greetings like, "Welcome to the end of the earth," to trade imports. But Mara encouraged him to go. He'd have loved for Lombardi to stick around and succeed Howell. But in all fairness, he could not tell his assistant when that would happen.

"When he came to me and told me about the offer from Green Bay, we sat down and looked at the situation there," Mara remembered. "The offer he had the year before didn't shape up as much of a chance, but this one did. There was a good deal of talent that could be developed. He had a chance to assume a position of authority, of command over his circumstances. It was the right job for him, and I advised him to take it."

He also apprised Lombardi of the Giants' situation.

"Jim Lee told me he was tiring of it, but that he wanted to stay for another year or so," Mara said. "I had to honor that request. I told Vince. I told him everything I knew about Jim Lee's status and about his considerations. I promised I would offer the job to Vince when Jim Lee finally told me he didn't want it any longer, but I also told Vince that until such a time, I was morally committed to Howell.

"He understood perfectly, though I think he was a little bit regretful. He would have loved to take over the Giants. It was his team and his town and his players."

Olejniczak undoubtedly had the laudatory words of George Halas ringing in his head when he made his formal presentation to the board. Halas was among the legion who had grown impressed with Lombardi. "I shouldn't tell you this, but he'll be a good one," Papa Bear had told the president. "I shouldn't tell you because you're liable to kick the crap out of us."

Convincing the board, of which only twenty-seven of forty-five members showed up to vote, wasn't easy. What had always been a contentious group grew even more disagreeable in the wake of the Scooter McLean fiasco. Many had their hearts set on Evashevski and openly questioned Olejniczak's efforts to land the iron-handed Hawkeyes leader. Some of the old guard let nostalgia get the best of them as they lobbied hard for a Lambeau redux. As far as Ole's choice went, one member piped up, "Who the hell is Vince Lombardi?"

Hours passed. The board argued.

Finally, the decision came in. The Green Bay Packers made Vince Lombardi their coach and general manager by a 26–1 vote in the early evening of January 28, 1959.

As the Wisconsin media scrambled to find out who, exactly, this Lombardi fellow was, New York newspapers reported the hiring with little fanfare. The *New York Post*, for instance, led with the correct speculation that Allie Sherman would succeed him the next day as Howell's offensive assistant, folding Lombardi's hiring in below that. The *Journal-American*, *Herald-Tribune*, and *Daily News* ran wire reports.

The leading columnists were silent on the subject, their attentions mostly taken up with heavyweight champ Ingemar Johansson's appearance in New York to promote his June encounter with Floyd Patterson.

Only the *Times* ran an extensive interview, conducted only minutes after Lombardi took Olejniczak's confirmation phone call at the Hotel Manhattan.

The understated coverage was somewhat surprising, even absent the lens of history. The New York writers and editors knew Lombardi well. Some may not have liked him because of his gruff manner when posed with simplistic questions, or worse yet, second-guesses. But he was the guy everyone went to for explanations of offensive strategy. He had provided important background and insight into how plays were run and why they were called. He often drew up the key play for the *Times*, which the paper ran as a sidebar and diagram next to the game story. Howell led them all to Lombardi, as he led them to Landry for defensive specifics. Jim Lee was the platitudes guy. For the real lowdown, one went to Lombardi or Landry.

Still, the hiring drew only the notice worthy of an assistant, one with no head coaching experience past the high school level at that. In essence, he wasn't really Vince Lombardi yet.

The *Times* continued to reflect his true importance in the hiring story. He told the newspaper of his plans for revitalizing the Packers.

"I'll take the Giants' offense with me and use it with the Packers as personnel allows," he said.

His power-based, "close end" attack, Lombardi said, was more effective than the more popular Split-T formation favored by most NFL teams of that era. By putting the end tighter to the offensive tackle and sending a flanker wide rather than lining up the halfback between a tackle and a wide end, the passing game opened up. And that kept defenses honest against the run.

"My attack is harder to defend against," Lombardi said. "I'm going to stick with what's been successful for the Giants."

The sweep and the halfback option were on their way to Green Bay, but so was a defensive philosophy Lombardi had picked up from Landry. While Landry's Legions' overshadowing of the offense had often rankled the offensive assistant, Lombardi had come to recognize the value of a dominant defense. As Gifford would say in later years, "Vince learned a lot from Tom Landry."

"I'll put the Packers' best players on defense," Lombardi told the *Times*. "It's best for a team and good for its morale."

Also, he said he would no longer divide his quarterback affections between two men. Strategic monogamy would replace the Conerly-Heinrich partnership.

"That was a thing peculiar to the Giants," he said. "I'd like to have just one man there."

Finally, the new coach predicted a quick turnaround.

"I've never been with a losing team in my life," he said, "and I don't think I'll start now."

To others, he expressed an eagerness to get to work, especially with a roster that already featured such promising talent as Bart

Starr, Paul Hornung, Jim Taylor, Jerry Kramer, Forrest Gregg, and Ray Nitschke.

"I know the Packers have a good nucleus of good veteran players," he told the Associated Press. "I intend to build around that nucleus."

"We're sure he'll make one of the best head coaches in the NFL," Jack Mara told the *Newark Evening News.*

While it wasn't front page news all over Wisconsin, the hiring drew adequate coverage for the state's only pro team. The *Milwaukee Journal* bannered the news story across the top of its lead sports page January 29, though the accompanying column greeted the move with only guarded optimism. Among other things, the column emphasized the twenty-year gap between Lombardi's last head coaching job—in high school—and this one. But it also said the problem of his inexperience paled next to the potential problems the board—"meddling little men who thus far have found it impossible to divorce themselves from the operation," as sports editor Oliver Kuechle put it—could pose. "Won't they please step aside now and give Lombardi a fair chance on the field?" the columnist pleaded. He had no idea how big a brush-off Lombardi would give those board members over the coming days, months, and years, even though he hinted at it the day he was hired.

"My word will be final," he said in the news story. When asked about taking the dual role, he said, "That's the only way I'd take the job. I doubt if I would have come just as a coach."

Lombardi saved one tidbit until he and Marie flew out to Green Bay February 2. He told the Wisconsin media that his yet-to-be-hired assistants would have only limited authority. He was going to be a more "active" coach than Jim Lee Howell.

"I'll work more with my assistants than Jim did with us," he said.

*   *   *

Gifford didn't know it as he settled into his steak at Schacht's that night, but the man he knew as "Vinny" was dying. Not physically. That wouldn't happen for another eleven years. But emotionally, Vinny was taking his leave, to be replaced by the man history came to know as "Vince."

That dinner was one of the last Lombardi would ever share socially with an active player on his roster.

The man who once asked Gifford and Conerly for advice on the types of plays they'd be comfortable running would turn into a "my way or the highway" despot in Green Bay. He had to. He was in charge now—of everything. The unprecedented authority he wielded as an assistant paled in comparison to the absolute power the Packers board of directors bestowed upon him. With that came immense responsibility.

He could no longer afford to be anybody's pal.

There would be no pizza at his home for Paul Hornung, the big halfback Gifford would describe as "me squared." Even the most free-spirited of Packers would never think about hiding his chalk before a blackboard session, as Gifford and his teammates often did to draw a rant, and then that rumbling laugh.

Lombardi would change, completely and necessarily.

All Gifford knew at the time was that he had to say good-bye to a friend and confidante.

"I had such respect for him, and I knew he did for me, too," Gifford said. "He wasn't the guy you read about in Green Bay."

10

HOME TO DALLAS

THE BEST PAIR of assistants any NFL coach could hope for were now divided between Green Bay and New York. Vince Lombardi had the head coaching job he craved. At least Jim Lee Howell still had Tom Landry to run the NFL's best defense, though as events would unfold, he wouldn't have him for long.

While he did, though, the Giants remained successful. So much so that in 1959 they'd put together the best record of Howell's tenure, 10–2, and return to the championship game for a rematch against the Colts.

Landry's genius continued to shine as the 1959 defense gave up a league-low 170 points (14.2 points per game), its lowest total since Landry played his double role as defensive back and chief strategy decipherer for Steve Owen in 1951. The Yankee Stadium crowds had grown since "The Greatest Game Ever Played," and Sam Huff would bring national recognition to the "Huff-Huff-Huff" mystique when *Time* magazine devoted its November 30 cover story to his violent world.

It was pretty obvious from the outset that the defense was in for a most special year, anointed by no less than Lombardi after the Giants pitched a 14–0 shutout in a September 5 preseason meeting with the Packers in Bangor, Maine. It was Lombardi's first contest against his old team, and he was blown away by the Giants' ability to shut down the running of Paul Hornung and Jim Taylor, and the passing combination of Bart Starr, Max McGee, and Boyd Dowler. "That Giants defense might be the best one in the history of the NFL," Lombardi said.

They didn't exactly start out that way, but they certainly ended like that. By then, teams searching for a new coach held the Giants' sole defensive assistant in higher regard than half the head coaches in the league.

Landry's profile soared far higher than Lombardi's ever had, even though the latter beat him into the head coaching ranks. Everyone knew he led the real stars of that team, and their very tangible results had put his name on the lips of many players, as well as coaches. Like Lou Groza in his post-conference championship game lament the previous year, they all knew who called the defensive shots.

That's not to say the defense didn't have its rocky times. The first two games of the regular season were anything but memorable. The opener in Los Angeles saw the eventual 2–10 Rams come back from a 17–0 halftime deficit with three third-quarter touchdowns to take a 21–17 lead into the final fifteen minutes. It took two Pat Summerall field goals to bail the Giants out with a 23–21 win, the last an 18-yarder with less than two minutes remaining.

The bumps the Giants survived in the opener turned into inescapable potholes in Game 2. For all his preparatory skills, Landry had absolutely no answer for the Eagles' Hall of Fame flanker Tommy McDonald as he caught three of Norm Van Brocklin's passes for touchdowns and scored a fourth on a punt return. The Giants would lose 49–21, their worst setback since their 62–14 loss to Cleveland in Owen's penultimate game as head coach.

Chalk it up to a transitional period. The unit had changed somewhat since that overtime loss to the Colts. Linebacker Bill Svoboda had retired, replaced fulltime now by free-spirited special teams wiz Cliff Livingston. Cornerback Carl Karilivacz had been traded to the Rams after just one year in New York, replaced in a trade with the Redskins by second-year player Dick Lynch.

Lynch went on to have an outstanding career, returning four interceptions for touchdowns and leading the league in picks twice. Both marks remain franchise records. He retired after the 1966 season, and from 1967 until his death from leukemia in 2008 he provided color commentary on Giants radio broadcasts. But during his playing days, he and roommate Livingston were just as well known for their night crawling as their on-field prowess, with special attention paid to their female admirers. Lynch actually dated Kim Novak, one of the hottest actresses in Hollywood. The news wound up in the gossip columns, and the gossip columns inevitably wound up on the locker room bulletin board.

As one might imagine, Lynch's teammates took great pleasure in poking him through scrawled anonymous messages. One that appeared beneath one of the clippings read, "In one date with Dick, Kim learned more defensive maneuvers than Lynch has been able to absorb in two years as a pro."

Lynch had his own fun, though, especially with the devoutly religious Andy Robustelli, who disliked swearing and public displays of affection. He often got down on one knee and asked if he could kiss "the Pope's" ring.

Faced with working in those new members and an opponent motivated by some unflattering comments from a Giants scout that drifted down to Philadelphia, the undoubtedly fired-up Eagles simply walloped the defense.

Landry had plenty of time to let it all soak in, between the train trip, subway ride from midtown to Yankee Stadium, and the return car ride to Stamford with travel-mates Robustelli, Livingston, and defensive back Ed Hughes. He was livid. Not screaming-wild livid as Lombardi might have gotten. Silent livid. Landry livid.

"Tom was really upset about the way the defense played," Hughes remembered. "Lombardi screamed and yelled and cut guys to pieces. Tom could do the same thing with just a look, making you feel about two inches tall."

Throughout the whole four-hour trip back, including a coffee stop, he uttered but four words to those players: "That'll never happen again."

It never did. That's where it stopped. Dead. Over the final ten games, the Giants gave up just 100 points, and never again allowed more than 20 points in any one game.

Over the next five, they allowed all of one touchdown. That came in a 24–7 revenge win over Philadelphia in which line-backer Harland Svare brought back a Van Brocklin pass 70 yards for his first career touchdown. Two weeks later, Lombardi got a regular-season taste of the defense. The meal went a lot like the one in preseason, with the Giants holding his cast of future All Pros and Hall-of-Famers to a mere field goal in a 20–3 victory. The Packers went 7–5 that year, and Lombardi won Coach of the Year honors for the one-year turnaround from 1–10–1. But on that November 1 afternoon, blockers Fuzzy Thurston, Jim Ringo, Jerry Kramer, and Forrest Gregg couldn't fend off a front seven that pounded Hornung and Taylor to under 100 yards of combined rushing.

Nor was the Packers' passing game of any consequence. But that was hardly a surprise, since Bart Starr wasn't Bart Starr yet. Players create their legends on the field, not the bench, and Starr still hadn't left that lonely locale by the sixth game. He had yet to impress Lombardi during practice, so the coach stuck with former Chicago Cardinal Lamar McHan. Starr, a clean-living but frustrated four-year veteran who once drowned his sorrow by downing three whole beers, would finally get his chance in the eighth game against Baltimore, after McHan was injured.

Not that the rookie coach's words held tremendous weight around the league, but in the postgame locker room Lombardi reiterated his preseason claim that the Giants were "the greatest defensive team in football. These guys just don't make mistakes."

It wasn't like Lombardi was breaking big news by then. If the roar of the capacity Yankee Stadium crowds as public address legend Bob Sheppard introduced the defense before every game didn't carry across the nation, the statistics reported in the newspaper accounts did.

The game after the Philadelphia debacle, the Browns lost their fourth straight game against the Giants in a defensive struggle. The same philosophy—disciplined, fill-the-gap defense—that held Jim Brown to two touchdowns in the three wins of 1958 remained intact. With Huff keying on him the whole game, Brown was a non-factor with 86 yards and no touchdowns on 22 carries. The 10–6 Giants win was decided when the offense capitalized on Lindon Crow's interception of Milt Plum.

Em Tunnell had been traded off to Lombardi's Packers, but amazingly the Giants secondary remained a top unit. Their effort against the Cardinals a week after Green Bay offered plenty of evidence as Lynch, Crow, and safeties Dick Nolan and Jimmy Patton held Chicago to just 68 yards passing in a 9–3 win.

The defense could not have peaked at a better time. The offense, now headed by Allie Sherman, went through a major drought in which it failed to score a touchdown in nearly three full games. But the Giants went 2–1 over that span because the defense held Green Bay, Chicago, and Pittsburgh to a total of 20 points, yielding two touchdowns to Pittsburgh in a 14–9 loss, the Giants final setback of the regular season.

Even the buttoned-up Landry found it appropriate to stand with Howell in joint displeasure over the offense's lack of production.

The defensive lineman and linebackers took their bow in the second meeting two weeks later, holding the Cards to zero yards rushing in a 30–20 victory. The offense now cured after the win over the Cardinals, the whole team contributed to a 45–14 win over the Redskins the next week that clinched at least a tie for first place in the Eastern Conference. To sweeten matters, it came on Charlie Conerly Day at Yankee Stadium. The thirty-eight-year-old quarterback had taken a beating in years past not only from opponents, but Giants fans, too. But on November 29, 1959, he was the beloved old man of the organization, in the midst of his best year. Obviously thinking he was headed toward retirement—he would actually earn the AP's MVP award that year and play through the '61 season—the crowd gave him a vocal group hug as the team showered him with $25,000 worth of gifts before the game, among them a ton of fertilizer and seed for his Mississippi cotton farm, a trip to Europe for him and his wife, Perian, a Cadillac for him, and a Corvette for her.

Conerly then went out and lit up the Redskins with three first-half touchdown passes. He sat out the second half.

A day later, *Time* magazine hit the stands with a cover story titled "Pro Football: Brawn, Brains, and Profit," centered around Sam Huff and illustrated by Huff's profile on the cover. Huff initially had declined to be interviewed for the story, since *Time* refused to pay him. He changed his mind when *Time* promised him the original copy of the cover art. Huff, taking Landry's 4-3 defense along for the ride, became a national figure.

"Let me put it this way," said defensive tackle Dick Modzelewski, who eventually coached as a Bengals assistant, "Sam Huff was the first (football player) to be on the cover of *Time* magazine, and we loved it. Nobody was envious of him. We loved to be with the Giants because we worked as a team. In my years of coaching, I've seen too many selfish guys. Too much 'me, me, me'. But with Landry, we were all together as a team."

Not that any of his celebrity went to Huff's head. He remained the tough, hard-hitting linebacker he always was, and he showed it the following Sunday when the Giants wrapped up the conference with a 48–7 demolition of the Cleveland Browns. In Paul Brown's worst defeat ever, Huff hit Jim Brown so hard that Brown had to sit out most of the second quarter. Once again, the Giants' defense dominated arguably the greatest running back in history, and Brown finished with just 50 yards and no touchdowns on 15 carries.

The Browns didn't score until late, but Landry, ever the perfectionist, dearly wanted the shutout and could be heard shouting, "Don't let 'em score! Hold 'em! Hold 'em!" from the sideline.

Apparently 3,000 of the capacity crowd had their minds on something else. They were intent on tearing down the goal posts. With about three minutes remaining, the mob stormed the field, not only going for their wooden targets, but throwing punches at the Browns as Paul Brown and his players high-tailed it to the safety of the visitors' locker room. Problem was, Ed Modzelewski was still caught in the riot.

Lucky for him, he had connections.

The Giants made a protective circle around Dick's big brother. One of them threw his cape over Ed to disguise him.

"Paul Brown took the whole team off the field, but I stayed out with the Giants," said Big Mo, now a backup to Brown. "They got in a circle and put me in the middle so they wouldn't start getting on me. I stayed there and stayed there, but the officials wouldn't end the game because we still had a couple of plays to go."

Bob Sheppard took it upon himself to announce that if the fans didn't retreat, the Giants would forfeit the game. It took police and security twenty minutes to clear the field.

"They held the game up and Paul Brown just sent enough guys out to finish the game," Ed Modzelewski said. "I ran into the locker room after that.

"We knew them all. Back then, it was more of a club thing. You respected each other and played like hell when you were against each other."

A meaningless 24–10 victory over the Redskins enabled the Giants to finish the regular season at 10–2, the NFL's best record since the Browns went 11–1 in 1953. Best of all, they would appear in the NFL Championship game for the second straight year against the Baltimore Colts, this time without the wear and tear of a conference playoff.

But Landry had already started to plan his future.

*　　*　　*

Tom Landry's name had gotten around the league well before the end of 1959. Jim Lee Howell had publicly complemented him. Paul Brown, eyewitness to the defense's constant abuse of his star running back the previous two years, had talked about him as a coaching genius. The only question was whether Landry wanted to become a head coach. His ego and success told him he had the goods. But the instability of any coaching career gave the husband and father of three pause.

As time went on, he eventually decided to try it. If he failed, he always had engineering as a fallback career.

"When he became a fulltime coach in '56, he realized he had the capability of being a coach," said Jack Cavanaugh, author of *Giants Among Men*, the definitive account of the franchise's golden years under Jim Lee Howell and Allie Sherman. "He was doing well, he liked it, and the more he got involved in the coaching and working with Lombardi and Howell, he was ready to change his mind and become a coach.

"By the late fifties, he was interested in becoming a coach. Never came out and said it. But that all changed with his success and the fact that he was being written up as an outstanding defensive coach, a very smart coach who knew how to handle men. He had all the characteristics to become a successful coach. He read that and he knew that, 'Hey, I can make more money.'

He was starting a family, and knew he could make more money as an NFL coach than as an industrial engineer."

He had opportunities. Rams general manager and eventual NFL commissioner Pete Rozelle never admitted it publicly, but the Rams put out feeler to him before they fired Sid Gillman. "He is one whom we obviously would have given serious consideration, but we have known he was committed," Rozelle told the media.

Detroit and the Chicago Cardinals had contemplated firing Pop Ivy and George Wilson, respectively, but didn't. Otherwise there would have been opportunity in both of those places.

Dallas didn't have a franchise yet, but it had a prospective ownership group in Clint Murchison Jr. and Bedford Wynne, and the league was ready to expand.

There is some confusion surrounding the Giants' own efforts to retain Landry. A promise to make him Jim Lee Howell's eventual successor probably would not have worked, since Howell had only hinted before 1959 that he had about had it with the coaching life. For sure, Landry wasn't about to stick around another year for a meager $12,000 assistant's salary. He needed to make a better living, whether it came through coaching or a private sector job.

Wellington Mara, who Landry kept in close touch with throughout the courting period, told some people he actually offered him Howell's job outright. Other accounts say he may have broached the subject generally, but never did make a solid offer.

But he told his son, John, that he did try to keep the quiet Texan in New York.

"He always said he tried to keep Landry," John Mara said. "Tried to convince him that at some point that he would be our head coach. But when [Landry] had an opportunity to go to Dallas, he said, 'I'm going home.' That was the quote he used.

'I'm going home.' There was no way we were going to be able to keep him."

Dallas intrigued Landry. The Cowboys, originally called the Rangers, had only a promise from Chicago Bears owner George Halas that if he could get an affirmative vote on a two-team expansion plan at the January 20 owners meeting in Miami, Murchison and Wynne would get one of the franchises. Expansion votes are always a crapshoot, even in this day and age, but especially back then. Landry knew that. But he also knew the prospective owners had hired Tex Schramm as team president. They had sent Schramm on a mission to sign some thirty college players to contracts that would be voided automatically if the owners voted down the Dallas franchise. The first of those players signed was Don Meredith, the All-America gunslinger quarterback from SMU Halas had drafted November 30 in the third round. But Halas let him sign a personal-services contract with the Rangers for a mere return of the third-round pick.

If he went to Dallas, Landry at least would not have to start with a bare cupboard, though its contents were still more paper and plastic than Lenox, Meredith notwithstanding.

Another factor was his and Alicia's desire to raise their children in Texas. They had enjoyed their time in New York, certainly. Always a tight family, Tom and Alicia had immersed Tom Jr., Kitty, and Lisa in the recreation and culture Manhattan had to offer, its parks and museums and such. But the kids were growing older now.

"We'd just decided that's what we were gonna do," Alicia Landry said. "I love New York, but I'm from Texas and Texas to us is like a club, not a state. And I wanted my children raised in Texas, just because I thought they deserved it. My family came from here, and his family.

"So we never thought about moving away to New York [permanently]. I loved New York, and I still see Ann Mara. But the defense was really great, and he got several offers to be a head coach. He decided that since he wanted to come to Dallas and he was offered the job, he'd do it for a year or so and then go on into engineering.

"We just knew what we wanted to do. We wanted to bring our children back to Texas."

Texas is a big state, though. Big enough to contain one other offer that nearly lured the Giants assistant. The rival American Football League had started, and teams had started to hire their coaches from the college and NFL assistant ranks. Dallas even had a team, and owner Lamar Hunt had just hired University of Miami line coach Hank Stram as the Texans' (soon to be the Kansas City Chiefs) first coach.

Houston Oilers owner Bud Adams Jr. had targeted Landry.

The Houston petroleum mogul had flown up to New York to speak with Landry in a hotel room. Actually, he had come ostensibly to try to sign two of Landry's players whose contracts were expiring. He first brought in Landry, which was fine. It was when the two players arrived earlier than expected that the whole thing turned into a scene out of a Marx Brothers movie.

Knock, knock.

"[Landry] said, 'Who's that?'" Adams recalled. "I said, 'That's two of your players that's contracts are up.' He said, 'I can't be seen here with you.' I said, 'Well, go in the bathroom. I'll get rid of them right away and postpone my meeting for later on today.'

"So he was in the bathroom, and I told the guys 'Really, I've got to go to another meeting, but I can meet with you in about two hours, and tell me where to go.' So they got ready to leave and one of them said, 'Well, I need to go to the bathroom. Is it all right to use the bathroom?' I said, 'Well, wait a minute. That door sticks. That door sticks. You might get locked in there.'

"He was already over there. He said, 'Let me try it.' He turned the handle and it wouldn't open. [Landry] had locked it. Thank God. I got out of that one pretty easily."

Adams would face much bigger predicaments in the near future, like fighting and winning the NFL's court challenge of his signing of LSU's Heisman Trophy running back Billy Cannon after Cannon had committed to the Rams. In this current issue, Adams gathered himself quickly and soon offered Landry a deal believed to be $65,000 per year. The amount, *Dallas Morning News* reporter Sam Blair wrote, made the Cannon contract "look like the contents of Tom Jr.'s piggy bank."

The sheer gravity of the numbers might have swayed another man, but Landry, in consultation with the staunchly pro-NFL Mara, moved cautiously. He told Adams that he might not make a decision until the NFL voted on expansion. Adams told him he probably wouldn't wait that long, and began interviewing other candidates.

On his end, Mara remained intent on keeping the best coach on the market away from the rival league. He lobbied Schramm hard on the merits of hiring his defensive coach.

Landry told nobody except those closest to him. His inner circle typically did not include nosey newspapermen.

"I need some help," Landry told *Dallas Morning News* columnist Charles Burton as he began preparations for the Colts. "How do you stop a team that has gained over 4,000 yards during the season?"

Burton expected to hear something about his decision, but Landry wouldn't bite. Landry acknowledged he'd had offers and was debating whether to stay in the NFL or jump to the AFL. But he went no further.

"I don't think it'd be fair to the boys or anyone concerned to reveal my decision before the game, even if I reach one," he said.

Seven days before the NFL championship game in Baltimore, Landry was more concerned with the present.

Unbeknownst to most, he already had the future in his pocket.

$$* \quad * \quad *$$

The snow covering the Yankee Stadium field forced the Giants indoors as they began their work week for the 1959 NFL Championship game in Baltimore's Memorial Stadium. Teams of the fifties did not have the atmospherically controlled practice bubbles and field houses of today, and the Giants were no different. They made do with the Squadron A Armory at Madison Avenue and 94th Street, which housed the best indoor polo field in the area.

The tanbark surface, basically tree bark crushed into a mulch-like composition, gave the Giants a nice, soft place to land, certainly more comfortable than the cold and now mostly naked Yankee Stadium field. But the dust it kicked up got in the players' eyes and mouths, making catching one's breath between snaps difficult. Rosey Grier took to wearing a white handkerchief around his face, creating the appearance of an Old West bank robber minus the six-shooter and ten-gallon hat.

If only tiny airborne particles were Tom Landry's biggest problem. The Colts were as big and nasty as they were in 1958, better even because the still-youthful team had matured by a year. As if it was even possible, Johnny Unitas had grown smarter while throwing a then-record 32 touchdown passes. Raymond Berry and Lenny Moore remained just as dangerous in their pass routes. And the Gino Marchetti-Art Donovan-Big Daddy Liscomb defense had mouthy second-year safety Johnny Sample, of future Jets fame, playing full time.

Making things tougher, the Giants would have to wage this battle in Baltimore, home of the rowdiest and most faithful followers of any NFL team. Between urgings of the cheerleaders, the Colts band, the stetson-hatted drum majorettes, and the player's neighbors who patronized the town's blue-collar bars, no group could make with the tonsils like Colts fans.

Landry was most concerned about the Unitas-Berry-Moore triumvirate that blew his defense apart in the final minutes the year before. His plan was to double-cover Berry and dangerous tight end Jim Mutscheller, leaving the speedy flanker Moore in single coverage. That basically meant leaving cornerback Lindon Crow on an island against Moore. Landry, in effect, was conceding Moore a touchdown in hopes of shutting down everyone else and winning a close one 17–14 or 21–17.

"He's your man, take him out," Huff said, recalling Landry's general, unbending philosophy. "Trying to cover Lenny Moore, he's one of the fastest guys I've ever seen. He says, 'You're a pro. Cover him.' He would not allow you to play zone defense. It was always man-to-man. 'He's a pro, you're a pro, you've got to take him.'

"That's what he said to me with Jim Brown. I knew him at Syracuse. That's how I broke my nose and shattered my teeth. And he said, 'That's your man.' And I said 'I got him. Don't worry.' You didn't make excuses to Tom. He was a genius."

Fully aware that this was their leader's last game as a Giant, the players desperately wanted to make up for the late blown lead of 1958 and send Landry into the next phase of his coaching life with a championship. But they had to settle for runner-up again on an unseasonably warm afternoon in Baltimore with Vice President Richard M. Nixon seated among the 57,545 noisemakers. Only a smattering of Giants fans showed up, a big contrast from the 20,000-plus Colts fans who appeared up at Yankee Stadium a year earlier.

The Colts proved Landry right about one thing. That touch-down he mentally conceded to Moore happened less than five minutes into the game when Unitas play-actioned to Alan Ameche, double-pumped to Berry, and fired a 22-yard pass to Moore, who had gotten past Crow, on the opposite sideline. Moore took it the remaining 38 of the 60-yard play into the end zone for a 7–0 Colts lead.

The Giants actually brought a 9–7 lead into the fourth quarter thanks to three Pat Summerall field goals. It wouldn't hold. A gamble Howell took moments before had changed the complexion of the game. Faced with a similar fourth-and-inches situation that caused Howell to punt near midfield in the '58 game, Howell went for it this time at the Colts' 29. Alex Webster, one of the most reliable short-yardage backs in the league, tried to run behind the great left tackle Rosie Brown, but the Colts had guessed right and stacked that side. They gang-tackled Webster for no gain.

From that point, it was as if the Giants were pulled under by a riptide of momentum and carried out to sea. The fourth quarter was all Baltimore as the Colts scored 24 unanswered points. Unitas marched his team downfield and scored the go-ahead touchdown himself on a 4-yard option around right end. Charlie

Conerly, who at thirty-eight had just become the oldest player ever to win the league's MVP award, then threw an interception to Andy Nelson that set up Unitas's 12-yard touchdown pass to Jerry Richardson. (The same Jerry Richardson who would bring the Carolina Panthers into the league in 1995.)

Sample, who badgered Frank Gifford with a day-long stream of trash talk, intercepted a pass and ran it back 42 yards for a touchdown, and then picked off a second throw to set up Steve Myhra's 25-yard field goal that expanded the lead to 31–9. The Colts had scored three touchdowns and a field goal in ten minutes.

The Giants offense scored its only touchdown with thirty-two seconds left on a 32-yard pass by Conerly to Bob Schnelker. Final score: 31–16. Unitas had gone 18-of-29 for 264 yards with two touchdowns and no interceptions, but Landry's front had sacked him six times, four of them by Robustelli. The Giants held Baltimore's running game to 73 yards. Given the short fields it encountered, the defense could hardly be blamed for this one.

The Giants came out of it with as many bruised bodies as egos, it seemed. Crow got knocked cold when he took a knee to the head on a fourth-quarter tackle on Moore. The trainers brought him around and he stayed in the game. Patton was done by halftime with a sprained foot. Kyle Rote suffered a concussion when he was nailed on a first-quarter end zone pass.

The biggest loss was still hours away. In the postgame locker room, Robustelli presented Landry with a going-away present—a silver football bought by donations Robustelli "solicited" from his defensive teammates. A championship game ball would have served better, but the silver consolation prize still became one of Landry's most cherished possessions.

The morning after the game, Monday, December 28, Landry boarded a plane with Rangers president Tex Schramm and signed a five-year contract to become head coach of the nascent Dallas franchise.

*   *   *

Bud Adams Jr. had an inkling his main target might stick with the NFL. And that became clearer in the hours after the Giants' second championship game defeat in two years.

"Landry was supposed to telephone me late last night or today," Adams told the *Dallas Morning News* early that Monday morning. "I haven't heard from him yet."

That's because Landry and Schramm were already on the airplane, headed 250 miles northwest of Adams's town.

The Dallas franchise would pay Landry $34,500 per year, a little more than half the fortune (for those days) Adams had offered him. Landry explained that he was really an NFL man at heart. The fact that he had been living and working in Dallas in the offseason also affected his decision, as did the challenge of building a brand new team.

Adams had already covered himself. A few days later, he hired Rams offensive line assistant Lou Rymkus as the first coach of the Houston Oilers.

The *Dallas Morning News* called the Rangers' move the NFL's second major coup over the AFL, right there with locking down Don Meredith, the quarterback the Texans' picked November 22 in the AFL's first draft.

Jim Lee Howell offered his plaudits on Landry's signing, crediting the success of the defense entirely to his former assistant.

"I've never given an order or made a suggestion," Howell said. "He's done it all."

But he also offered a glimpse into Landry's silent, often off-putting, ways.

"Tom is a warm person, but not so much with his players," Howell said. "Sometimes he gets impatient with them, doesn't pat them on the back. He expects them to go out there and do their jobs.

"One thing is, he's so much smarter than most of them. Maybe he should be more of a dope like me. He's like Paul Brown, a perfectionist. But he's smarter than anybody."

All Landry needed now was an active franchise. He knew the day he signed he had the makings of one, what with Meredith already committed and an expansion draft coming after the expansion vote.

"All we got is a coach and a pitcher," Landry said. "But that's a start. Now we're going to be able to get some more players."

Landry was under no illusion that the other teams would flood his roster with stars, but "they won't be the worst, either. The league doesn't want any weak clubs, either. That hurts everybody," he said.

As he waited for the vote—a month, it turned out—he busied himself with the details of starting up a team and making speeches to groups such as the 200-member Region III Texas High School Coaches Association.

Much happened in the interim. The simmering feud with the upstart AFL turned into all-out war. And the NFL owners engaged in an intimate battle of their own at their January 20 meeting. Bert Bell's sudden death of a heart attack in October as he viewed an Eagles game at Franklin Field made it necessary to appoint a new commissioner. Marshall Leahy, team attorney for the 49ers, was the favorite of those wanting to maintain current league policies, but couldn't get the necessary 75 percent of the vote. Vince Lombardi's name was thrown out there. The idea of making Medal of Honor winner and AFL commissioner Joe Foss a super-boss over both leagues was put forth in the press. It took seven days, a fight between old-guard owners and the more forward-thinking, and twenty-three ballots to settle on thirty-three-year-old Rams general manager Pete Rozelle.

The main expansion proposal—Dallas, because it already had a roster going, would come in 1960 and Minnesota would enter in 1961—was for the most part tabled.

Some owners dug in deep against the expansion plan, anyway. George Preston Marshall of Washington was vehemently anti-expansion unless the league grew by four clubs: Dallas, Minnesota, Miami, and St. Louis, all to be admitted for the '61 season. Wellington Mara said he'd only vote yea to the preferred two-team format if Baltimore, then in what was considered the big-money Western Conference, was moved to the East.

They settled their differences on January 28, after they voted in an amendment to the bylaws that reduced the threshold required to pass the expansion proposal from unanimous to 10 votes. The final vote was 11–0, with the Chicago Cardinals abstaining. Baltimore moved east. Dallas came in the West as the league's thirteenth franchise, but would play a non-divisional "swing" schedule. The renamed Cowboys would face every team in the league in 1960.

Landry had no problem with superstitions or odd schedules.

"Being number thirteen doesn't bother me at all," Landry said. "I'm elated that we're definitely in for 1960."

The date Dallas entered the NFL union held great significance, for it also marked Tom and Alicia's eleventh wedding anniversary.

"I guess this is the day great things happen for me," he said.

A couple of weeks after Landry's departure, Howell dropped his bombshell. The strain of coaching had left him a cranky, snappish wreck at home. The agony of the few losses so overshadowed the thrill of winning that it just wasn't worth it anymore.

He was ready to quit. Burned out. Cooked. Well-done.

Mara, his brain trust permanently scattered to Green Bay and Dallas, was not happy with his head coach for putting him in such a bind. Had Howell announced his intentions during the season, the owner might have made a bigger push for Landry. Had Howell offered to step down after 1958, Vince Lombardi certainly would have stuck around.

Now Mara was in a pickle. Brother Jack convinced Howell to honor the final year of his contract. Howell would coach the 1960 season, and then move into the front office to help Wellington with the draft and trade matters.

Landry filled the rest of his first roster in the expansion draft. Each team was allowed to freeze twenty-five of their thirty-six rostered players. Dallas could pick no more than three from every other club. After a team lost a player, it could pull back three others.

The Cowboys had twenty-four hours to make their picks. Landry had made an intensive study of the league's talent, however, and was well-prepared to deal with the process. A deal with the Giants that allowed them to freeze more players brought him Don Heinrich, who eventually became a player-coach. Schramm's additional trade of a future draft pick brought

Redskins quarterback Eddie LeBaron, who came out of retirement out of respect for Landry.

The new coach knew the talent wasn't at an ideal level. He didn't even know most of the thirty collegians under the personal-services contracts. But that didn't lessen his enthusiasm.

"We may even get another Roosevelt Brown," he said optimistically of his unknown flock. "The Giants drafted him [in the twenty-seventh round], but look at him now."

He had his own team now. Landry was officially gone, and with him went the first half of a golden era in New York Giants football.

Things would never be the same.

11

WHERE IT ALL WENT

A **S PRESIDENT AND** CEO of the Giants, John K. Mara
runs one of the NFL's oldest franchises. The 56-year-old Mara
actually took over the team's day-to-day operation in 2003, two
years before his father, Wellington, passed away from cancer.

Mara has been personal witness to his team winning three
Super Bowls in four appearances since 1986. He saw the Bill
Parcells era from afar, ensconced in the offices of Shea & Gould,
where he served as a labor and litigation lawyer until he officially
boarded his father's ship in 1990. He, along with co-owners Steve
and Jonathan Tisch made the decision in 2006 to extend head
coach Tom Coughlin's contract despite a failed playoff season, the
rewards for which came with a Vince Lombardi Trophy in 2007.

Born on December 1, 1954, as the first year of the Jim Lee
Howell–Vince Lombardi–Tom Landry triumvirate neared its
conclusion, he is the oldest of Wellington and Ann's eleven children. John Mara would not become of conscious sporting age
until years after the separate pieces of that partnership drifted
away. The accoutrements of early childhood such as rattles and

toys and tricycles occupied the son far more than the evolution of power sweeps and 4-3 defenses.

He learned soon enough about the importance of Vince Lombardi and Tom Landry to the Giants, however. The barbs his elementary school, Iona Prep, and Boston College classmates threw at him as his father's team wandered through the wilderness of the 1960s and '70s reminded him every Monday of the greatness that was, and what could have been, had his father hired either man as his head coach.

"When I think back on it, I think about how much more pleasant it would have made my childhood as opposed to what we went through," John Mara said. "Up until the time I was ten, it was pretty good. But from the period where I was ten up until the age of twenty-seven, it was mostly pretty difficult going to school [and work] on Monday morning."

Wellington knew he had lost tremendous talents in his two departed assistants. But he didn't mourn because Howell was still in charge and Allie Sherman, though hardly the communicator Lombardi was, had a wealth of offensive knowledge. The common perception is that Sherman sent the team spiraling down the drain once Howell retired after the 1960 season. But the fact is the Giants went to the championship game in 1961, '62, and '63 before the bottom fell out.

"We were still very successful at that point," John Mara said. "There were still some frustrations involved, losing five championship games in a six-year period. But we were still in the championship game. Allie Sherman was Coach of the Year a couple of times during that era, so at the time we hadn't lost a beat.

"Now, years later, when things went downhill for us, there was a lot of second-guessing. Why didn't you keep Lombardi?

"The interesting thing was, when Lombardi was on the staff at West Point in '53, Steve Owen gets fired and we're looking to hire a head coach, and we offered the job to Red Blaik and he didn't want to leave. And we asked Blaik for permission to talk to Lombardi to bring him over as an assistant. I think Lombardi thought at the time we were asking him about the head coach. You can second-guess that. If Lombardi was the head coach back then, he would have stayed and I would have had a very happy childhood."

Even if Landry had stayed instead, it still could have been very happy. Stories conflict on whether Wellington Mara actively sought to keep Landry from bolting to Dallas. John Mara said his father often spoke about his attempt to hire Landry. But Landry's wife, Alicia, said that was never a consideration because the dyed-in-the-wool Texans simply wanted to go home. Besides, at the time of Landry's departure in February 1960, Jim Lee Howell still hadn't made known his plans to retire after the upcoming season. Mara wasn't about to get rid of a coach who had just taken his team to a third championship game, and it wouldn't have been fair to Landry to make him a head-coach-in-waiting with a sure opportunity at hand in Dallas.

Whatever the case, Landry soon made a sport of beating the daylights out of the Giants. After the Cowboys' break-in period in which the Giants held a 5–1–1 advantage from 1960–63, the Cowboys steamrolled them. Between 1964 and 1981, Landry put up a stunning 29–8–1 mark against his old team.

This was the man Wellington actually steered toward the Cowboys after the upstart Houston Oilers of the AFL had approached him. But John said his father never had any regrets, though the son might have thought differently as Landry rolled up an 11–1 record against the Giants from 1973–79.

"I remember Dad talking about that once," John said. "If we were going to lose him, he wanted to lose him to our league instead of theirs. In retrospect, I wish he let him go to Houston so he wouldn't have kicked our ass all those years.

"[Dad] was very protective of the NFL. This [new] league was a threat to us. Keep in mind where we're sitting at this time. We've been in all these championship games, we're pretty confident about our team and our future. We're not worried about an assistant, even one as highly thought of as him, going to another team in the NFL. That didn't bother us at the time.

"We didn't want the AFL to be successful at that time. So there was never any thought in [Dad's] mind. He wanted [Landry] in the NFL."

John Mara was not bitter over what had occurred when he was young. But for some of the players who were there, losing Lombardi and Landry one season apart foreshadowed a death knell of sorts.

"The thing that always got me was, how in the world did we end up with Tom Landry and Vince Lombardi? And let them go?" Frank Gifford said. "The Maras were always so loyal. Wellington regretted enormously letting Lombardi go because they were classmates at Fordham. And Tom, there was a franchise developing and it was a great opportunity for him.

"I'm sure Wellington felt, 'What the hell are we going to do now?' And he was right. He hired Allie. Allie knew a lot of football, but he was not a communicative guy and he pissed people off a lot. The defense didn't care for him much, either, and it turned into a big mess."

Sam Huff never got over it. To this day, he makes no effort to hide his bitterness over the Allie Sherman era. He loved

Lombardi, and actually convinced the then-Redskins coach in 1969 to allow him to come back one more year as a player-coach for the linebackers. And he never lost his affection for Landry, the man who turned him from struggling guard into a Hall of Fame middle linebacker.

"If Jim Lee was going to go inside, why didn't they have Lombardi or Landry coach the Giants?" Huff said. "That's where the house fell in . . . It went to hell."

*   *   *

Allie Sherman was the ultimate second choice. He knew it. Wellington Mara told him so.

The road to Allie Sherman's hire had actually begun in 1959, right after Jim Lee Howell informed Wellington and Jack Mara in a private meeting that 1960 would be his last year of coaching.

Howell indeed stepped down to assume a spot as the team's player personnel director after an injury-ridden 6–4–2 mark in 1960. Wellington Mara had wanted Lombardi to succeed Howell, not only because of their close personal friendship, but also because Lombardi had immediately started to prove himself with a 7–5 record in 1959, the Packers' first winning season since 1947 which his former star and radio host Frank Gifford hailed as "the best reclamation project since the raising of the Normandie." The turnaround earned him Coach of the Year honors.

Packers president Dominic Olejniczak granted Mara permission to speak to Lombardi after that season, but only in private. Eventually, the sides agreed to table the matter until after the 1960 season in recognition of Lombardi's contractual obligations to the Packers.

By the time the subject came up again, however, Lombardi had taken the Packers to the championship game against the Eagles. On the Packers' end, Olejniczak was not about to let his coach out of his five-year contract. "I'd just as soon lose both legs as lose Lombardi," Olejniczak said before the Eagles game. "But I know one thing, he's a man of integrity."

Lucky for Olejniczak, Lombardi not only had integrity, but a conscience. George Halas and Paul Brown had warned him that jumping his contract could trigger a trend where other coaches would routinely break contracts for more lucrative jobs in the NFL or, heaven forbid, the rival AFL. That's the last thing Lombardi wanted.

On a more personal level, Lombardi had grown accustomed to the all-encompassing power the Packers gave him. He grew close to his players and knew they had the stuff of champions.

Despite his not-so-secret yearning to get back to his big-city roots, Lombardi told the Maras before the championship game that he'd decided to stay in Green Bay.

"I know dad believed he could get Lombardi back," John Mara said. "Let him go to Green Bay for a couple of years, and if necessary, we could get him back. After all, he was a New Yorker. Dad had a very close relationship with him. I think he underestimated the pull that Green Bay had for [Lombardi] after he goes in there and has them in the championship game after the 1960 season."

Mara had apprised the offense-savvy Sherman, then a Giants scout, of his desire for Lombardi, but also told Sherman he would be the man if Lombardi balked. Sherman had replaced Lombardi as offensive assistant in 1959 and had become a desirable commodity in a very short time. In a former incarnation as Steve Owen's backfield coach from 1949–53, he had helped convert Charlie Conerly from a college tailback to a T-formation quarterback. And he became one of the first coaches to put men in motion in the NFL.

Sherman had left the Giants to coach three years in Canada before returning to the Giants in 1957 as a scout.

A former quarterback with the Eagles, drafted by Greasy Neale in 1943, the little (5-foot-10, 160 pounds) Jewish kid from Brooklyn was also up for the Pittsburgh Steelers' head job. And Lombardi wanted him to coach the Green Bay offense, making him the offer in a men's room.

As it happened, Pittsburgh proved not to be as attractive at second glance, so Sherman eliminated that possibility. And when Lombardi refused to leave Green Bay, Wellington Mara offered the ex-quarterback the job at the Senior Bowl in Mobile, Alabama.

Sherman had one of the sharpest offensive minds in the league. He was innovative, incredible with game plans. He had a tremendous eye for offensive talent, but had absolutely no interest in defensive football.

He left it to Landry's playing successors, Andy Robustelli, Harland "Swede" Svare, and Jimmy Patton to handle the defense. Robustelli coached the line, Svare the linebackers, and Patton the defensive backs. Aside from some cursory instructions early in the week, Sherman basically left the defense to coach itself.

"It was like he hated the defense," Sam Huff said. "He'd come into our meeting and say something like, 'Okay, so how you guys gonna screw it up this time.'"

There was no doubting his offensive mind, however. One of the first players he had Mara procure for him was San Francisco's nimble quarterback, Y. A. Tittle. The trade, to this day one of the greatest in NFL history, sent the Giants' top offensive lineman, Lou Cordileone, westward in a straight-up deal that left Cordileone stunned. Not because he was traded, but because the Giants' top draft pick of 1960 thought he was worth more than a thirty-four-year-old quarterback.

"Is that all?" Cordileone asked incredulously.

Split end Del Shofner, the player the Rams took with the 1957 first-rounder the Giants sent them for Robustelli the year before, came that same season for another No. 1. Tight end Joe Walton and defensive back Erich Barnes were also added in trades.

Almost immediately, it didn't matter whether Sherman was interested in the defense or not. His offense became a gridiron slot machine, churning all sorts of numbers and yielding huge payoffs in points. Lombardi's offense was certainly competent, but Sherman's became a juggernaut.

Sherman started the 1961 season with a two-quarterback rotation, starting Charlie Conerly—forty and aching—who had given his blessing to the break-in of a new starter in what would be his final season, and following with Tittle. But by the eighth game of the league's new fourteen-game schedule, Sherman made Tittle the fulltime starter. That 53–0 win over Washington marked the beginning of a three-year period where Tittle and Shofner became the NFL's premier passing combination. The Giants scored more than 30 points in four of the last seven games en route to the first of three straight championship game appearances, all losses.

Tittle had three of his greatest seasons from 1961 to 1963. He put up a then-record 33 touchdown passes in 1962, then broke that the following year with 36, which still stands as a club record.

Shofner caught 185 passes, 32 of them for touchdowns, as he terrorized defensive backfields for 18.5 yards per catch over that same period.

Sherman's offense made Lombardi's look like kid's stuff. From 1961–63, Tittle, Shofner, Kyle Rote, and company put up 368, 398, and a still-standing franchise record 448 points in succession, good for second, second, and first in the league. Even adjusting for the two fewer games Lombardi's group played each year, his totals of 293, 267, 264, 254, and 246 didn't come close to Sherman's production. Those offenses never ranked higher than third, and Lombardi's final team in '58 finished ninth.

In his best year, 1954, Lombardi's unit averaged 24.4 points per game. In Sherman's best, 1963, it averaged 32 points per game.

The offense was the star of the Giants' show now, even though Sherman's less-favored unit continued to draw the now familiar chants of "Dee-Fense!" and "Huff-Huff-Huff" from the Yankee Stadium faithful.

But all was clearly not well. The defense gave up more points and yardage. And Sherman, in his few forays into defensive game planning, tinkered with the 4-3 alignment Tom Landry had made so successful. It might have been ego; a need to put his stamp on both sides of the ball. Whatever the case, things changed on the defensive side, and not for the better. The veterans who swore by Landry's philosophies never bought into Sherman's schemes. More than once, the unit unilaterally trashed his game plan and reverted to Landry's old 4-3 techniques to stanch offensive onslaughts.

In one particular alteration in 1962, Sherman anchored Huff on the strong side, assigning him to plug the gap between the center and guard rather than allowing him to sit back and flow to the ball. As a result, Huff wound up shackled, caught up in traffic, and unable to roam sideline-to-sideline for the tackles he used to make as common practice. The defense suffered because of it in the exhibition season. But when Huff went to Sherman with his complaints, Sherman exploded.

"You know, Sam," Sherman said, "you're always bitching. Why don't you just play the defense the way it's designed? That's the way I want it, and that's the way you'll play it. If you're going to play on my team, you're going to play my defense!"

Sherman wasn't nearly as reluctant about suggestions from his offense. Tittle could talk to him. So could Conerly's former partner-in-crime, Don Heinrich, now Sherman's offensive coordinator following his retirement after spending the 1960 season in Dallas. On one occasion in 1961, he even took some advice from Yankee Stadium clubhouse attendant Pete Previte.

Previte had told Heinrich and defensive assistant Svare about a common practice in baseball where a manager would bring in his fastest men to pinch-run. Heinrich and Svare brought the concept back to Sherman, and Sherman liked the idea, especially since he had Erich Barnes, one of the fastest men in the league, playing in his secondary. And fellow defensive back Jimmy Patton was no slow-poke either. So Sherman devised a play where Barnes and Patton would replace running backs Bobby Gaiters and Alex Webster; basically a five-wide receiver gadget with Barnes and Shofner running deep patterns on left side, and Joe Walton, Patton, and Kyle Rote running medium and underneath routes on the right.

They only practiced it a few times, but it came in handy when the 6–2 Giants met the 7–1 Eagles in a battle for the Eastern Conference lead. Up 17–7 in the second quarter, Sherman called for the Previte Special.

Each man did his job as Tittle took the shotgun snap. Seeing that Shofner had drawn double coverage, he looked to Barnes as the cornerback-turned-receiver ran a post pattern against overmatched linebacker Maxie Baughan. Tittle, Barnes's regular teammate in the team's weekly touch football game, hit Barnes in stride, and the pinch-runner went 62 yards untouched for the score to give the Giants a decisive 24–7 halftime lead.

That kind of imagination, plus consecutive trips to the championship game, won Sherman Coach of the Year honors in 1961 and '62. Unfortunately, both of those championship games were against Lombardi's Packers, and Lombardi easily got the better of Sherman in 37–0 and 16–7 wins. Then the Giants traveled to Wrigley Field and lost to the Bears, 14–10, in the '63 title game.

"You look back at the trades that were made, we made some pretty good trades to add some players, Y. A. Tittle being one of them," John Mara said. "Y. A. didn't start until '61. Then we made some bad personnel decisions after that. We felt we'd reached the peak with some of the guys we had and we had to shake things up, and it wound up being disastrous. Traded Sam Huff."

Whether Sherman was out to deliberately destroy the old defense is up for debate. But gradually, and quite systematically, that is exactly what happened.

Cliff Livingston, a popular though ethereal strong side linebacker, was traded in 1962. Rosey Grier, still productive, went to the Rams before the '63 season for 6-4, 275-pound defensive tackle John LoVetere, who never did become comfortable in Sherman's system, got hurt in 1964, and was done by the end of '65. Grier, on the other hand, made himself right at home in Los Angeles and starred for the next four years on the Rams' fabled Fearsome Foursome front with Deacon Jones, Merlin Olsen, and Lamar Lundy.

The final blows came after the 1963 championship game loss to the Bears. Sherman and Wellington Mara shipped off tough, reliable defensive tackle Dick Modzelewski to Cleveland on

March 4, a move that left Huff in stunned disbelief. A couple of days after the trade, Huff paid a visit to Mara in the Giants' Columbus Circle offices for some straight talk.

"I told him, 'You've traded Livingston, you've traded Rosey. Now it's Mo,'" Huff recalled. "What about me? Am I next?"

"Nothing's going to happen to you," Mara said.

Mara may have believed that at the time. But a month after the conversation, Huff, on a business trip to Cleveland, received a tearful phone call from his wife as he ate dinner in Ed and Dick Modzelewski's restaurant.

"Allie Sherman just called," Mary Huff told her husband that April evening. "You've been traded to the Washington Redskins."

The demolition was complete. Sherman's trade of a New York football icon brought down a rain of criticism from fans and media. But even worse than that, it brought only a smallish halfback and kick returner in Dickie James and a defensive end in Andy Stynchula in return, along with Huff's undying dislike for his former coach.

"I know he's sick," Huff said years later. "I know he's not in good shape. But I hate the guy. Always will, 'til the day he dies."

Huff had four more productive years with the Redskins. James and Stynchula made zero impact on the Giants.

Mara reflected on those trades in Gerald Eskenazi's book *There Were Giants In Those Days* and admitted that he was too easily led by Sherman. "It's easy to look back now," Mara said. "Allie believed the team was never going to be good enough to win the whole championship. He said we'd never be better than second best. I think he felt that maybe they were jaded or had gone about as far as they were going to go. Obviously, I did [agree to the trades after 1963] because I could have stopped any of those deals. But I didn't sense the era was ending."

It did, though, with a resounding crash. The year after his team put up a league-leading 448 points, motored through the schedule at 11–3, and lost the championship game to the Bears 14–10 only because they returned two of a busted-up Tittle's five interceptions deep into Giants territory, the Giants went 2–10–2.

Thus began a seventeen-year meander through the NFL desert. Sherman, the offensive genius who compiled an off-the-charts 33–8–1 mark his first three years, would go 24–43–3 in his last five and would lose his job after a humiliating preseason loss to the AFL Jets in 1969.

A succession of coaches that included Lombardi's old pile-driver Alex Webster would have no better success. The only three winning years before Ray Perkins took the 1981 team to the playoffs came in 1970, '72, and '80.

The range of negativity the Giants would pass through was mindboggling, starting with Sam Huff's revenge in a 1966 game with the Redskins. The Giants, in the midst of a franchise-worst 1–12–1 season, the vaunted defense dismantled, gave up a team record 72 points. Huff had predicted a 60-point output to end-turned-interviewer Kyle Rote. Redskins coach Otto Graham eventually was criticized for running up the score with a field goal in the last seven seconds of the 72–41 blowout. But Huff said the media totally misplaced the blame.

"You know who sent in the field goal team for those last three points?" Huff asked. "Ol' Sam Huff. Otto was busy with something or other, and I told them to get in there and kick. Seventy-two points!"

They would experience embarrassment in "The Fumble" of 1978, as quarterback Joe Pisarcik inexplicably tried a reverse handoff to Larry Csonka in a kneel-down situation against Philadelphia at

Giants Stadium. It was the lowest moment in franchise history, one that truly saw them snatch defeat from the jaws of victory. Two games later, fans burned their season tickets in the parking lot as a show of protest. During the final home game that year, a plane flew over the stadium with a banner that read: 15 YEARS OF LOUSY FOOT-BALL—WE'VE HAD ENOUGH. The game had 24,374 no-shows, and fans hanged Wellington Mara in effigy in the parking lot.

Tragedy came in 1979 when defensive tackle Troy Archer died in a traffic accident before the season.

And finally, the high anxiety of an internal feud between Wellington and his late brother Jack's son and co-owner, Tim Mara, threatened the very existence of the franchise. Only the intervention of commissioner Pete Rozelle, who suggested that George Young come on as general manager with very specific duties in running the day-to-day operation, put the Giants back on track.

While the Giants wandered infamously through the wilderness, Lombardi and Landry each found the promised land.

*   *   *

Vince Lombardi's first words to the publicly owned Packers' board of directors after he accepted the team's head coaching job went something like this: "I'm the boss."

"I want it understood that I am in complete command," he told the forty-five-man board in his first official meeting. And then he proved it by taking president Domenic Olejniczak's parking space.

The spot proved only a mild metaphor for what came later. Lombardi took over everything—player personnel, strategy, the operation of City Stadium (soon to become Lambeau Field), uniform design, and contract negotiations, if the one-sided discussions were in those days could be called such. Lombardi set about changing the very culture under which the Packers operated, turning predecessor Scooter McLean's losing, devil-may-care squad into a militaristic, disciplined winner.

He had no time for idle banter, as the man who hired him learned when he called the coach's office a few days after Lombardi took command. Olejniczak wanted to come by, just for a friendly chat about the roster.

"Make an appointment," barked Lombardi. "I'm too busy to just sit and talk. I have work to do!"

He ordered that the sign to his office read MR. LOMBARDI instead of COACH LOMBARDI. Players would wear jackets and ties on the road, not T-shirts and sweats. Various pubs that proved trouble spots for players were deemed off-limits. And everything—*everything*—operated on what became known as Lombardi Time. If a meeting was announced for 9 a.m., a player not seated and ready to go by 8:50 risked a fine and a good airing out.

When he assisted Howell, Lombardi would often have players over his house to review film, eat pizza, and enjoy a few brews. In his first year, 1954, he asked Frank Gifford and Charlie Conerly for advice on adjusting his West Point offense to the pro game.

He changed as a head coach. Lombardi no longer asked. He told. He ordered. And drove his players under a philosophy where the pursuit of unattainable perfection would allow his team to achieve excellence.

Whatever chumminess Lombardi had with his Giants players, it never traveled with him to Green Bay.

"Lombardi changed dramatically from the guy we got from [Army]," said Gifford, who became a great friend of Lombardi once he entered broadcasting fulltime. "When he left us, [Paul]

Hornung couldn't believe the Vince Lombardi they got was the Vince Lombardi I'd told him about. When Vince went up there, he turned into the head coach, and there was no more of this buddy stuff. Either you do it my way or [it's] the highway."

Part of his way involved practices far more grueling than he, Landry, or Howell ever conjured up in New York. His vomit-inducing, up-and-down grass drill exhausted players as they ran in place, knees pumping high, and then on command dropping to their bellies or back and popping back up again, Lombardi barking through the ranks the whole time. "Get those knees up! Get those legs moving! Front! Dive on your stomach! Up! Pop back up!"

The Nutcracker punished. Lombardi's favorite drill pitted blocker against tackler head-on. Two blocking dummies were placed on the field five yards apart, forming the boundaries of the violent drill. The quarterback would hand the ball to the back, running between the dummies, as the blocker drove at the defender full speed while the defender tried to shed the block and make the tackle. Its pain-inflicting violence made it a test of manhood, but it also helped make the Packers one of the toughest, most well-conditioned teams in the league. Once Lombardi got done with them, they looked nothing like the 1–10–1 group he inherited from the laid-back McLean. And that was saying something, because McLean's group had talent. Embedded in the roster were future stars such as Ray Nitschke, Bart Starr, Paul Hornung, Jim Taylor, Fuzzy Thurston, Jerry Kramer, Max McGee, Forrest Gregg, and Jim Ringo. But it was undisciplined.

Lombardi tied it all together, ridding his squad of divisive forces and substandard players while adding quality through draft and trades. His ever-growing friendship with Paul Brown, the Cleveland coach who urged the board to hire Lombardi, came into play in his 1959 trade of end Billy Howton to the Browns for defensive end Bill Quinlan and halfback Lew Carpenter. Quinlan became a key member of Lombardi's defense. Hall of Fame defensive tackle Henry Jordan also came from Cleveland that year for a mid-round draft pick.

Hall of Fame defensive end Willie Davis came from Cleveland in a similar fashion in 1960.

Brown and Lombardi made a habit of exchanging extraneous talent, forming a sort of talent pipeline between the teams.

"My father would send players up there," Paul Brown's son Mike said. "He'd take guys at the end of our roster—you had good players every year, like Henry Jordan and Willie Davis—and we had a set team.

"Early on, as Vince was coming on, we were ahead of them. We would send players up, and [fullback] Ernie Green he sent to us [in 1962]. They'd talk on the phone and my dad would tell Vince about them, and they trusted each other. It turned out their trust was well-placed and their judgments were very accurate on these guys.

"There was a time when the Cleveland team went two years and didn't add a player. You get the loyalty to some guys who stay with them and you stick with them a little longer than what's good. But a lot fell into the Willie Davis–Henry Jordan category and he sent them up to Green Bay. And if Vince had more than he could use, he'd work with my dad and send them up to us. That's just how they worked with each other."

Ernie Green became one of the league's top fullbacks, not only as an able ground-gainer and pass-catcher, but as a lead blocker for Jim Brown.

Lombardi and Brown went to great pains to make their transactions beneficial to both teams.

"What it showed was a mutual respect," Mike Brown said. "It was unusual. I don't think my dad did that with anyone else. It was a relationship of respect."

To top it all off, there was The Sweep. Now fully realized from his time with the Giants, Lombardi told his assistant coaches and players that The Sweep would be "the play we'll sleep with"—the bread and butter play of the Lombardi Packers. He taught it endlessly, noting the twenty-odd options for each position that covered everything from the most basic defenses to the totally unexpected. He practiced it relentlessly, coaching guards Jerry Kramer and Fuzzy Thurston as they pulled right to lead Paul Hornung around the corner—Kramer stepping from his right guard spot to take on the first alien uniform he saw; Thurston arcing deep into the backfield from left guard to lead Hornung through the next block, Hornung trailing so close that he often had his hand on Thurston's hip; right tackle Gregg laying out the defensive end first on high-low block with fullback Jim Taylor, and then gleefully heading downfield in search of the middle linebacker.

Lombardi called Gregg the greatest downfield blocker he ever saw.

For Hornung, Lombardi was a lifesaver. As Steve Owen had used and abused Frank Gifford before Lombardi told him "You're my halfback," so, too, had Scooter McLean tortured Hornung with undefined responsibilities. Quarterback, halfback, fullback—Hornung played them all. But that ended after Lombardi studied the films of the previous season and saw the former Notre Dame option quarterback skirt the corner. He called Hornung, then making real money in real estate and contemplating retirement, and said, "I want you to know one thing. You're not going to be my quarterback. You won't have to worry about playing three positions anymore. You are my left halfback. You're my Frank Gifford. You're either going to be my left halfback, or you're not going to make it in pro football."

Lombardi had his pieces: Hornung, Taylor, Kramer, Thurston, Gregg, Ringo, McGee, Boyd Dowler on offense, the madman Nitschke, Em Tunnell (brought from the Giants), Quinlan on defense. Now he just had to win with them.

Nineteen fifty-nine was as good a start as any. The Packers went 7–5, their first winning season since 1947. They won three, lost five, and then won their final four games. That last stretch was key, however, as it marked the beginning of the Bart Starr era. Starr had underachieved in his three previous seasons, at first playing behind Tobin Rote as a rookie and then splitting time with Babe Parilli his next two years. Scooter McLean's wordy play calls confused him, and he struggled to learn the coach's 4 ½-inch-thick playbook.

When Lombardi came along, the light went on. He cut the playbook back drastically, as simplicity was a quality he carried over from the Giants. So was brevity. The end sweep went from "49 Bill O Grace Ed" to simply "49," the 4 identifying the formation, the 9 the hole. The offensive linemen made the blocking calls.

Suddenly, Starr understood. And by the eighth game, a 28–24 loss to Baltimore, Starr had taken over the starting job from an injured Lamar McHan, the old Cardinals quarterback Lombardi had imported to hold the fort while Starr developed. From that point until Lombardi's departure after the '67 season, Starr went on to compile a 78–23–4 regular season mark and a 10–2 post-season record that included three NFL championships and wins in the first two Super Bowls, in both of which Starr was named the MVP.

That first 7–5 record sufficed to earn Coach of the Year honors. But Lombardi really hunted only two things in his head coaching life, and subjectively awarded hardware wasn't one of them. The NFL championship trophy came first. The absolute, unbridled joy he took in beating the Giants and the Dallas Cowboys ran a close second.

Lombardi never let his preparation lag for any team, but he took special care in studying the franchises of his former boss and his former defensive cohort. His lifelong friendship with Wellington Mara always took a backseat on game day to the resentment he felt about the Giants' failure to make him their head coach. Despite his personal regard for Tom Landry, he never let that innovative genius forget who the real alpha dog was.

He lost to the Giants once in three regular-season meetings, and never lost to the Cowboys in their three encounters. But it was his postseason battles with those two that raised his passion to a different level. Before those confrontations took place, however, he had to suffer one more important, but painful, passage at Philadelphia's Franklin Field the Monday after Christmas in 1960. The Packers' 17–13 loss to the Eagles in the 1960 championship game proved a solidifying moment for Lombardi's squad. It made the players believers in his hard-driving, relentless ways. And it brought to the surface the love Lombardi had, not just for winning, but for his men.

"That was a pivotal game in our relationship with Coach Lombardi," Kramer said. "He had come in '59, worked our butts off. We weren't sure about him. We went 7–5 that year;

WHERE IT ALL WENT

everyone's attitude was, 'We ought to win, as hard as we worked, but is this guy really able to take us all the way?'"

Right after that game, a contest in which Lombardi eschewed a pair of easy field goal opportunities, the coach assured them that they would reach the NFL summit.

"This will never happen again," he said after the game. "You will never lose another championship."

They never did. Championship number one came in 1961 when the Giants traveled to bitterly cold Green Bay for the first title game the Packers ever hosted.

Lombardi took a group of friends, priests, and former Giants associates led by Wellington Mara out to dinner the night before. As the festivities ended, Lombardi got up and announced, "Well, that's it. You're on your own now," and turned around and walked out the door, leaving the group without rides back to their hotels.

His friends had turned into the competition. Their friend had gone into coaching mode.

Lombardi handed the league's top defense a 37–0 whacking.

The teams met again for the title in 1962, this time in 13-degree, 40-mph wind conditions at Yankee Stadium. The Packers won again, 16–7, in a game so rough that Jim Taylor actually dented Sam Huff's helmet when they met on an outside run. That helmet now resides in the Hall of Fame in Canton, Ohio.

Those games started Lombardi's success. But his second NFL championship game against Landry's Cowboys made him and his team a legend. The "Ice Bowl" of 1967 was played in Green Bay, in minus-13-degree weather with a minus-46-degree wind chill factor. In what would be his final game at Lambeau Field, Lombardi saw his squad fall behind 17–14 in the fourth quarter as Dan Reeves tossed a 50-yard option pass to Lance Rentzel for a go-ahead touchdown.

The Packers had two possessions after that and didn't score. But on their final one, they methodically moved over the frozen field to the 1 as the clock ticked away the final five minutes to an almost certain defeat. The goal line, shadowed by the scoreboard, was a sheet of solid ice. "Like a marble tabletop," Starr said.

Two handoffs to Donnie Anderson didn't work, as Anderson slipped on the ice and nearly fumbled. Starr called Green Bay's final timeout with sixteen seconds left, went to the sideline, and suggested the simplest play in Lombardi's playbook, Brown Right, 31 Wedge. Guard Jerry Kramer would chop down the lanky Jethro Pugh in the middle, and Starr would hand the ball to fullback Chuck Mercein, a former Giant, who would plow though the middle to the end zone.

"Let's run it and get the hell out of here," Lombardi said.

Only, Starr had other things in mind. What if Mercein were to slip and never make it to scrimmage? With no timeouts left, the Packers would be doomed. So Starr took it himself, riding Kramer's block into the end zone and a most legendary 21–17 victory.

For as long as Lombardi coached, he never let Landry get the better of him. Nor would any AFL opponent. In the first two Super Bowls, Lombardi beat the Kansas City Chiefs 35–10 and the Oakland Raiders 33–14.

He retired after the second Super Bowl to become the Packers' general manager, handing over the reins to defensive coordinator Phil Bengston. But idleness didn't agree with him, and he gained his release from Green Bay to take on the head coaching job at Washington in 1969.

That reclamation project lasted one season, just long enough to bring the Redskins back from 13 straight non-winning seasons to a 7–5–2 mark.

Though the signs existed, Lombardi didn't know then that his future as a coach, and as a man, had grown short.

*   *   *

As Vince Lombardi showed Landry who was boss, Landry was just beginning the second phase of his career in Dallas—the "Can't Win the Big One" era.

Lombardi never went through that. He had instant success, which only bolstered his legend as the list of championships grew. But Lombardi operated in a different atmosphere than Landry.

Lombardi had gone to a losing franchise with an existing roster, which just happened to be chock full of misused future stars. Landry had to build his team from the ground up, and experienced the typical growing pains of expansion teams of that era.

Lombardi, as Wellington Mara put it, was a law unto himself. He ran the team from top to bottom, even to the point of authorizing an $80,000 expenditure for an electric blanket to keep the Lambeau Field warm in the icy Wisconsin weather. Ironically, it was that blanket's mechanical failure that created the conditions for the Ice Bowl. Landry worked from the beginning within a hierarchal framework, with president and general manager Tex Schramm in charge of contracts and player procurement, and Gil Brandt the chief talent scout as vice president of player personnel.

Landry coached.

He had his assistants, but Landry kept his thumb on the pulse of every unit throughout the week. That was a commonality between he and Lombardi. Though both benefited from Jim Lee Howell's delegation of duties, neither man would give his assistants that kind of power. At least Lombardi let Phil Bengston handle most of the defensive operation, though the head coach always had a firm hand on everything. If such a thing is possible, though, Landry was even more controlling than Lombardi when it came to running the strategic operation.

"He's the only coach I've ever known that was just involved as much on offense and calling his own plays, as with the defensive game plan," Landry disciple Dan Reeves said. "Most of us are one-sided. You might have a little input on the other side, but he was in on every meeting of the game plans. We'd meet on Mondays and Tuesdays, and we'd finish the offensive game plan and he'd call the defensive coaches in and he'd start working on the defensive game plan.

"The time it took, I don't know how in the world he did it. When I look back on my twenty-three years as head coach and working with the offense, I can't imagine coming out of an offensive meeting and all of a sudden saying, 'Okay, defensive guys, let's meet.'"

Along with endless stamina, a certain hard-headedness marked Landry's twenty-nine years as head coach. Just as he preached faith in his system to his Giants defenders, he did the same with his Dallas players. If he said something would happen, it would, simply because his analytical mind had gone over the possibilities and permutations of keys and tendencies thousands of times. That was a blessing and a curse, as it turned out. Against most teams, it worked. Once Landry had real talent on his roster, the Cowboys could dominate a game defensively by each player simply handling his responsibility, over and over again. But it proved counterproductive against Lombardi's Packers, simply because Lombardi understood Landry's mind so well.

"Look, I know this guy and he's not going to change," Lombardi would say. "Sixty-five percent of the time, his defense is going to stay the same. If we beat it the other 35 percent of the time, we win."

The Packers did just that, outscoring Landry's teams 99–31 in three regular-season and two postseason meetings.

There was a parochial nature Landry's system, born of his religious epiphany of 1958. His Bible studies taught him that, like a football team, life had its chain of command. Believe in Jesus and he will lead you in the right direction. Believe in Landry's system, and you will win. Understanding the whys and wherefores was never as important as unquestioningly following the edicts handed down from on high, be it from God or the head coach. Faith in God will carry you through life. Faith in Landry's offensive and defensive systems will carry you to victory.

Unlike Lombardi, who showed great tolerance for alternative religious views despite an unflagging devotion to the Roman Catholic Church, the Methodist-born Landry often implored his players to follow the Bible's teachings. He read them bits of Scripture during tough times. He ran a prayer session before every game, and a nondenominational service before each road game. Each was optional, but his religious piety caused a certain amount of friction between himself and some of his stars, including his hard-partying quarterback Don Meredith. He never did rescue running back Duane Thomas from the sex, drugs, and rock 'n' roll lifestyle, or defensive lineman Thomas "Hollywood" Henderson, either.

Landry's many successes and his unheard of longevity as the Cowboys' head coach overshadowed all that. But, as with most expansion teams, it took him a while to get going. Six years, actually, including an 0–11–1 maiden voyage in 1960.

For a while, the denizens exhibited patience with Landry's growing program. They really didn't expect much from old Redskins quarterback Eddie LeBaron and a bunch of no-names and castoffs.

"The people in Dallas are really polite and we didn't ever get harassed," Alicia Landry said. "It was no problem. We didn't win at first, but they knew he was brand-new and that he had to build a team. It didn't take him that long. And then we were always good."

The winning wouldn't come until folks like Bob Lilly, Bob Hayes, Don Meredith and later Roger Staubach developed. In winless 1960, they had to be satisfied with a 31–31 tie with the Giants at Yankee Stadium. Landry, his old defense still the darling of Giants fans, received a huge ovation when he stepped onto the field before that December 5 game. The Cowboys surprisingly stayed with the Giants on three LeBaron touchdown passes. With the Giants up 31–24, Joe Morrison fumbled, and LeBaron followed with his fourth touchdown throw of the day to Billy Howton, the wide receiver Lombardi had sent to Cleveland for Bill Quinlan and Lew Carpenter in 1959.

Stunned by the Cowboys' performance and preparing to step down, Howell called Landry "the best coach in all of football."

The Cowboys record over the next few years disguised that pretty well. And when the Cowboys went 4–10 in 1963, one win less than they'd had in 1962, the natives became restless. Cries for Landry's head rang out in the media. But Clint Murchison, showing Wellington Mara-like loyalty, signed Landry to a ten-year extension, which began the year his original contract ran out in 1965.

Murchison probably saw something the fans didn't, namely Landry's genius as a strategist. Of course, he had come to the Cowboys with a reputation as a defensive mastermind, the father of the modern 4-3 defense. But what the fans didn't see was that, almost from the time he took over, Landry began to develop offensive strategies to beat his revolutionary brainchild. By 1960, the 4-3 had become a commonly used defense around the league, but it was Landry who truly figured out how to exploit its strategic tradeoffs.

Motion and shifting formed the bedrock, all to create defensive confusion. One of the simplest things he did was to have his offensive linemen rise straight up from a crouch, and then fall into their stances after a 1-2-3 count. Though many linemen thought the maneuver needless, even foolish, it shielded the backfield from the defense's sight for a split second. That gave the opponent less time to recognize the formation and its keys. The backfield could then begin a shift to present an entirely different alignment.

There were plenty of alignments, too. The playbook looked voluminous, especially when compared with the handful of perfectly-executed plays his rival Lombardi relied upon. An NFL release noted that Landry would throw ten or eleven offensive formations out there each game, with up to six variations off each.

Landry was also among the first to make motion a regular part of offensive strategy. This created coverage problems, as defensive backs and linebackers had to chase backs and ends across the field.

A lot of the older vets on his early squads bristled at Landry's philosophy. And many didn't have the talent or mental wherewithal to execute his finely timed maneuvering. Some perceived a futility in all of it as the losses mounted and asked him to simplify things. But Landry stuck to his guns, reasoning that he was installing an offense for the future, one that would beat the Giants and the Browns once the real talent arrived.

At least in an offensive sense, Landry never thought simpler was better.

"The trouble with simplistic football is that if every team concentrates on perfecting routine plays, the best athletes are going to win," he said, turning Lombardi's whole philosophy on its head. "If the whole emphasis is on repetition and execution and cutting out mistakes, the game comes down to one thing only—personnel. Well, I reject that as the idea of football. To me, it's a great deal more than trying to out-personnel the other team."

As he tinkered with the offense, he also revised his defense. Noting Lombardi's Run to Daylight tendencies that exploited the natural gaps in the 4-3 defense, Landry came up with the Flex, which debuted in 1964 and became an integrated part of the defense a year later. It was still the 4-3, only several defensive linemen would set themselves two feet off the line of scrimmage. Future Hall of Famer Bob Lilly had settled nicely into his role as the right defensive tackle and became the key to the Flex, which basically disguised the gap responsibilities of the 4-3 inside and 4-3 outside alignments.

The Flex became the hallmark of the Dallas defense throughout the glory days. But the Cowboys had to pass through the Lombardi era before they hit legendary status. The two NFL title games, including the Ice Bowl, marked Landry as the fine coach who couldn't win the big one.

"Vince Lombardi was the monkey on Tom Landry's back," offensive lineman John Wilbur said. "Landry never did conquer Lombardi's world. Lombardi always outsmarted him."

Once Lombardi retired, the Browns got in Landry's way. Despite the Cowboys finishing first in what was then called the Capital Division in 1968 and '69, Cleveland beat them twice in the conference championship games. When Landry finally did reach Super Bowl V in 1970, Baltimore beat him 16–13 on Jim O'Brien's 32-yard field goal with five seconds remaining.

But Landry finally had his players. Staubach became the scrambling master of the two-minute drill. Drew Pearson, Calvin Hill, Duane Thomas, Lance Alworth, and Mike Ditka became offensive forces. The Doomsday Defense, featuring Lilly, Lee Roy Jordan, Jethro Pugh, Chuck Howley, and Mel Renfro, dominated the league.

From 1970 to 1978, the Cowboys appeared in five Super Bowls, winning twice in Super Bowl VI against Miami and XII against Denver. Twice, 1970–71 and 1977–78, they appeared in consecutive Super Bowls. The last one against the Steelers was considered by many the best matchup in Super Bowl history because the winner would become the first team to capture three Super Bowl championships.

The Steelers, in the midst of their own history-making run of four titles in six years, won 35–31 in a game Drew Pearson called the biggest disappointment of his career. "We wanted the back-to-back Super Bowls so badly that we could taste it," Pearson said. "We could feel it. We lived it. It took a lot out of myself and a lot of players."

Apparently so. The only other Super Bowls Landry attended after that was as a guest of the league. The pieces began falling away, starting with Ed "Too Tall" Jones's announcement in 1979 that boxing had replaced football as his first love. Hollywood

Henderson got into drug problems that year, and five concussions forced Staubach into retirement.

Landry still won for a while; even got to the NFC championship game in 1981, where he lost to Bill Walsh's emerging 49ers team. But in 1984, after ten straight playoff seasons, they failed to qualify at 9–7. A 10–6 mark in '85 that included shellackings against the Bears (44–0), Bengals (50–24) and the 49ers (31–16) produced a first-round playoff exit via 20–0 shutout to the Rams. Landry battled factionalism in the locker room, an ownership change, and front-office upheaval.

Three straight losing seasons, an unheard of happening since the franchise's infancy, followed along with yearly calls for Landry's retirement. Arkansas oilman Jerry Jones took care of that with his first act after he bought the team in February 1989.

He fired Tom Landry.

The end came in Austin, in a forty-minute meeting near the golf course where a stoic Landry had just finished a round. Twenty-nine years, 270 wins, and it was over. Just like that.

After the meeting, Landry headed back to the golf club in time for dinner with his family.

*   *   *

Should the Giants have kept either Lombardi or Landry? Could they have?

History says yes, were there a will, there was a way. But that's the beauty of history. It's full of what-ifs.

At the time, Wellington Mara had simply lost a couple of assistant coaches.

Valued assistants? Yes.

Can't misses? That's another story.

"That's the hardest decision you have to make in this business, deciding whether the successful assistant can make the step up to be a successful head coach," John Mara said. "There's many more failures than there are successes.

"Lombardi was a high school coach, followed by being an assistant coach in college. It's easy to look back now and say, 'Shit, you should have hired him.' But the only way [my father] could have kept Lombardi was to have fired Howell when Green Bay came calling for permission to speak to him. [Winning the] '56 championship, then being in the championship game in '58 in The Greatest Game Ever Played, and you're going to fire your head coach to promote an assistant who's highly thought of as an assistant?

"You tell me, looking back in NFL history, how many highly thought of assistants fail as NFL head coaches. He ended up becoming the greatest head coach of all time.

"To lose them both in the course of a year. Pretty good pair of coordinators."

Wellington Mara never forgot that he had them on the same staff at the same time, and lost them both. In fact, he referenced them when Jim Fassel's defensive coordinator John Fox left to coach the Carolina Panthers after the 2001 season.

"When John Fox left us to go to Carolina, my father actually wrote him a letter saying how sorry he was to see him go," John Mara said. "He said it feels like we're losing Lombardi or Landry again."

But there again was the choice. Fire the head man, who a year before had taken your team to a Super Bowl, or keep what seemed to be working.

The question hadn't changed since the late fifties.

"We're in the Super Bowl in 2000, and we're not so good in 2001," John Mara said. "But we still feel pretty good about our team. We've got a great, young assistant coach who goes to Carolina. We do pretty well in 2002, and Fox goes on to take his team to the Super Bowl.

"You have situations like that all the time. You have to make that decision. Are you going to blow up what you have on the basis that this young assistant coach is going to become a great head coach, or do you stick with what you have? It's a tough decision."

Had the Giants a definite inkling as to Jim Lee Howell's future plans, things might have worked out differently.

"The only part of the story that might have been better is if Jim Lee had quietly retired like everyone thought he was gonna do," said Frank Gifford. "No one knew what he was going to do. But had he done it a couple of years earlier, and Vince had taken over as head coach, God knows what might have been.

"Then again, who knows?"

Wellington Mara knew.

"On a number of occasions, he said letting Lombardi go was the biggest mistake he ever made," John Mara said.

EPILOGUE

ONE DAY NOT long after Sam Huff rejoined the Redskins as a full-time assistant in 1970, he ran into Vince Lombardi in the hallway of the team's downtown offices.

Noting how gray, worn out, and sick-looking his boss was, the old linebacker suggested Lombardi pay a visit to the team doctor. Lombardi agreed, suspecting he had the flu. But tests at Georgetown University Hospital revealed something far more dire.

Colon cancer.

That explained the gallons of antacid he had downed over the last few years to ease an ever-growing abdominal pain. It explained the recent bouts with constipation, the sweats, the fevers. Doctors might have found it early had he consented to a proctoscopic exam, the best diagnostic test in those pre-colonoscopy days, but a natural squeamishness caused him to decline, and not so politely at that.

The biopsy revealed anaplastic carcinoma in the rectal area, a fast-moving, aggressive form of cancer. A two-hour and fifteen-minute exploratory operation on June 27 removed two feet of colon. Some minor complications kept him in the hospital longer than expected. But once Georgetown released him July 10, Lombardi publicly expressed his hopes that he would "beat this thing" and return to coaching the Redskins.

Privately, though, he told friends he was dying.

He turned over the coaching job to his old Giants guard Bill Austin, by then Lombardi's second in charge.

Exactly one month after his original operation, July 27, he re-entered Georgetown after his symptoms escalated. More exploratory surgery found the cancer had spread to his liver, peritoneum, and lymph nodes. Doctors sewed him up, ordered radiation, and handed down the prognosis to his wife, Marie—it amounted to a death sentence.

He died in his hospital bed on September 3, 1970, at 7:20 a.m.

Huff wasn't there near the end. He last saw the coach at a rookie scrimmage with the Colts the day before Lombardi went in for the second surgery. Forty pounds lighter, the coach gathered the rookies he had drafted around him for a short speech, his voice strained and weak.

"You're my people. I selected you," Lombardi said. "You're going to wear this uniform with pride. You're now a member of the Washington Redskins, and there's a lot of responsibility that goes with that. Don't you ever forget it."

Right up to his final interaction with his team, Lombardi espoused the ideals that began back at Fordham, continued through his high school and college coaching days, and blossomed in his New York Giants apprenticeship. Responsibility—an all-encompassing word that, to him, meant duty, discipline, execution, and accountability to each other and oneself.

He had pounded that into each one of his players, the great and not-so-great. And though many of them detested him for his hard-driving ways, most of them felt his adherence to that one word made them better people. In his final days in the hospital, they showed him just how much.

The line of visitors seemed unending. His old Packers, NFL executives, priests, nuns—they all came to the hospital to bid farewell to the coach, his body withered and frail from the futile cobalt treatments. His good friend and former boss Wellington Mara called almost every day at 2 p.m., just before heading out to practice. One day he forgot, and Lombardi was heard to say, "What the hell's the matter with Well?"

Frank Gifford also paid his respects.

"Took the train down and he was actually alone," Gifford remembered. "He knew who I was and he kind of laughed and I squeezed his arm. We kind of talked about the weather. What do you say?

"I remember grabbing him by the arm as I was leaving and he said, 'Frank, it really hurts.'"

Pat Summerall didn't remember where he was the day one of his two greatest teachers died. But he remembered his reaction upon being apprised that cancer had killed his friend: "Cancer wouldn't dare."

Lombardi's funeral was held September 7 at St. Patrick's Cathedral in Manhattan. Wellington Mara served as an honorary pallbearer. As the hordes of fans would gather across Fifth Avenue thirty-five years later to bid the Giants' patriarch adieu, so did thousands line up as Terence Cardinal Cooke presided over Lombardi's Mass of Christian Burial. In his homily, Cooke intoned the writings of St. Paul, knowing well how deeply those epistles influenced Lombardi's life as man and coach.

Especially St. Paul's first letter to the Corinthians.
"Run so as to win."

*   *   *

Getting fired from a head coaching job that spanned the terms of eight presidents, from Dwight D. Eisenhower to George H. W. Bush, didn't send Tom Landry into a life of idling between golf rounds, autograph shows, and celebrity lectures. Far from it. But he did need an adjustment period.

He hadn't really seen it coming, even though he knew the dangers any ownership change posed to an employee's future. As he headed back to the golf club for a typical dinner with family after he parted from Jerry Jones in the late afternoon of February 25, 1989, his external stoicism belied the churning emotions inside.

"I don't recall [Jones's] exact words," Landry recalled years later, "but he went on to say he'd bought the Cowboys and he was bringing in Jimmy Johnson to be his head coach. I don't remember anything he said after that. A jumble of feelings crowded my mind. Anger. Sadness. Frustration. Disappointment. Resignation."

Really, the five stages of grief. Before he could move on, he first had to reconcile himself with the death of his coaching career, with losing part of his family. For all his emotional detachment from his players, always designed to present a calming, controlled image during the chaos of the games, he loved those who shared his competitive drive. He told his players that as he bade them a final farewell two days after his firing.

And then he broke down and cried, right in front of everybody.

He wasn't the only one. His Hall of Fame defensive tackle Bob Lilly told the media, "A lot of old Cowboys are crying tonight," when he heard of Landry's dismissal. Commissioner Pete Rozelle said, "I feel like I did when Vince Lombardi died."

His players gave him a standing ovation. So would many others. A Tom Landry Day was planned for April 22, 1989, even as Landry questioned the wisdom of it. He wondered to both family and event organizers whether anyone would bother showing up. "He only missed by a few hundred thousand people," his son, Tom Landry Jr. would say at his father's memorial service.

The son might have exaggerated the numbers a bit, but Cowboys fans did line up five and six deep in many spots along the mile-long parade route through downtown Dallas.

President Bush and evangelist Billy Graham wired him. Bob Hope called. Ex-players, friends, and religious leaders spoke at the podium. But just as important were the city fathers, for it was the city of Dallas which benefited the most from Landry's success. Until Landry started going to championship games and winning Super Bowls, Dallas had the bleakest image of any American city. In many people's minds it was, simply, the place where Lee Harvey Oswald killed John F. Kennedy in 1963. A city of hate.

As odd as it seems, winning football games helped turn that around. The expressionless man with the snap-brim fedora who turned a rag-tag expansion squad into "America's Team" brought new life to a city blighted by assassination. "There's no doubt the Cowboys' image around the nation and even the world helped rebuild the image of Dallas," former mayor Wes Wise said at the Tom Landry Day ceremonies. "Tom had a lot to do with that."

Landry and Lombardi were a lot alike in that respect. They both transformed the image of their towns. At the time Lombardi took over the Packers, Green Bay was *the* backwater locale of the NFL; a cold, forbidding place in God's blind spot where coaches threatened to send their loafers and locker room lawyers. Lombardi and his championships turned it into Titletown, USA, where small-town values and local fervor met in the luncheonettes and saloons and made it all right to come from the heart of dairyland.

Landry took a city still reeling years after Oswald set up his sniper's nest in the book depository, years after Jack Ruby plugged Oswald in the belly in TV's first live murder, and elevated it into a winner.

Other honors awaited. Canton came calling in 1990—another thunderous, standing ovation from the thousands in attendance. In 1993, the Cowboys inducted Landry into their Ring of Honor, the silhouetted image of his fedora placed above his name, since he didn't have a number. It marked one of only three times Landry ever went back to Texas Stadium after his firing. The Ring ceremonies for Randy White and Tony Dorsett were the other two.

Jerry Jones never invited him to a practice. He never watched a game there. Landry left football behind, forever.

But he wasn't done with being Tom Landry, coach of the Dallas Cowboys. His name recognition remained sky high, and that allowed him to stay busy the remaining eleven years of his life.

"When I moved on, I found it very enjoyable," Landry said. "I started getting into different projects and my mind wasn't on the Cowboys or football. I was fortunate. The good Lord took that away from me and put me in another category. I got a different outlook."

He ran an investment firm with his son. But mostly, he used his time to spread the gospel. Always willing to give witness for a Billy Graham crusade or a fund-raiser for his favorite organization, the Fellowship of Christian Athletes, during the offseason, he now spent one weekend after another traveling to FCA functions around the country.

Always a great golfer, he enjoyed the FCA benefit outings. In one such event, he was paired with then-Dallas Mavericks owner Don Carter. The self-described hacker confided to Landry that he'd sent up a little message skyward that he at least wouldn't embarrass himself in front of such an accomplished player. Carter stepped up to the tee and proceeded to smash his ball down the middle of the fairway.

"See there?" Landry said. "Prayer works."

He chaired numerous Billy Graham crusades, often going to each city weeks ahead of the main speakers to address and encourage the event leaders. He spoke at many other crusades, offering witness to spellbound crowds.

He created a Bible-study group and became part of the official board at the Highland Park Methodist Church, the largest Methodist church of its kind in the country, where the Landrys remained members for forty-three years. He participated in a prison ministry.

And, of course, Tom Landry signed autographs. Whether the request came during an informal meet-and-greet at a Super Bowl party in Tampa or a formal gathering, his pen was always at the ready. Even when such a request was unexpected. Mary Martin, a Dallas housewife, found that out just before Valentine's Day in 1999. Thinking the coach's autograph on a *Life* magazine cover that featured him and Roger Staubach would make an ideal gift for her husband, she ventured over to Landry's Preston Center office and asked the secretary if she could procure a signature. The secretary said that with all the obligations and engagements

Landry had to attend to, it could take up to three months to get the periodical signed. So Martin left it there.

Two days later, the secretary called Martin to say the magazine, which became one of her husband's prized possessions, was ready. On the day of Landry's public memorial service, the housewife pulled her young son out of school early so they could attend.

Landry's life remained full until May 1999, when doctors diagnosed him with acute myelogenous leukemia. He took chemotherapy at the Baylor University Medical Center, his only major complaint being that the disease and its treatment prevented him from working out every day.

His wife, Alicia, his son, Tom Jr., and his daughter Kitty were at his side were at his bedside when he died nine months later, at 6 p.m. on February 12, 2000.

He was seventy-five years old.

The crowds came out again five days later. A thousand of his ex-players, coaches, and friends and family members gathered at the Highland Park Church for a private service. Two thousand fans and admirers began lining up at 7:30 a.m. for a 6 p.m. public service at the Myerson Symphony Center.

The *Dallas Morning News* blanketed its front page and news section with coverage of his death and the memorial services. Timelines and quote boxes containing the words of friends such as Billy Graham, Cowboys executives Tex Schramm and Gil Brandt, and former players Roger Staubach and Everson Walls bordered picture essays of Landry's life.

Reverend Mark Craig, senior pastor of Highland Park, said a brief visit to Landry's hospital room in December 1999 stood as one of the greatest Christmas presents he'd ever received. "Most of it was a blur to me," Craig said in his eulogy. "I just stood there and cried. And I asked myself, 'Why am I crying?' And I realized it was because I was standing in the presence of greatness, and when you do that, it's a very emotional thing."

*   *   *

The span between the deaths of Vince Lombardi and Tom Landry bridged two different eras of the NFL and, in a way, spared both men from what was to come.

Lombardi died at a time the country and its mores were undergoing great upheaval. The Vietnam War was at its full height, and the questioning of iron-fisted authority had become the norm, not the actions of a few renegade youths. Landry not only shepherded the Cowboys through that era, but also a period where access to sex, drugs, and the hard-party celebrity lifestyle made it ever harder to motivate and discipline players.

Yet, neither had to contend with the millionaire star, the one that signed contracts ten times more valuable than any head coach's deal and thus decided he could go his own way. Neither had to deal with a salary cap that penalized teams for prematurely cutting a player, no matter how disruptive that player may be to the locker room.

So the question becomes, would either have been successful in the current atmosphere of the NFL?

The answer is uncertain. What is clear is that each would have had to do a significant amount of bending—even abandoning—of the leadership principles that took root during their apprenticeship with Jim Lee Howell's Giants.

Rule by fear no longer applies today, for players are protected by their Players Association, the salary cap, and in many cases large guaranteed portions of contracts. While neither had so-called hiring and firing power under Howell, both Lombardi's and Landry's opinions of their charges carried great weight.

If a player couldn't do, or refused to do, what Landry demanded, he sat. No chewing out. No warning. He simply found himself on the bench on game day. And if that player sat long enough, he soon found himself out of a job, his paycheck gone. The bombastic Lombardi might have handled things a bit differently, certainly in louder terms, but his criticisms could produce the same results.

Their stock in trade under Howell was the teaching of fundamentals. Lombardi may have adjusted his strategy from the collegiate T-formation to a pro-style offense, but the teaching that got the Giants to execute it remained basic—details like first steps, exact measurements for offensive line splits, the number of steps in pass routes, the length of hesitation of the running back before heading out on the sweep. All were covered in endless blackboard sessions, and then drilled relentlessly on the practice field.

For all of Landry's defensive innovation, the 4-3 inside and 4-3 outside came down to Sam Huff's pursuit and sure tackling.

"That was a time in sports when coaching was fantastic," Huff said. "I can remember every down, every play, every move Tom Landry ever made. Unbelievable person."

"They were both sure that their way was the way you had to do it," Pat Summerall said. "They imparted that knowledge to you in such a confident way that it bred confidence in us. We figured, if they said it, that was the way it was going to make us win and that's the way it should be done.

" I'd never experienced anything like that with coaches before; never with the confidence in what they said, and the details they went into, both of them. They were so sure their way was the winning way . . . I think I'd never had coaches who were so knowledgeable and so thorough. They both presented it in different ways, but Landry was so confident in what he said and Lombardi was so confident in what he said."

These days, it takes a lengthy losing streak for coaches to fall back on such mundane teaching points. Simplification, it's called. With Lombardi and Landry, football began with the simple and expanded outward to the complex.

One can only wonder how either would have handled the steroids era. Landry dealt with drug issues, but marijuana and cocaine hurt the athlete's performance. Steroids offered a competitive advantage.

Cheating. Neither Lombardi nor Landry could abide that.

St. Paul may have beseeched his followers to "Run so as to win," but he never wrote anything about better strengthening through chemistry. In his speech, "What It Takes to Be Number One," a motivational oration many consider Lombardi's greatest, he called winning "not a sometime thing. It's an all the time thing." But he also added that the object was to win "fairly, squarely, by the rules."

Landry also believed in limits in the chase for victory, though the cold and often calculating way he coached the Cowboys would seem to contradict that. Some of his more liberal players criticized him for seeming uncaring. Others saw it as a win-at-all-costs mentality.

But Landry said he never considered his approach as such.

"I believe winning is important," Landry said. "The real danger is when winning becomes the only thing. If you forsake your honesty and integrity to win a football game, it's wrong."

Lombardi and Landry

Lombardi and Landry both became winners. But they may never have ascended to the heights if not for their joint apprenticeship with the Giants.

Lombardi learned about defense from Landry. Landry learned about the winning attitude from Lombardi.

They were a head coach's dream.

"This is a vision I will always have about those two," Sam Huff said at Landry's public memorial service. "Vince Lombardi sitting at one hand of God, and Tom Landry at the other, saying, 'Let the game begin.'"

BIBLIOGRAPHY

Interview Subjects:

Mike Brown: Son of Cleveland Browns coach Paul Brown; Cincinnati Bengals president (2010)

Jack Cavanaugh: Author, *Giants Among Men* (2010)

Frank Gifford: New York Giants 1952–60, 62–64 (2010)

Rosey Grier: New York Giants 1955–56, 58–62 (2010)

Sam Huff: New York Giants 1956–63 (2010)

Johnny Johnson: Trainer, New York Giants 1948–2007 (2010)

Alicia Landry: Widow of Tom Landry (2010)

Dan Lauria: Actor, *Lombardi* (2010)

Professor Louis Leonini: Curator, Garibaldi-Meucci Museum and Italian Cultural Society (2010)

Vince Lombardi Jr.: Son of Vince Lombardi (2010)

John Mara: President and CEO, New York Giants (2010)

Wellington Mara: Co-Owner, New York Giants 1937–2005 (2002)

Dick Modzelewski: New York Giants 1956–1963 (2010)

Ed Modzelewski: Cleveland Browns 1955–59 (2010)

Keith Nobbs: Actor, *Lombardi* (2010)

Dan Reeves: New York Giants Head Coach 1993–96 (2010)
Don Smith: PR Director, New York Giants 1958–72 (2010)
Pat Summerall: New York Giants 1958–61 (2010)
Ray "Whitey" Walsh Jr.: Director of Research and Development,
    New York Giants (2010)

Books:

Of the many books, newspaper clippings, films, and websites used in researching this project, I leaned heavily on two masterworks in particular for chronological and philosophical clarity: *When Pride Still Mattered*, by David Maraniss, is the definitive biography of Vince Lombardi. *Giants Among Men*, by Jack Cavanaugh, is the all-encompassing story of the Giants' golden era of 1954–1963. Their labors, along with those of all the other authors listed here, made mine that much lighter. I thank them all.

Backseat Quarterback; Perian Conerly, University Press of Missis-
    sippi, 1963.
The 50 Greatest Plays in New York Giants Football History; John
    Maxymuk, Triumph Books, New York, 2008.
*Giants Among Men: How Robustelli, Huff, Gifford, and the Giants
    Made New York a Football Town and Changed the NFL;* Jack
    Cavanaugh, Random House, New York, 2008.
*Giants: What I learned about life from Vince Lombardi and Tom
    Landry;* Pat Summerall with Michael Levin, Wiley & Sons,
    Inc. 2010.
*The Glory Game: How the 1958 NFL Championship Game Changed
    Football Forever;* Frank Gifford with Peter Richmond, Harper,
    2008.

The Holy Bible

Joe DiMaggio: The Hero's Life; Richard Ben Cramer, Simon and Schuster, New York, 2000.

The Landry Legend: Grace Under Pressure; Bob St. John, Word Publishing, Dallas, 1987.

Landry's Boys: An Oral History of a Team and an Era; Peter Golenbock, Triumph Books, Chicago, 1997.

The Most Memorable Games In Giants History: An Oral History of a Legendary Team; Jim Baker and Bernard M. Corbett, Bloomsbury, New York, Berlin, London, 2010.

New York Giants Information Guide; New York Football Giants, Inc.

NFL Record and Fact Book; National Football League, 2010.

The Official Vince Lombardi Playbook: His Classic Plays and Strategies, Personal Photos and Mementos, Recollections from Friends and Former Players; Phil Barber, The Lyons Press, Guilford, Conn., 2009.

Once A Giant, Always . . .: My Two Lives with the New York Giants; Andy Robustelli and Jack Clary, Quinlan Press, Boston, 1987.

PB—The Paul Brown Story; Paul Brown with Jack Clary, Atheneum, New York, 1980.

There Were Giants In Those Days; Gerald Eskenazi, Prentice Hall, New York, 1987.

Total Football: The Official Encyclopedia of the National Football League; Ed. Bob Carroll, Michael Gershman, David Neft, and John Thorn, Harper Collins, New York, 1997.

Tough Stuff: The Man in the Middle; Leonard Shapiro and Sam Huff, St. Martin's Press, New York 1988.

Vince: A Personal Biography of Vince Lombardi; Michael O'Brien, William Morrow and Company, Inc., New York, 1987.

Vince Lombardi on Football; George Flynn, New York Graphic Society Ltd. & Wallyn, Inc. 1973.

The Vince Lombardi Story, Dave Klein, Lion Books, New York, 1971.

Wellington: The Maras, The Giants, and the City of New York, Carlo DeVito, Triumph Books, 2006.

When Pride Still Mattered: A Life of Vince Lombardi, David Maraniss, Simon and Schuster, New York, 1999.

When The Grass Was Real: Unitas, Brown, Lombardi, Sayers, Butkus, Namath, and All the Rest, Bob Carroll, Simon and Schuster, New York, 1993.

The Whole Ten Yards, Frank Gifford and Harry Waters, Random House, New York, 1993.

Newspapers and Periodicals:

Bergen Record

Cleveland *Plain Dealer*

Cleveland Press

Dallas Morning News

Giants Extra

Green Bay Press-Gazette

Life magazine

Los Angeles Times

Milwaukee Journal

NEA Dispatch

New York Daily Mirror

New York *Daily News*

New York Herald-Tribune

New York Journal-American

New York Post

New York Times

Newark Evening News
Newark Star-Ledger
News-Herald, Willoughby, Ohio
Philadelphia Inquirer
Portland (Maine) *Press-Herald*
San Francisco Chronicle
San Francisco Examiner
Sports Illustrated
Time magazine
Washington Post

Films, Websites, etc.
Speech by Bud Adams Jr., Tennessee Titans archives
Bengals.com
The Complete History of the New York Giants, NFL Films, (2004)
Giants.com
Lombardi (documentary) HBO Films
NFL.com
ProFootballHOF.com
Pro-Football-Reference.com
Wikipedia.com

ACKNOWLEDGEMENTS

PROJECTS SUCH AS this do not come together naturally or without help. This book would not have happened if not for the aid and support of family, friends, colleagues, associates, and strangers alike. I am indebted to all.

When I first mentioned the idea for this book to New York *Daily News* Giants beat writer Ralph Vacchiano, he immediately sent this first-time author to his editor at Skyhorse Publishing, Mark Weinstein. Ralph's generosity in giving me advice and counsel throughout, and his personal recommendation to Mark paved the way for a pleasant and exciting experience in a world far outside my longtime comfort zone. Mark afforded me the space and time to execute the manuscript, and his invaluable insight as a lifelong Giants fan led me to several sources that enhanced the storytelling.

The Giants' public relations staff of Pat Hanlon, Peter John-Baptiste, Avis Roper, and the true power behind the throne, Phyllis Hayes, provided invaluable assistance by giving me access to the team archives. Whether my task involved poring over long-yellowed newspaper clips or sifting through box scores, they always welcomed me regardless of the time of year. A special thanks goes out to Joe Scacciaferro and Christine Baluyot of the Giants' broadcast production crew for holding this technologically challenged writer's hand as he muddled through some old game tapes. They were particularly patient with my request for still pictures pulled from the grainy film, a couple of which are featured here.

Pat Walsh, Andy Robustelli's right hand, afforded me insight into the mind of the late, great defensive end, and author Jack Cavanaugh's generosity of time helped lead me in the proper direction on both Vince Lombardi and Tom Landry.

Joe Favorito kindly allowed me access to the cast of *Lombardi* on Broadway, thereby opening my eyes to a different view of the legendary coach.

Richard Fox and Denise Sanders of the Cleveland Public Library Microform Center helped fill in some gaps created by the New York Newspaper strike of 1958. And Brian Smith of Cleveland Browns public relations department filled a factual hole in Jim Brown's stats.

Matt Lutts of AP Images was instrumental in researching and finding many of the photos you see before you.

None of this happens without support from family and friends. Tom Canavan of the Associated Press was there for me with many encouraging words whenever outside forces threatened to undermine this project. Alex Raskin of CBS Sportsline was never above bending the truth toward the positive as he critiqued several raw chapters for me. Frank DeRose, Paul Abramowitz, Joe Malara, and John Schwint were always there to root me on whenever circumstances turned bleak.

Finally, my family. To Diane, Andrew, Liz, and Kathleen, thanks for putting up with me. This one's for you.

ABOUT THE AUTHOR

Brill De La Merced

ERNIE PALLADINO is a sportswriter with nearly forty years of experience. He spent thirty-three of those years at the *Journal News* in Westchester, New York, including twenty covering the New York Giants as a beat reporter. Presently, he publishes, writes, and edits *Ernie Palladino's "The Giants Beat"* for Scout.com, part of the Fox Sports.com Network. He lives in Staten Island, New York.

INDEX

Lombardi and Landry